THE NEW COLUMBUS

BY FREDERICK J. POHL

Security • Dupont Press 617 Sibley Tower Bldg. Rochester, New York 14604

First Edition - First Printing 1986

ISBN: 0-9611422-4-3

Library of Congress Catalog Number 86-060784

Printed in the United States of America

ACKNOWLEDGEMENTS

Knowledge of ships and problems of navigation were given me by fellow members of the Ship Lore and Model Club of New York City. Awareness of the many fallacies in widely accepted history came from historians in the American Revolution Round Table through many years of dinner meetings at Fraunces Tavern, New York City. From the Andiron Club of New York came awareness of the central problem of biography, which must hold to all known facts, and can stand only to the extent to which its presentation of ambition, personality, motivations, consequences of desires and actions, build a character who is entirely convincing. Most valuable information was given me by Mr. W.R. Anderson, President of the Leif Ericson Society of Chicago. My feeling of deep gratitude extends to the attendants at the New York Public Library, the Library of Congress, the Brooklyn Library, the National Library of Scotland, the Library of the British Museum, and especially at the Newberry Library in Chicago.

I am grateful to Professor Noemí Escandell and Professor Napoleon Sanchez at Westfield State College for help in translation from 15th century Spanish. Many helpful suggestions were given me by readers of the manuscript: Moulton H. Farnham, Frank O. Braynard, Winthrop H. Root, Howard E. Shaw, and Newton F. Miller. Most closely of all, my wife Loretta helped me to perceive and keep ever foremost an awareness of the never-ending interraction of character and achievement.

MAPS

ILLUSTRATIONS

CONTENTS

At the end of each chapter, the reader questions facts at variance with many widely held errors, and the biographer replies.

1

MAJORCA

The boy asked his mother: "Who was my father?" Having foreseen that he would someday ask, she had often pondered how she could most safely reply. She dared not let him know while he was so young. She must postpone the telling. All she dared let him know at his age was that his father was no longer living. When she told him that his father and he had never seen each other, she ventured to explain that his father had left their island in the year in which he, her son, was born.

She hoped she had satisfied his curiosity. She believed she had, until he repeated his question. Then she told him he must not know who his father had been until he was old enough to keep it forever a secret. Even to hint that much was perilous. His knowing that there was something which must be kept secret might cause the child to say something that would start people's minds working. That there was a secret must not reach the ears of their maid servant, for she might gossip. If by a single word her son let it slip out, disaster would swiftly destroy the whole family, him, his uncles and herself.

When his mother told him that he himself would be killed by his enemies if anybody knew who his father had been, he wanted to know who those enemies were. She dared say no more than to tell him that his father had ruthless enemies who would want him, his father's son, to die. And so, Margarita admonished him. He must never answer any questions about his father. She would tell him everything when he was old enough never to let drop the slightest hint.

Like the man he was to become, a man who could and did keep secrets, the boy, who was named Juan, had a glib and persuasive tongue. He may have boasted to his playmates, as he probably did, and may have told them his father had been a ship captain who fought pirates until in a big storm he had been drowned at sea, his body never recovered. Juan's inventive imagination in creating such a likely story, a splendid and convincing fiction which could be plentifully adorned with harmless details, would have made his mother feel he might be old enough to be told who his father had been and what had actually happened. But her brother Bartolomeo, cautious business man that he was, would have counselled otherwise. He would have advised waiting until Juan realized fully what their family was up against. Even if Margarita called on Jehovah to save them, Bartolomeo would have said that Jehovah might not be able to save them if they let the boy know his father's identity before he was old enough to realize why it must be kept secret. He reminded his sister that they had left Felanitx and had come to where they now lived because in Puerto Colóm* it would be less likely that anyone would guess from Juan's face and figure who his father had been. Everyday now Juan was looking more like his father, with the same features, a long nose and same color of eye and hair. In Felanitx, people might already have begun to guess. Here, Juan would be naturally accepted as son of one of their ship captains who had come from a mainland country, and who nobody here remembered.

* On the island of Majorca, the Spanish name
Colon (Columbus) was in this instance spelled Colom.

The more his uncle and mother thought about it, the better they liked it. It was a clever avoidance of the perilous reality. They told Juan to hold to his appealing story of his being the son of a deceased captain of one of the Colón ships. They assured him that his father had not been a criminal, had not been in hiding for anything he had done, but had been an honorable man of whom Juan would be proud. They promised him he would be told everything when he became a man. That would be on the day when he was thirteen and was a bar mitzvah.

With his blue eyes looking as though they were staring into the distant future, Juan accepted their decision, as he had accepted others.

He learned two alphabets, and began to read in two directions, from right to left in Hebrew, from left to right in Catalan Spanish. When, about twenty-five years later, he had become the famous man known as Cristóbal Colón, his speech was diagnosed by a shrewd observer as not Castilian, but Mallorquin (Catalonian Spanish).[1]

His reading brought many questions. Those his mother could not answer, his uncle did. If, before he was thirteen, he ventured to ask if his father had been a pious Jew, he was told his father had been a Gentile.

As soon as Juan knew his letters and could write as well as read, his uncle devoted much time to his education, and became his rabbi, his teacher. He gave him much more than book learning. He took him often to the wharves in the harbor, where the boy saw the ships, some gaily blue and yellow, some green and red. All had differently colored gunwales, with large eyes painted on both sides of the bow. Bartolomeo explained the reason for these. Sailors thought such painted eyes would see reefs ahead and would avoid the danger of running too close to whales. He had the sailors show Juan how to coil a rope, always with the sun. They showed the boy how a ship was steered. Bartolomeo said that for many years the Colón family ships had carried spices, perfumes and carpets from the eastern end of the Mediterranean, and had brought from Africa ostrich feathers and ivory. He proudly told Juan that Puerto Colóm got its name from their family. That Majorcan port had carried their family name for more than 200 years, from the thirteenth century, and perhaps earlier. The family had always owned some of the ships which came into Puerto Colóm.

The Colón ships traded between Majorca and the mainland. Some went to Marseilles laden with almonds, olive oil, wine, embroideries, furniture and pottery. Others took timber and hogs to Barcelona. When

3

Bartolomeo told Juan that they carried passengers between Puerto Colóm and the great port of Genoa, Juan, at first hearing the name Genoa, asked in what country Genoa was. Bartolomeo would have told him it was in Liguria. When Juan asked where Liguria was, Bartolomeo would have said it was in Italy.

Juan learned that Genoa was on the near side of Italy, from Puerto Colóm in the direction of sunrise, and that on the other side, the principal port was Venice. That was where Colón ships went to get mirrors and glassware. When he was told that Venice was the city of Marco Polo, and asked who Marco Polo was, like everyone of his time, he was fascinated to learn that Marco Polo had been a far traveler who went, or said he went, all the way to the end of Asia — to what they called Cathay, the Kingdom of Kubla Khan. Bartolomeo said Marco Polo came home in the year 1324, as Christians count. But Marco Polo told so many marvels of things he claimed he had seen that the people of Venice, not believing him, dubbed him "Il Milione," — the million — the teller of a million lies.

If Juan asked if they were lies, as he probably did, his uncle may have replied that he believed Marco Polo exaggerated, but nobody could prove that he had. Curious as to what incredible things had been told, Juan read his uncle's Marco Polo book. It made him glad he had learned to read.

Bartolomeo saw to it that he learned many things outside of books, especially how to swim. On a day when the wind was right, he had no doubt taken Juan in a boat which had a sail, and taught him how to use the wind in getting across the harbor not only with the wind, but partly sideways to it.

When his other uncle, Uncle Juan, came to visit, his uncles took the boy with them to Palma. They rode on muleback. It was a long ride, eight miles to Felanitx, and from there thirty miles to the west. In Felanitx his uncles pointed to the Castle of Santueri, and when Juan said it seemed most grand, they told him he would see a much more lordly palace in Palma. Before they came in sight of the capital city, the road was for a long distance flanked by a high wall which his uncles said had been built by the Muslims. They told him to get off his mule and climb up on a high bank to where he could look down on the wall. Up there he was surprised to see what the wall had on top of it, a runnel in which water was flowing. The water was kept running by a waterwheel turned by mules. He saw with his own eyes how clever the ancient Moors had been.

In Palma they passed through a street named Colón. Soon after, they came to the great palace. It was the building in which Muslim rulers had resided until King Jaime I of Aragon conquered Majorca with a Christian army brought to the island in 143 ships. It took King Jaime a year of hard fighting to subdue the Moors. Juan saw the street in which a decisive battle had occurred, and he saw a church where the Moorish mosque had stood.

He and his uncles of course attended a service in the cathedral. On the way home, Juan's uncles asked him what in Palma had impressed him most. He said two things. One was the Arab baths, because they showed that the Moors washed themselves. The other thing was the cathedral, which they had been building for 150 years. He liked especially the Portal of Del Mirdor, which they had finished building 20 years before. But the most thrilling was inside the cathedral, the colors in the stained glass windows. When he told his uncles how religiously stirred he had felt while listening to the music in the cathedral, Bartolomeo said feelings are the same in all religions. Jews, Christians and Muslims all have the same feelings. Every man feels love or hatred or awe and reverence — the same in every religion. What makes religions differ is not feelings but ideas. Those different ideas prejudice people against each other. Juan learned that eight years before he was born, or to be precise, in the year 1453, as Christians count, all Jews in Majorca were compelled to become Christians. Those who refused had been fined or imprisoned, or had their property confiscated, or they had been exiled. Bartolomeo said that every religion makes its followers believe they have the best vision of truth, a better knowledge of God than anyone else has. Juan, a Jew who must also be a Christian, would discover for himself that this was how it was in both religions. Jews and Christians each think they understand God better than the others do. As converts worshipping with Christians, Jews are in a position to see this more clearly than Christians see it. If Christians worshipped with Jews, they also would see it. Bartolomeo said Gentiles feared Jews who were more successful in business. He said the reason why some Jews were so successful was because their boys were taught to read, and even some of their girls. Perceiving that he would always have to appear to be a devout Christian, Juan saw he must watch his every step, and he saw why his uncles had taken him to

Palma. It was so that he could talk with enthusiasm about the cathedral and Christian worship. He declared that he really liked the music and singing in the cathedral service, and had loved the colored windows of orange, purple, red and green, and blue like the sky, and that wonderful Portal of Del Mirdor, which they said was the best of its style, what was called Gothic. He had also admired, as everyone did, the tombs of the kings, and the tomb of the anti-pope Clement VIII.

Bartolomeo, advising him to use to his advantage both religions, told him he could use both more easily and naturally than either of his uncles could, because in physical appearance he seemed to look more like a Gentile, with shape of face and hair and eye coloring like his father's.[2]

It was in character for Juan to demand what he felt to be his. If he fought with a playmate, as he no doubt did, and his mother asked him why he had to fight, he may have given answer which made her gasp, telling her that the other boy had called him a bastard. If she asked why the other boy had called him that, his reply may have eased her, since it would probably have been that the other boy had tried to take a leadership which Juan would not allow him.

In 1469, when he was nine years old, everyone was talking about the princess and the prince who had become leaders and were said to be fighters. One was Isabel of Leon and Castile, and the other was Ferdinand of Aragon. Those two had been married in October of that year. Bartolomeo said there would be a great future for Spain if Leon and Castile were linked with Aragon, though it did not seem likely, since the king, Isabel's brother, had recognized his daughter, Princess Juana, as his heir, and had thus denied his kingdoms to Isabel. But Isabel's becoming Queen of Leon and Castile was a possibility. If she did gain the throne, anyone could see what would happen. She and her husband together would rule over all of the Spanish Kingdoms, except what the Muslims still held in the southern part of the country. Bartolomeo often remarked that those two, Isabel and Ferdinand, would bear watching.

The gossips were saying that Princess Juana was not the daughter of the king, but was the illicit offspring of the queen, and that her real father was Don Beltrande de Cueva, who had been elevated by King Henry IV to be Duke of Albuquerque. It would not be the first such case.

Commending Juan for using his long arms and firm fists in fighting, Bartolomeo advised him also to use his wits. He said wits are trained by good reading. He named some books he had for Juan to read, books printed in Catalan. Catalan was one of nine Romance languages, a Spanish variant of Provençal.

One of the books was *Libre del Feyte,* (Book of Deeds), which dealt with the history of Majorca. Another, by a Majorcan islander, Raymond Lully, was *Libre de contemplacia,* and was a climax to its author's mystical experiences. While Juan got a taste of it, he was far more interested in Lully's *Libre de maravelles,* which told of the Catalan conquest of Majorca. From it he learned that Catalonia included not only the Balearic Isles but Gerona, Barcelona, and Tarragona. He took pride in being a Majorcan islander, for in cities in mainland countries, if a grownup person went out of his house after dark, he needed to have an armed guard go with him, and should himself go armed. But it was not so in Majorca.

The book which thrilled him as a boy was *Cronica,* the heroic deeds of King Pedro III (Pedro the Great), which told of how Aragon had taken possession of the south of Italy, and how Catalans fought against French invaders. He learned from his reading not to be completely prejudiced against any country, but to be as openminded in political relations between countries as he had to be in religions.

The book which undoubtedly interested him most was printed in 1460, the year of his own birth. It was Roig's *Spill,* a verse novel, in some respects a forerunner of the picaresque novel, in its telling of a young man who has adventures with bandits and suffers marital misfortune.

King Ferdinand of Portugal (1402-1443) who had fought against the Moors in Africa and had died as their prisoner, was popularly called "the Constant" and "the Standard Bearer", and a saint. His cult was approved in 1470, when Juan was ten. The only oath Juan Colón used throughout his life when he was provoked enough to swear was "by Saint Ferdinand!"

When Juan was eleven, he heard of an invention made the year before — an improvement for firearms — the matchlock for muskets. A matchlock was a slow match fastened to a serpentine or cock, to be activated by a lever or spring which would bring the match in contact with the powder in a flashpan under the touchhole. Juan learned that gunpowder was made half of a potassium mixture and one-quarter part each of charcoal and sulfur. In discussion of the matchlock invention, Bartolomeo said that a man must know how to handle other weapons which

7

can be used faster than setting off a charge of gunpowder by matchlock. A man should be skilled in wielding a sword and throwing a javelin, and should be able to shoot straight with bow and arrows.

Bartolomeo not only had books for Juan to read, but sea charts which were brightly colored and fascinating to look at. One of them on a parchment showed many countries. On it one could tell one country from another by the coloring, yellow or green. Red dots were towns and cities. What was colored blue was the Mediterranean Sea, with a narrow strait at its western end, a strait called the Pillars of Hercules. When Juan asked what was outside the Pillars of Hercules, his uncle told him it was the ocean. Juan wanted to know how large the ocean was, but his uncle did not know. He may have said it was as large or almost as large as all of Europe. It was unusual for him to admit ignorance, and when Juan asked him why he didn't know how large the ocean was, Bartolomeo said it was something nobody knew.

Along the northeast side of Majorca, only one long day's walk from Puerto Colóm, was a sky-roofed mountain range, the Sierra de Artá. Juan's playmates may have more than once gone to climb that sierra, and if they did, Juan Colón surely went with them. Almost anywhere before they reached the base of the sierra, the boys could have lain down in a meadow behind a hedge to sleep out under the stars. Doing so, they may have heard from a nearby house a peasant woman giving voice to a plaintive song with intonations of Arab music.

The path up the sierra went through the olive groves, where the older trees had grey trunks gnarled with age, but were bearing olives as plentifully as younger trees. From the groves, climbers could look down over yellow and brown rock terraces. They could see below them the farm lands heavily dotted with algarroba and fig and almond trees. Further up they would come to evergreen trees, on the acorns of which hogs were feeding. Further up, there was scrub, and there where there were no trees, the view was breathtaking. Far below lay the terraced farm lands showing varied tints of color. Far-off beyond them all along the northwest side of the island was the majestic Sierra Alfabía, three times higher than the Sierra de Artá. That loftier mountain range gleamed blue in the distance. It was all of Majorca in one look — all of it south of the two sierras which shielded it from the dreaded tramontana, that fierce north wind that blew hard and cold in the winter.

Looking down on his native island, Juan Colón would have thought of how Majorca had been occupied ages past by Carthaginians, and after them by the Romans, and then by the Vandals, and then by the Vikings, those long-armed tall fighters who had made themselves masters and rulers of every country in Europe. After the Norsemen, Moorish Muslims had swarmed in. They had erected the watch towers and forts which stood on the crags along the shore. They had ruled Majorca until King Jaime came with his 143 ships and recaptured the island, and brought in Catalans.

The most stupendous part of the view from the Sierra de Artá was the sea, the immense spread of sea meeting the horizon. Minorca, the other sizeable Balearic island, lay within view to the northeast. From Bartolomeo's chart, Juan knew that to the north of him was the Balearic Sea, across which was the great port of Barcelona, but too far away to be visible. The view from the Sierra would have appeared to him of unimagined magnitude. To him, if perhaps only for a moment, the vast silence spoke of the God of Mt. Pisgah and the Prophets. On the height looking down upon the land with which he was familiar, he may have felt a freedom such as he had never known, and might never feel again. One thing sure. The view from the Sierra showed water much wider than the land. If to Juan's young mind his native island had seemed vast, it was dwarfed by the sea, the wide expanse of it accentuating the smallness of island life. Bartolomeo's chart showed mainland countries very much bigger than Majorca, and we can well imagine that Juan Colón was eager to sail out on that blue sea to some distant port, with dreams of a larger life.

We do not know whether the boy who would one day become known to the world as Columbus was told who his father was by his mother or by his uncle. We are guided, therefore, by what we know of mothers and uncles. Also, by what we know of a woman's point of view and a man's point of view. We feel that Bartolomeo, being the kind of man we know he was, believed he should be the one to tell Juan who his father was. In arguing the matter with his sister Margarita, Bartolomeo would have felt that he, better than she, could impress on young Juan that if he ever let slip any slightest hint as to his father, he and all the family would have to go into hiding and be mercilessly sought out and slain. He felt this the more urgently because he knew better than she what trouble was brewing in Majorca. Margarita with feminine feelings and intuition would have insisted that she loved her son so deeply that she could im-

Majorca

part the dangerous knowledge without Juan's taking hurt from it. She had seen him growing closer to his uncle through their discussions of his reading and their sharing of interest in charts and maps. But Juan had been her baby. She naturally felt she could steer her son's reaction through the telling, however embarrassing it might be to herself. She felt she could foresee what his reactions would be. She therefore must shape the telling. She would present the whole story so that Juan would not be injured, but would gain stature from it. If the telling were as a mother's love could make it, it would be a great thing for Juan. It would be an advance in his education and understanding of life. It would be a determinant in his character.

Margarita did not find it as easy as she had imagined it would be to tell him who his father had been. She felt instinctively that her son should not hear of his father from anyone except herself. But how to begin the telling? At first she could not see how. Then she thought of a way to ease her embarrassment. To prepare him for the revelation of his father's name, she would relate some history. Much of it he already knew. It was what everybody had heard. She told him that Prince Juan of Aragon, brother of King Alfonso V of Aragon, had married Queen Bianca, Queen of Navarre. In 1421, Queen Bianca bore him a son, Carlos, Prince of Viana. The title of the crown prince of Navarre came from a district, Viana, in the western part of Navarre. If the grandfather of Prince Carlos, King Alfonso, died without issue, as appeared likely, the father of Prince Carlos would become King of Aragon, and Prince Carlos, as his eldest son, would then be heir also to the throne of Aragon.

With these prospects in mind, it had been arranged that Prince Carlos would marry Princess Isabel, sister of King Henry IV of Castile. This was when Isabel was only eight years of age. Prince Carlos, at age 39, said he would marry Princess Isabel as soon as she reached the age of puberty. But these high hopes were dashed.

When Prince Carlos was 20 years of age, his mother, Queen Bianca, had died. His father, Prince Juan of Aragon, had then married Juana Enriquez. She bore him a son, Fernando (Ferdinand).

Margarita could not speak with any kindness of Juana Enriquez, but only with bitterness. Juana Enriquez was indeed a ruthless woman. Ambitious for her son Ferdinand, she had schemed for him against Prince Carlos. When King Alfonso V of Aragon died and her husband became

11

King Juan II of Aragon, and she became Queen, she had persuaded her husband to stand with her against Prince Carlos.

For centuries the Kingdom of Navarre had suffered from royal family maneuverings. It had been partitioned. The kings of France had taken a part of it. Queen Juana now planned to have Aragon get possession of all that remained of it, the Spanish portion. The people of Navarre continued to dream of regaining their kingdom's lost power. Their hopes centered upon Prince Carlos, who as son of Queen Bianca and King Juan of Aragon was now rightful heir to the thrones of both Navarre and Aragon. But the amibitious Queen Juana stood in the way. She was determined that her son should become King of Aragon, and eventually ruler over Navarre as well. To this end, she persuaded her husband to oppose the claims of his eldest son, if necessary with active warfare. Prince Carlos suffered this humiliation. Regretfully, he prepared for a struggle that was distasteful to his temperament. He sought to avoid civil conflict. He wrote three letters to his father in an attempt to keep peace. Throughout Navarre, which boasted the cities of Barcelona and Saragossa, and throughout the Balearic Isles, all Catalonians were for Prince Carlos. There were battles, and a temporary peace, and then more fighting. Determined to win what she wanted for her son, Queen Juana persuaded her husband to resort to treachery.

Prince Carlos was in Sicily. King Juan invited him to come to Majorca to have a peace conference and set up a permanent peace. Prince Carlos was suspicious of what his father and Queen Juana planned to do, but he set the restoration of peace above his personal safety. He had imperturbable confidence in the justice of his cause. He knew the people were with him. Of greater concern than his personal safety was what he meant to all Catalonians, as rightful heir to the two thrones. But his father and Queen Juana were firmly entrenched against him. King Charles VII of France announced that he would support King Juan and Queen Juana in any open struggle against Prince Carlos. Therefore, to go to Majorca seemed to Prince Carlos to be the only thing to do. And so, he took ship from Palermo to Palma.

In August of 1459 he landed in Majorca. When he made his formal entrance into Palma, everyone was there to see him. He rode on a horse, wearing a robe of pink fustian, a purple hat, a flowing black cape, and a gorgeous collar of gold set with precious stones and pearls.

We can imagine Juan Colón's asking his mother why she was telling him all this tedious history. Whether or not she told him why at once, he soon guessed. We can be sure he gave full attention to the rest of what she told him about Prince Carlos of Viana.

She had thought Prince Carlos the most handsome, most glamorous man who ever lived. He was tall, with red hair like Juan's, and eyes as blue. He was a royal-looking man whom no woman could resist. Her family was living in a house in Felanitx close to Santueri Castle. To that palace Prince Carlos came. When he saw her, Margarita, he had eyes for no one else. For a time she held him off. The love affair which ensued most probably took place in the Alqueria Rossa, today called Son Ramonet, at the foot of the Castle of Santueri.[3]

We do not know the physical appearance of Margarita Colón. She was very likely a blond and fairly tall. In any case, she was a girl whose extraordinary beauty attracted and captivated the heart of Prince Carlos. She was ensnared by his ardor. She probably never knew of the letter recently brought to light, the letter in which Prince Carlos wrote to the Governor of Majorca on October 28th, 1459, two months after he had arrived in the island. In the letter he alluded to his "success" with Margarita Colón.[4]

To Juan, what he had heard from his mother was at first almost overwhelming. No doubt he said over and over to himself: Don Carlos, Prince of Viana, was my father![5] I am the grandson of Queen Bianca of Navarre! I am son of a prince who was the rightful heir to royal thrones!

We can imagine his wanting to know how large Navarre was, and the thrill he felt at finding on his uncle's chart that it was three times the size of Majorca.

He listened with full mind to his mother's telling him that Prince Carlos had been heavily in debt for the cost of the voyage from Sicily. In Majorca, lacking money and having no means of getting any, he realized he had put himself in his enemies' hands. After seven months in Majorca, he managed to take ship to Barcelona, where he felt safer. All this time, Queen Juana, jittery at the idea that he might marry the probable heir to the throne of Castile, the Princess Isabel, was determined that her son, Prince Ferdinand, her husband's second son, should be the one to marry Princess Isabel. It was said she wept copious tears at her feeling of frustration. To persuade her husband to do what she wanted, she accused Prince Carlos of fomenting revolts. She kept on this tack until King Juan decided to finish with his eldest son. And so, when Prince

Carlos was about to leave Barcelona to go to Lérida, King Juan secretly sent soldiers in advance to Lérida, which was in a strong defensive position and would serve as a secure prison. When Prince Carlos arrived there on December 2nd of 1460, he was disarmed and imprisoned.[6]

The Catalonians refused to accept the situation and made many protests. Three weeks later the prince was taken by his captors to Saragossa, and everyone feared that King Juan intended to kill his son. Realizing how the people felt, he publicly announced that he would rather die himself than have it believed that the life of his son, the Prince of Viana, was being menaced. In spite of the urgings of Queen Juana, he committed himself to keeping his son alive, and at Saragossa on the 25th of February, 1461, he signed an order for his son's release. Church bells rang throughout all of Navarre.[7]

Queen Juana now had to dissemble her feelings. She met publicly with Prince Carlos, and there was a great show of reconciliation. It was said that in the vestibule of the palace the prince offered to kiss the queen's hand, his offering of which she at first refused, before she consented, and then he kissed not only her hands but her deceitful mouth. The king and queen, declaring that the establishment of lasting peace was their nearest heart's desire, announced an invitation to Prince Carlos to make a formal entry into Tarragona. When the prince entered that city, a thousand persons came out to meet him with cries of joy. Bombards were shot off. All the clergy were in the procession, as were also the City Councillors in grand costume, the Archbishop of Tarragona, the Bishop of Barcelona, abbots, priors, canons, the Count of Prades, knights, officers with lances, men in armor, and standard bearers. There were trumpets and drums. Children brandished wooden swords and waved little flags, and cried out: "Carlos! God save him! The first-born heir of Aragon and of Sicily!" Again and again they shouted: "Long live Don Carlos!" They reveled in the music, singing hymns and motets. There was a triumphal arch, and all the houses were decorated with tapestries, and a Te Deum was sung in the Cathedral. That night there were illuminations and discharges of artillery. Thus the people did all they could to make their prince a hero and to show how much they wanted him.

After that Prince Carlos reentered Barcelona on March 10th of 1461. The Catalonians had succeeded in rallying to their cause all the States and the crown of Aragon. But Prince Carlos, for all the intense enthusiasm, was without real power, since he had no financial credit. He had no means of recovering Navarre or of marrying Isabel. The demonstration, however, had carried an unmistakable message to King Juan and Queen Juana, and the king signed a peace treaty with his son.

It meant nothing to the king and the scheming queen, for they were on the throne of Aragon and firmly held Navarre. Prince Carlos had no illusions. Without real power, without soldiers, without credit, he had no hope of gaining the throne of Navarre. Disheartened, he thought of entering the religious life and of becoming a monk. The Abbot of Poblet dissuaded him. It was said that the abbot did so because he saw the physical condition of the prince, who was daily weakening with some illness. Knowing his condition and that he had not long to live, the king and queen did not need to hasten his dying. Six months after his grand entry into Tarragona, when he died on September 23rd of 1461, there were many who believed he had been poisoned, murdered. He could have been given slow poison, though it seems unlikely. If Queen Juana had killed him by slow poison, she was punished for the crime by a cancer which killed her soon after the death of the prince.[8]

Margarita Colón naturally did not enlarge upon any criticism she herself had faced from her family for having had an affair with a Gentile. After all, her lover had been a prince of royal blood.

Young Juan had heard enough of royal families to realize how ruthless they could be in killing each other off to win or keep a throne. He now saw why his uncle and mother had not told him until he was old enough to keep it all and forever an absolute secret. If his father's half-brother King Ferdinand had any hint of their relationship, he would be a merciless enemy. But to Juan Colón just entering manhood, the thrill of it! To know himself to be grandson of a queen, grandson of a king, son of a prince who had been heir to the thrones of Navarre and Aragon!

But now, all he was actually was himself, Juan Colón. It made him know himself to be different from all his playmates, from all his acquaintances. He was set apart. His father had been a merciful man. He would strive to be always worthy of his father. Even if he could never avenge his father for what had been stolen from him, he would do all he could to make himself a somebody.

He thought of what might lie ahead. He said to himself that his father had been a Christian, and therefore he himself was as much Christian as

Jew. This realization would have a great bearing on everything he would ever say and do. His noble father would loom ever larger in his mind. He would think of his father in any situation in which he found himself. He would live up to his father in any meeting with anyone. If it should be his lot ever to meet with a king, he would act like the equal to the king. He would always play the part of a prince. He would acknowledge no superior.

❋ᚲᚲᚲᚲᚲᚲᚲᚲᚲᚲᚲᚲᚲᚲᚲᚲᚲᚲᚲᚲᚲᚲᚲᚲᚲᚲᚲᚲᚲ❋

You say Columbus was born in Majorca?

Yes.

Not of a peasant family in Genoa, Italy?

All evidences recently unearthed point to Majorca. His many surviving reports and letters show him ignorant of Italian idiom. He sent a letter to Italy in Catalan Spanish and asked to have it there translated into Italian. How explain what has hitherto perplexed his biographers, the assumption that amnesia blotted out what they have believed was his native language which he had spoken for his first twenty-five years?

So you deny to Italians the honor of discovering America.

I do not. America was discovered by an Italian.

You have me confused.

Read on and you will not be.

You do say that Juan Colón, Majorcan-born son of Carlos, Prince of Viana, became known as Columbus?

Yes. A princely man.

My guess is you are going to say that Columbus does not deserve the attention that has been given to him.

I shall never say that! He deserves immortal memory. I shall show that he does, and why he does, though for a different reason from the one generally believed.

Then he is a new Columbus.

That is what I call him.

2

REVOLT

Being a red-head, Juan had no doubt been singled out among the other boys as hot-tempered. He was indeed daring and unabashed. But now that he knew who his father had been, he felt a new reason for being self-controlled at the same time that he was forthright and domineering. Knowledge of his father had planted within him a compelling ambition which would shape all his future years. It initiated in him audacity, aggressiveness, an urge to be recognized as somebody of importance. He was no longer content to be merely Juan Colón, a Jew conforming to opinions of the majority of Majorcans in everything he let them hear him say or see him do. His father had been a Christian. As his father would want him to be, he would be a Christian wholeheartedly. Knowing his origin, he reconsisdered all his preconceptions. Under compulsion from what he now knew about himself, he would no longer be aiming to do what was expected. Conscious of his royal blood, he would think and act in a way which would win his father's approval. As son of a crown prince, as grandson of a queen, as grandson of a king, he would hold to the feeling of privilege. He would act as one of the God-appointed highest, as one called to supreme command. Having been told that in physical appearance and eye and hair color and facial features he resembled his father, he felt immense pride. He became determined always to behave, carry himself, and speak as a man among the greatest, as though he bore a title of nobility. He vividly recalled having seen in Palma the tomb of the most highly honored Majorcan, Raimond Lully, who died in 1315, having lived to the age of eighty, and who, at request of King Jaime II, had written *Laws Governing a Prince,* a manual for royal behavior. Juan would apply such laws to himself. He would conduct himself like a prince.

He decided never to argue about religious doctrines. He understood, or thought he understood, the differences between the Jewish and Christian theologies. Christians boasted that their faith had won out against the polytheism in the ancient Roman Empire. Based upon the monotheism of Abraham and David, Christianity had destroyed all the old gods and goddesses, but still held to a belief in a man-god, a tangible god. Jews were tied back from this by the divine injunction, "Thou shalt have no other god." But such theological differences were not for him to ponder. He would close his mind to them. He would be an orthodox Christian. In action and purpose he would be as much a Christian as his father.

His uncle Bartolomeo was voicing complaints of the excessive taxes which were taking all profits out of shipping between Majorca and mainland countries. Most Majorcans could no longer pay the prices he was compelled to ask for the merchandise which the family's ships brought to the island. He commented on the luxury being enjoyed by the rich in Palma. Some there were living in palaces, women with fans of ostrich feathers or lace, with dresses of velvet, or of brocade with oriental patterns of gold and silver. There was wasteful extravagance, drinking from flagons of gold. There was gambling, hunting, hawking. Everywhere else on the island there was the pinched poverty of the peasants. Fishermen were living in huts or in caves. The taxes were crushing the people.

Those who had imposed the taxes were of the same royal family in Aragon to which Juan felt antipathy for having denied the throne to his father.

Juan first learned of the involvement of his uncle in plans that were afoot when he caught the whispered name "Simon". He would have assumed that Simon was merely a business acquaintance of his uncle. But one night after dark, when the man Simon Ballester came to their house with precautions having been made to keep their neighbors from knowing of his visit, Juan learned what was brewing. Plans were making for more than mere protest against the heavy taxes.

Majorca was seething with a spirit of revolt. Bitter rebellions against feudal injustices had from time to time risen in various countries — in England, in Florence, in the Netherlands. Now resistance was being planned in Majorca. Bartolomeo left the house suddenly one night. Then came word that a revolt had broken out near Palma. Its leaders were Simon Ballester, Bartolomeo Colón, and Bartolomeo's brother, Juan Colón. Palma was being surrounded by men who came from the vineyards and olives groves. Soldiers under the pay of Aragon were defending the city against them. For a time it looked as though it would be only a matter of days and those soldiers would be compelled to surrender or be slain. One of the Colón ship captains brought word of revolts on the mainland. In Barcelona there were two rebellious factions — one called "La Gabela de la Busca" and the other, "La Viga".

The rustics who were besieging Palma were being sneered at as "churls." But they were being well led by Simon Ballester and the Colón brothers, Juan and Bartolomeo. They were maintaining and tightening the siege. Their cause looked promising. For thirty days they held the siege against the city. Success seemed almost won, until unexpectedly, 2,000 well-equipped Aragonese troops arrived, and quickly crushed the revolt. Many who had taken part in the revolt were being slaughtered.

Margarita at first could learn nothing about her brothers. She feared that they had been captured and slain. Then word came that Simon Ballester and the Colón brothers had escaped the slaughter and had fled into hiding. But a tremendous search for them was being made. All Margarita could do was pray for their safety. Several days went by. Then came the terrifying news that Simon Ballester had been captured. He had at once been savagely tortured, and most horribly executed. He had been quartered, his legs and arms pulled off by four oxen driven in four different directions.

Then came the news that an edict of indulgence had been issued. It pardoned all who had taken part in the revolt, except three persons: the brothers Juan and Bartolomeo Colón, and the young son of Simon Ballester, Miguel Ballester. Those three were still in hiding. Everyone was saying they would soon be caught.

Juan and Bartolomeo Colón were named in the record as the *tios* (uncles) of young Juan Colón.[1] This is the only mention of an Uncle Juan. That uncle does not appear in any subsequent record. Could it be that there has been a mistake in identity in naming him? Years later, Juan Colón let everyone think that his Uncle Bartolomeo was his brother, for he then had good reason for doing so. It seems unlikely that Juan Colón at age twelve or thirteen was one of the leaders of the revolt in Majorca.[2] Nevertheless, as we shall see, in another activity which involved hand-to-hand fighting, he had at the age of fourteen or fifteen become a leader.

What we know definitely is that Juan Colón and his uncle Bartolomeo and Miguel Ballester escaped from Majorca. Bartolomeo's property had been declared confiscated. Presumably on some dark night Bartolomeo seized possession of one of the ships and sailed out of the harbor before dawn. He could not go to Barcelona. He could not go to any port in Spain .

We do not know what happened to Margarita. As a woman who had not participated in the revolt, she may have remained in the island, presumably with permission to work for her living. There may have been for Juan an emotional parting from his mother. He probably never saw her again. He may never have learned when she died.

❀⅔⅔⅔⅔⅔⅔⅔⅔⅔⅔⅔⅔⅔⅔⅔⅔⅔⅔⅔⅔⅔⅔❀

You say that a red-headed youth from Majorca became the world-famous Columbus?

I do.

You ignore racial pride.

The Creator of the Universe does not play favorites.

What do you mean?

Racial pride is often in error.

How so?

Since anthropologists tell us that human beings originated in Africa, it seems fair to say that the ancestors of Europeans were Africans, and presumably black.

You're suggesting that white Euopeans have negro blood in them?

Just as every European has in him the blood of Julius Caesar.

How can you say that?

Arithmetic, and law of chances. Double your ancestors for each generation. In twenty generations you would have a billion ancestors, except for intermarriages. But there are eighty generations back to Julius Caesar — a far greater number of ancestors than all the people on earth in his day. Therefore, the chances are millions to one that you have Caesar's blood in you.

Fantastic!

By the same arithmetic, every Jew has some Gentile ancestry, and every Gentile some Jewish blood.

And Italian and Spanish also?

And also Majorcan.

3

SEVEN-MILE SWIM

The ship in which Miguel Ballester and Juan Colón and his uncle Bartolomeo escaped from Majorca went to a seaport where both ship and
they were warmly welcome. Before telling what harbor that was, we
look for a moment at the relations between kingdoms and nations in the
fifteenth century. At that time it was not the prejudices and whims of
kings which decided alliances in peace and war. It was primarily geography. Proximity caused mistrust. Countries with common borders
were natural enemies. Friendships existed only between countries which
were many leagues apart. Portugal and Spain, being contiguous, were
rivals and potential foes. France and Spain likewise. Italians, far from
Spain, were friendly to Spain. They were not so friendly to France.

Italians were welcome in Spain because Spain and Italy were far enough away from each other not to feel enmity.

Bartolomeo knew that the ship in which they escaped would be a welcome addition to the fleet of King René of Anjou at Marseilles, and so to Marseilles they steered. They had no other choice, international antagonisms being what they then were.

The Kingdom of Anjou had been prominent in history. Stemming from Anjou had come the Angevin (Plantagenet) kings of England. Only after King René died in 1480 was Anjou permanently incorporated into France.

Rene of Anjou was a vassal of the King of France. He opposed those who had prevented Juan Colón's father from ascending the throne of Navarre. Catalonians, opposed to Aragon, had offered the crown of Aragon and the County of Barcelona to René of Anjou, who was also Count of Provence and King of Naples and Jerusalem. This offer was forwarded by René to Barcelona to his son, the Duke of Lorraine, who was lending aid to the rebellions in that city.

Marseilles was the base of operations of René's naval forces. In the service of René were mariners who, in the custom of those times, acted as privateers. The Spanish author, R. Llanas de Niubo, tells us much of their activities in aid of the Barcelonians who were being besieged by King Juan II of Aragon. He tells of their performances in the destruction of Aragonese galleys near Alicante.

Privateering was a surreptitious activity. It was done with a commission to raid as if a state of war existed. If a privateer was captured, he was summarily executed. Privateering under René of Anjou was from René's point of view as legal as was that by Admiral Sir Francis Drake and Admiral Sir John Hawkins under Queen Elizabeth of England a century later. Spaniards called the English privateers pirates, which from their point of view they were. Italians, whose merchant ships were being attacked, made the same charge against those who served King René. The cruelty with which the troops from Aragon had crushed the rebellion in Majorca and so fiendishly tortured and executed Simon Ballester, gave Simon's son Miguel and his friends of the Colón family justification for becoming privateers against Aragon. For Juan Colón, there was the added desire to fight against his grandfather, King Juan II of Aragon.

In early adolescence, Juan had acquired a man's stature. He was sturdy, strong in limbs from swimming and other sports. At age fifteen he became a leader, outstanding in battle, more daring than most.

When not actually privateering, he continued his studies of ships and seamanship, how to hold a course and make reckonings of directions and speed of sailing. He got to know the stars as guides. As he observed the working of the log, the casting into the water of a chip of a log at the bow and the estimates by ship's officers of the time elapsed when the stern of the ship passed the floating chip, he saw that varying estimates were much in dispute as to the speed of sailing. Estimating speed by the log often led to error. He gave thought to making a more accurate estimate. He discovered how to do it. Having observed that his heart beats came at a steady pace, he counted his heart beats during the time it took the length of the ship to pass the floating piece of log. He thus found a fairly accurate means of estimating the speed of a ship. He developed superior skill as a navigator.

He was active as a privateer at age fifteen. When sixteen, he was a leader in perilous enterprises. While we know of only two specific incidents in which he was involved, since his biographer, his son Ferdinand, was never told "where or under what circumstances he first went to sea," we do have several facts which hint at the extent of his privateering activities.

In a letter in January of 1495, he wrote of his having been sent in 1472 to capture the galleas *Fernandina* belonging to King Juan II: "When I was off the island of San Pietro near Sardinia, a vessel informed me there were two ships and a caravel with the said galleas, which information frightened my people, and they resolved to go no further but to return to Marseilles to pick up another ship and men. I, seeing that I could do nothing against their wills without some ruse, agreed to their demand, and changing the point of the compass, made sail at nightfall, and at sunrise the next day, we found ourselves off Cape Carthage, while all on board were certain we were bound for Marseilles.[1]

A bit of boasting? Perhaps. Or let us say it was boasting. Whether or not young Colón was captain of a ship in the Mediterranean is almost beside the point, since we know he had experiences which made him the best navigator of his time.

Another fact like a flashlight on him as a privateer is that the Doge of Venice sentenced Juan Colón in absentia to pain of death, and offered a reward for his head "for acts of piracy at sea in the service of the king of

France."[2] That the Genoese Cristoforo Colombo appeared before a notary several times in Genoa during the years in which Juan Colón was a privateer against Italian ships has been cited as an argument for Majorcan origin of Columbus. But an unprejudiced scholar, Tertius Chandler, who accepts the Majorcan origin, wrote me: "Nectario Maria supposes Colón couldn't be sailing for René of Anjou and be a merchant in Genoa in the same years. But of course he could; raiding was not full time . . . . His case is stronger, in my opinion, if he leaves out such dubious claims."

Everywhere in Europe there was much talk of how Princess Isabel, the sister of King Henry IV of Castile, and whom he had disclaimed as his heir, had made herself Queen of Castile. Her doing it was the more sensational in that she did it directly contrary to the wishes and hopes of her husband Prince Ferdinand and in defiance of those who wanted the king's daughter to inherit the throne. At 23 years of age, Isabel showed her shrewdness and daring. Having heard that her brother the king in Madrid was dying, she took up residence in nearby Segovia. She did this for two reasons. One was that the royal treasure of Castile was in Segovia. The other was that Segovia was near enough for her to get news from Madrid quickly. In Segovia she waited. The moment the news came of the king's death, she seized the royal treasure, and with it in her possession, had means to pay soldiers to support her. She immediately had the soldiers proclaim her Queen of Leon and Castile. When the news of the king's death reached her husband Prince Ferdinand, he came, spurring his horse, but he arrived too late. He had hoped to mount the throne which she now firmly held.

He was so furious at her having beaten him to it that he wanted to break off their marriage.

Queen Isabel clearly knew her own mind. She was a clever and determined woman. She was one to be watched. She knew what she wanted. She would be ruthless in getting it. She, as Queen of Leon and Castile, with her husband as ruler of Aragon and other kingdoms, would together make a strong, unbeatable fighting team. They would be what Spain most needed, a bond of unity. For many centuries, Spain had been a mere conglomeration of kingdoms, but Queen Isabel and King Ferdinand together would unquestionably be able to conquer the Muslims of Andalusia. Until they did, however, as Bartolomeo Colón saw it, the French and the Portuguese would continue to take advantage of Spaniards. Catalonians were Spanish in spite of their good reasons for opposing the grab-all plans of Aragon which had driven many of them to poverty.

While Juan listened to his uncle and gave heed to his advice, he decided to stay clear of political arguments. Bartolomeo Colón was looking at the growing Castile-Aragon power in two different ways. He desired to oppose it for business reasons. But he also saw the advantages that would come to all Spaniards if Queen Isabel and Prince Ferdinand were successful in what they were obviously planning to do.

Bartolomeo became deeply concerned with the reported growing anti-Semitism in Spain. It threatened to become worse than that in Majorca. The "Catholic Kings," as Isabel and Ferdinand were later called, were blaming Jews for the rise in taxes. Bartolomeo saw that the anti-Semitism was intensified by the more than 750 years of war between Christians and Muslims in Spain, in consequence of which there was an unavoidable shortage of everything throughout that country. With the crying need for every kind of article, shipping men were importing things and charging high prices. Successful business men were being regarded with increasing jealousy by nobles who were striving to maintain their feudal privileges.

Since privateering was an occasional occupation, engaged in when spies reported opportunity to make a surprise attack, Juan Colón and Miguel Ballester in Marseilles had time to continue their education with reading of books. It was widely known, by those interested in learning, that Prince Carlos of Viana had possessed a remarkable library. In it he had the five books of Moses, the New Testament in French, and the Evangels and Epistles in Greek. Only one-fourth of his books were in the field of theology. His library was strong in ancient literature: Demosthenes, Aristotle, Josephus, Plutarch, Marcus Tullius (Cicero), Pliny, Eusebius, Oroso. He had six books in Catalan Spanish which were "in paper." This probably meant they were printed books, and were incunabula. Since printing in Europe began with the *Gutenberg Bible* about the year 1451, and Prince Carlos died in 1461, most of the books in his library must have been in manuscript on vellum. His library contained 59 Latin volumes, 5 Greek, 29 French, 1 Italian, 6 Catalan, and only one of Castilian Spanish. It was a library deserving the detailed listing of the books in it given in histories of the period.[3]

Prince Carlos had recorded the estimated value (or purchase cost?) of each of his books in French money — a total of 1408 livres. The most costly book he valued at 130 livres. It was a manuscript translation he had himself made from Latin into Spanish. It was the *Ethics* of Aristotle.[4]

When Juan Colón learned that his father had a library of treasured books, he was stimulated in his reading of ancient authors, several of whose books he acquired, and from whom he quoted in later years. The books he acquired were the beginning of a library which was expanded by his son Ferdinand into the greatest private library of the Sixteenth Century, the so-called Columbiana — 20,000 volumes. Book collecting was in the family's blood.

When Juan heard that his father had made a translation of the *Ethics* of Aristotle, he naturally wanted to read that author. He had no doubt heard what was generally known, that Aristotle had been the teacher of Alexander the Great. He now learned that Aristotle had taught Alexander how to become great. He of course wanted especially to read the *Ethics*, but he had no access to his father's translation, since it was not published until about 35 years later. He most probably read the *Ethics* in a Latin version.

We can fairly surmise how deeply the *Ethics* influenced him, since his lifetime habits and several traits in his character exemplified what Aristotle had said were the characteristics of a great man. These are passages which Juan Colón evidently took to heart:

"A great man is gentle and temperate. People who overeat are called mad-bellies."

"The claims of pleasure to being the prize of high excellence is not true wisdom. — Better to be happy as a result of one's own exertion than by the gift of fortune."

One thing in the *Ethics* of Aristotle struck Juan Colón directly. As a privateer he had many a brush with danger. Risking his life in sea fights, he was especially interested in Aristotle's description of a great-souled man: "The great-souled man does not run into danger for trifling reasons. He is not a lover of danger, but he will face danger in a great cause. . . . The traits of a great-souled man are a slow gait, a deep voice, and a deliberate utterance . . . . When great honors come to him he will feel he is receiving only what belongs to him."

Quotations such as these from the *Ethics* of Aristotle inevitably drilled deep into Juan Colón's consciousness and would mold him as a man. It is certain from all we know of his character that he cultivated the great-souled feeling.

His uncle Bartolomeo now saw two things clearly. One was that printed books were becoming the fashion. Since he had knowledge of charts, he decided to go into the business of making charts, some of them to be put into printed books. He also saw that since the Portuguese were claiming control of the ocean to the south and were aiming at getting around Africa to India, the most flourishing place of business might in a few years be the city of Lisbon. He decided to open a chart shop in Lisbon.

Privateering under King René against ships belonging to or serving Castile and Aragon had been a reaction to a royal change of mind. Henry IV, King of Castile, who had at first declared his daughter Juana illegitimate and had recognized his sister Isabel as his heir, had annulled recognition of Isabel and declared Juana his heir. He did this because he disapproved of Isabel's marriage to Ferdinand. This is why, after his decease in 1474, and Isabel had seized the throne, the partisans of Juana, called by them "La Beltraneja," organized their opposition to Isabel and Ferdinand. In April of 1475 they proclaimed Juana Queen of Castile. In doing this they had the support of King Alfonso of Portugal. War at once began. The King of France, backing King René's giving aid to Portugal, sent corsairs into battle. With them went Juan Colón.

Between Sagres and the Port of Lagos, near Cape St. Vincent, at a distance of two leagues, or about seven miles from the southern coast of Portugal, the French corsairs closed with Italian ships which were serving Castile and Aragon.[5] This of course was not how Columbus told the story years later in Spain.[6] In Spain he had to make a telling that put him on the pro-Spanish side.

A naval battle called for skill in outmaneuvering the enemy. The rolling of a ship at sea made almost impossible any accurate aiming of a cannon from the side of a ship. Only cannon pointing forward at the bow could be hopefully fired on target. Only rarely did one of them rake the enemy's deck or bring down a mast. A sea battle therefore usually involved courageous grappling with an enemy ship and boarding the enemy for hand-to-hand fighting. Juan Colón was on a ship which threw out grappling hooks and chains to hold tight to an enemy vessel.

In this encounter gunpowder caught fire or exploded, and both ships began to burn. There was no time to free the ships from each other. Men from both vessels began jumping into the sea, preferring death by drowning to death by fire.

This was on the 13th of August, 1476. Juan Colón, just turned sixteen, had received in his flesh a gunshot wound, a lead bullet the size of a tooth filling, about one ounce in weight. Bleeding, he saw much blood in the water, and very likely sharks were busy attacking the men who had leaped into the sea. He had to jump or burn. Would the sharks attack him? There was so much blood from the others he might escape. With mind set on the direction of the nearest Portuguese coast, he dove overboard and began swimming as fast as he could away from the blazing ships. Luckily he found an oar floating, and with it began his long swim. With his eyes only an inch or two above the water, he could not see the distant land, nor any horizon. He could see no further than perhaps twenty or thirty feet of waves. He had begun swimming away from the ships in the right direction, but soon he could not even see the ships, and so could not take direction from them. Though the oar gave him partial support and opportunity to rest occasionally, he would have drowned if he had not been able to hold direction to the nearest land. Fortunately his wound was in a fleshy part, not in an arm or leg muscle. The salt water eased though it did not close his wound.

When he felt his strength ebbing and feared he would never reach the distant land, he must have asked himself: Was it for this I fled from Majorca? Was it for this I took to sea as soon as I became a man? Was it for this I have been ambitious and have read books and studied arithmetic and geometry and astronomy? Was it for this I have made myself knowledgeable about maps of lands and sea? If I fail to reach shore, if this is to be the end of me, I might better have stayed at home.

Clinging to hope though desperately weary, he forced himself to keep on swimming. When at last he heard breakers and soon after felt his toes touch bottom, he struggled to rise to his feet, staggered, fell, crawled out of the surf, and lay panting on the shore. His landing was on the coast of Portugal at Lagos.

❋✿✿✿✿✿✿✿✿✿✿✿✿✿✿✿✿✿✿✿✿✿✿✿✿✿✿✿✿✿✿✿❋

You have told your readers that Juan Colón got to the Portuguese shore at Lagos.

So he did.

But how did he get there?

As I said, by swimming.

But you haven't told how he held direction when his eyes were only two or three inches above the water, and he could see no more than thirty feet of waves.

Haven't you been swimming where there were waves?

Often.

Then you know how Colón steered himself. He kept at the same angle to the wave direction.

Yes. At first. But he had to have another means of holding direction.

Why?

Undoubtedly he began swimming by the wave direction. But seven miles is a long swim, and he was slowed because with one hand holding to the oar, he could use only one arm in swimming. Holding to the oar delayed him for hours, and so he had to swim far into the night. In the dark he could not clearly see the direction of the waves.

Then how do you think he did steer?

You should have told us how.

How do you think he did it?

By the stars. Or, if the moon was shining, by the moon.

Since we don't know, I can't say, but I think you may be right.

4

EXPLORING THE ATLANTIC

The people of Lagos found on the shore the young man who had saved his life by a long swim from the distant naval battle. They closely questioned him. They soon learned for whom he had been fighting.He had been serving under King René and France allied with Portugal. He had been a supporter of "La Beltraneja" claimant to the throne of Castile. Since he had been fighting against the Spanish, the people of Lagos gave him a hearty welcome. When he told them his name was Juan Colón, they informed him that in their language it was João Colom or João Colum.

He told them he had an uncle in Lisbon who was named Bartolomeo. They told him that name was Bartolomeu in Portuguese.

As chart maker, Bartolomeu was in touch with shipping men. João Colom soon obtained a berth as a minor officer on a trading ship. This was not just his uncle's doing, though his uncle undoubtedly helped. It was primarily because of his impressive physical appearance. We have eighty portraits of him, but none painted during his lifetime. Since no two of the portraits seem to be unmistakably of the same man, they fail to tell us what he looked like. But the contemporary physical descriptions of him are in agreement. That by Las Casas is the most completely detailed:

> His form was tall, above the median, his face long and his countenance imposing, his nose aquiline, his eyes clear blue, his complexion light, tending toward a decided red; his head and hair were red when he was young.

Here we have the description of a young man of typical Viking type. Since the Vikings had established themselves as the ruling families in every country in Europe, the man's physical appearance, to observant contemporaries, hinted at royal blood.

The ship on which João Colom was a junior officer sailed from Lisbon to Galway in Ireland, and from there to Reykjavik in Iceland.

At the port of Galway in western Ireland, where the people today point to the Church of St. Nicholas as the one in which they say he attended mass, Colom with enquiring mind listened to what Irishman had to say. They were constantly telling of their Saint Brendan who early in the sixth century had sailed to the West. They did not know how far Saint Brendan went out in the ocean or what land he reached, but they told what he and his men reported having seen — a marvel the likes of which no sober Irishman had ever seen in the waters near Ireland — a marvel indeed. From their description we know what it was: "A column in the sea the color of silver and as hard as marble and of the clearest crystal." An iceberg, of course, and therefore it is most likely Saint Brendan had been within sight of the coast of Greenland.

At Reykjavik in western Iceland, Colom acquired definite information of the glaciers of Greenland. As a mariner, he was more interested in relative positions of islands and in their distances from mainland ports. He was learning all he could about the movements of ocean water. Years later he told his son, who put it into his biography of him: "I sailed myself a hundred leagues beyond Thule (Iceland) . . . . To this island, which is as big as England, the English trade, especially from Bristol. At the time I was there, the sea was not frozen, but the tides were so great, that in some places it swelled twenty-six fathoms, and fell as much."

A surviving record tells us that the harbor of Reykjavik, the chief port of Iceland, was as Colom said, free of ice that February of 1477. Colom said he sailed "a hundred leagues beyond Iceland." This was more likely to the west than to the north. Colom's statement that "in some places" (obviously not at Reykjavik) there were tides of "twenty-six fathoms," has often been cited as an error on his part. But it could have been a most precise report by waterfront gossip of a region of which Icelanders had heard. The fathom length at that time familiar to Colom was twenty-two and nine-tenths English inches. Twenty-six of such fathoms are forty-eight and six-tenths English feet. On the west side of Ungava Bay in Labrador, where Thomas E. Lee found numerous evidences of Norse settlements, the tides are fifty feet, the highest in the world. The tides in the Bay of Fundy are twenty-eight feet, but get a reputation for being higher than that because in the Minas Basin in Nova Scotia there are several estuaries in which the tides funnel in and the water level rises about fifty feet. Colom picked up in Iceland a correct "twenty-six fathoms" information.

Tall, blond, looking like a Norseman, he was fully accepted in waterfront gatherings at Reykjavik, and he heard waterfront gossip of a vast land that lay to the southwest of Reykjavik — several days' sailing distance from Iceland — a land to which Icelanders said their ancestors had sailed centuries before and which they had named "Vinland." Icelanders knew by heart the sagas (tales) of the voyages to Vinland made by their Viking ancestors, and they repeated those tales for their winter entertainment.

Listening to the talk of mariners in Reykjavik, Colom heard that the shore of the vast land to the southwest of Iceland ran a great deal to the southwest, to a region where there were cities, temples, and knowledge of gold and silver. The Norsemen said this region was farther south than Portugal. Clearly we see it was Mexico. Colom may also have heard it said by some Icelanders that to the south of where there were cities, the coastline of the southwestern land turned back eastward and was the north coast of Africa. This turn of the far land toward the eastward was an idea born in the minds of some Norsemen who had sighted the north coast of Cuba or the north coast of South America.

Colom knew positively that the Norsemen who thought this were mistaken. It could not be. Just recently, only the year before he saved his life by swimming two leagues of ocean, Portuguese ships had succeeded in exploring the west coast of Africa as far as to the equator. All Portugal was full of talk of it.Colom thus knew that those misinformed Icelanders did not know what he knew about Africa.

After he returned from Iceland to Lisbon, he sailed on other extensive voyages in the Atlantic. One of his voyages was to very near the equator, for he piloted a ship or captained a ship to El Mino, the gold mine on the African Gold Coast (now Ghana) where the Portuguese began building Fort St. Jorge in the year 1481. Some historians believe he made two voyages from Lisbon to the African Gold Coast. One was enough to give him opportunity to learn what he did. His sailing to the site of Fort St. Jorge was of necessity by a course that ran far out to westward into the Atlantic to avoid heading into the northward-running current near the African coast, a current which painful experience had taught Portuguese pilots not to buck. Colom's course southward was certainly well off the African coast, far out of sight of land. He later wrote: "I observed carefully the course." He undoubtedly observed that winds blow westward at the latitude of the Canary Islands.

The voyaging Colom did for Portugal in what we call "pre-Columbian" years has significance for us when we see what he learned from it. Keenly observant, in his voyaging in the far north and far south, he acquired a knowledge of ocean currents and prevailing winds' at all latitudes from near the equator, at 4° North to the far north, 64° North, off Iceland. This was knowledge he would someday use. While for the moment he did not foresee its full value, he did not speak of it to others. He had acquired proficiency in keeping secrets. He would not tell anyone except his uncle Bartolomeu what he had learned about the Atlantic Ocean, until there came the time when he could no longer conceal it — until it was unavoidably revealed in 1493.

Most people have thought of Columbus as a discoverer of land. But he was a seaman. Winds and water currents were his primary concern. Sailing in Portuguese ships, he made his unique discovery, his only unique discovery, the discovery at what latitude winds and currents were strong and steady toward the west and could be counted on to car-

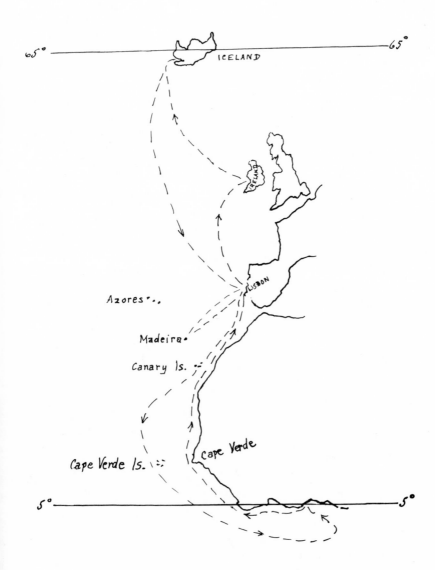

ICELAND

Azores

Madeira

Canary Is.

LISBON

Cape Verde Is.

Cape Verde

65°   65°

5°   5°

Voyages in Atlantic by Columbus previous to 1484

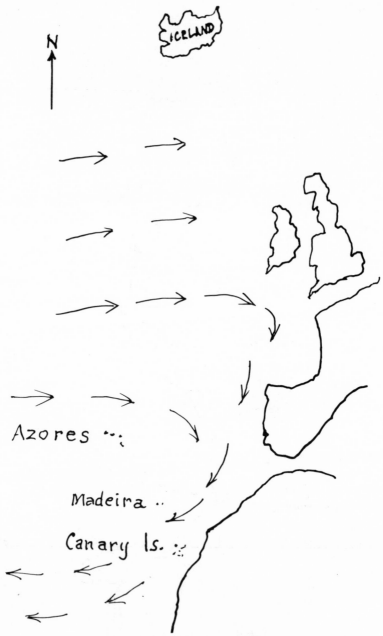

Prevailing winds known by Columbus before 1484

ry a ship across the Atlantic, and at what other latitude winds and currents could be counted on to bring a ship back home. To a landsman this may not seem so important as discovery of land. But it was the vital thing a pilot needed to know, for in his day ships could sail effectively only with a following or what is called a fair wind. Though the Portuguese were beginning to learn to make headway by sailing into the wind, advance in a direction contrary to the wind was too slow and time consuming for an ocean crossing.

In his south-north and north-south sailing in the Atlantic he conquered that ocean mentally long before he conquered it physically in east-west and west-east sailing. His observation of winds and currents gave him a clear grasp of two-way sailing across the Atlantic, and would someday enable him to open the ocean which had been held locked for all but fishermen by fears, superstitions, and ignorance. This priceless knowledge would be his trump card. He would not reveal it to anyone until it had served his purpose a dozen years later.

❀☙☙☙☙☙☙☙☙☙☙☙☙☙☙☙☙☙☙☙☙☙☙☙☙☙☙☙☙☙❀

You say that João Colom had unique knowledge of prevailing winds and currents in the Atlantic Ocean. Surely many Portuguese mariners who had sailed to the Azores and back and to the Canary Islands and back knew the winds and currents as well as he did.

Of course they did.

Then how can you say only Colom knew those winds and currents?

I do not say it. What I say is that he, and no one before him, no one who crossed the Atlantic in ancient times, none of the Vikings, none of his predecessors gave the world the knowledge essential to acceptably brief crossings of that ocean in both directions by ships which could not sail effectively into the wind. I believe fishermen already knew, but they of course weren't telling. The ultimate revealing of that essential knowledge was the unique contribution made by Columbus. That revelation of winds and ocean currents can never be denied to him. It is the basis for fame rightfully and forever his. It is for that he deserves immortal memory.

5

GO WEST
TO THE EAST

When he was not voyaging in the Atlantic, João Colom worked in Lisbon with his uncle Bartolomeu at making and selling maps and charts. Near Bartolomeu's shop was a convent which had belonged to the military order of St. Iago and had sheltered the womenfolk of warriors who had been off somewhere fighting. It had now become a fashionable school for the daughters of the leading Portuguese families. With demure propriety those females had devised a pious way of finding suitors. They invited the public to attend mass in their chapel. Young men who sought God and girls in that chapel were exposed to husband hunters. Whether João Colom went to that chapel to pray, or to see and be seen, he captured the heart of a patrician girl. His face, stalwart figure and good manners won the fancy of Doña Felipe Perestrello e Moniz, whose deceased father, Don Bartolomeu Perestrello, had been captain and governor of Porto Santo, one of the Madeira Islands. On the Moniz side, her mother's side, Doña Felipe was descended from one of the oldest and most respected families in Portugal.

The Colom-Perestrello union was a match of disparate ages. It was like that of Wiliam Shakespeare at 18 marrying Anne Hathaway of age 26, João Colom was 18 or 19. Doña Felipe, who admitted to being at least 25, was probably older than 26. Unusual men seem to find older women more appealing. Or is it that older women are more discerning? Doña Felipe, like Anne Hathaway, appears to have been the more active in the wooing. As Colom's son Ferdinand put it in his biography of his father: "For as much as he behaved himself honorably, and was a man of comely presence and did nothing but what was just, it happened that a lady whose name was Doña Felipe Moniz was so taken with him that she became his wife."

Samuel Eliot Morison in *Admiral of the Ocean Sea,* in ardent combat against anything which makes his biographical concept of Columbus unconvincing, yet finding himself forced to recognize the inconsistency in his picturing of Columbus, says: "To some writers this marriage appears to be a great mystery. How could a foreign chartmaker of low birth marry into one of the noble families of the kingdom?"[1] Morison makes no attempt to answer his own question, for the very good reason that with acceptance of Genoese peasant origin of Columbus, he could find no answer to it.

We now know what it was in João Colom that captivated the aristocrat, Doña Felipe. It was his patrician appearance, tall, red-headed, blue eyed, with cheeks somewhat full yet neither fat nor lean. It was also his obvious breeding which matched his princely quality — his moderation in eating and drinking, his being always exemplary in his dress, unusual in every way, among strangers affable, without presumption quietly forceful in speaking to servants and underlings. He was not alarmingly book learned. He spoke with commanding voice, and acted with modesty and easy gravity. Doña Felipe sensed in him something beyond what other men of her acquaintance had — a capacity for achievement, as though he had been selected by deity for a great purpose, and had inklings of it — a man who would someday write: "God hath given me a genius . . . . He hath given me the spirit of understanding." Above all else, what won Doña Felipe's heart was the imperial quality of the young man, his magnificent carriage, regal traits, and unmistakable nobility.[2]

For a brief time the married couple resided in Lisbon with Doña Felipe's mother. She heartily approved of him as a husband for her daughter, and she gave him the journals and sea charts which had belonged to her husband. Then Colom and his wife went nearly 200 leagues far out into the ocean to dwell on the island of Porto Santo in the Madeiras, in the house which had been her father's.

On that island less than three leagues (less than 10 miles) long and only one league (less than 3 miles) wide, João Colom soon knew, or was known by, all its inhabitants. He could not expect anything of great importance to happen on so small and remote an island, but he was for a while contented to live there quietly with his wife who was pregnant. He of course was in touch with the ship captains who entered the harbor, and with merchants who came to the island to buy sugar and wine. Sailors and traders kept him informed of events in the mainland countries. From them he heard that King Juan II of Aragon had died. To himself he must have said, my unsaintly grandfather has reaped his heavenly reward. And that ugly second son of his, that foul Ferdinand, has become King Ferdinand, King Ferdinand II, King of Aragon. João Colom was deeply stabbed with resentment that the second son of King Juan was on the throne which had rightfully belonged to Prince Carlos. If it hadn't been for the wicked ambition of that Juana Enriquez who was now Queen Juana!

While King Juan II had been failing, the Prince Ferdinand from the age of twenty-two had been active ruler of Aragon. For five years his wife Isabel had been Queen of Leon and Castile. The two of them together were now masters of all Spain except the southern part, that Vandal land, Vandalusia, or Andalusia, as it was now being called.

It was emotionally easier for João Colom to be on a Portuguese island far away, 200 leagues away from Cabo Santo Vicente, the nearest point of Portugal, and farther than that from the nearest point of Spain. He was well away from mainland troubles caused by royal ambitions. He felt permanently removed from Spain and all its affairs. Better so for his peace of mind. But he could not avoid thinking often of the Kingdom of Navarre which King Ferdinand would no doubt someday acquire.

Dwelling in the house where his wife's father had resided as Governor of Porto Santo, he acquired direct acquaintance with Portuguese voyagings from the former governor's journals and charts which his wife's mother had given him. From them he obtained intimate knowledge of some of the discoveries which the Portuguese did not want anyone outside of Portugal to know about.

On the small island there seemed little promise that any event would occur which would change the even tenor of João Colom's life or stir him to great action. But his wife, with patrician push, wanted him to be at least as knowledgeable and as prominent as her father had been and as her brother now was. She no doubt often reminded him that her father had been Governor of Porto Santo, and that her brother was now Governor of Madeira, a much larger island. João of course wanted his wife to think him as capable a man as her father had been, and as her brother was, and as he felt himself to be. He no doubt welcomed the dream she stirred in him, the innocent and permissible dream of becoming the governor of an island, a larger island than Porto Santo, larger than Madeira, hopefully as large as the Kingdom of Navarre. Whether she knew or did not know that he had been a privateer who had fought in a naval battle against Castile and Aragon, his daring spirit and strong body and length of arm promised him leadership. But now at age twenty he had the responsibility of parenthood, for his wife gave birth to their son Diego in 1480. And in that year he heard that Queen Isabel and King Ferdinand had begun a war to wipe out the last remaining infidel strongholds in Andalusia, where the Muslims were still powerfully entrenched.

The next year, late in the sailing season, a ship with no member of her crew standing visible, drew slowly into the harbor of Porto Santo. She barely made it. To shore observers, she seemed to have no able-bodied sailor on board. Her coming, since it would shape João Colom's career, was an event which would through him affect the history of the world.

She had on board only her captain and four men of the crew. They were sick, too feeble to rise to their feet. They were in a pitiable state. The moment João Colom saw their condition, he knew they had been too many days without sighting land, too many days without fresh water and fresh provisions. They were sick with the too-long-voyage disease, what we now call scurvy. Obviously, they had been out of sight of land for more than six weeks.

The captain and crew were Spaniards. Their coming to Porto Santo showed them to be far off course. The home port of their ship was Huelva, a fishing port in western Spain. How and why had they come to a Portuguese island? Where had they been? When they began to fall sick, why did they not sail directly to their home port? Why had they come to Porto Santo? As João Colom estimated it, they were four degrees of latitude south of where they ought to be. They must have been storm-driven.

The captain said he had been trying to make it home to Huelva. He spoke in Spanish, and João Colom conversed with him in that language. The captain said he had been delayed by head winds, and unable to make it home at the latitude that would bring him there. His illness had been intensified by anxiety. He was too ill to talk much. João Colom and his wife took him into their house, intending to nurse him back to health. He was too far gone to be saved. He died in their house.

He did, however, write an account of his voyaging, and with some rambling and much verbosity, what he wrote tells the tale:

Alonso Sánchez Master of the caravel which God save which has for its name *Atlante,* I, with great respect for the grace of Your Highnesses and impelled by the great goodwill and relish with which I hold to your service, and understanding that Your Highnesses find much pleasure in knowing that which is hidden to others, it occurs to me to tell of the lands now found by me in this journey and voyage which with the aid of God and the glorious Saint Mary Our Lady I made through the ocean, and the magnitude of the realms and provinces and cities which were seen and the multitude of people with their laws and doctrines, and customs and tribes which are found in yonder regions. But I declare that my intention is not to write anything which I did not see and did not know for sure of the many marvelous things I saw, and so many and such other things which no Christian had seen, keeping separate that which I know from having seen with my own eyes, from that which I did not, and what I did not know for sure of information of those natives in such manner that this report will be always held to be accurate and true. The which, if it be God's will, it is my intention to place before Your Highnesses, humbly requesting that you receive it in your royal hands, and if I can not, to send it by one of my men already instructed for it. But if the will of God Our Lord is that by neither in one or the other manner, that my intention has been achieved, I beg and entreat and demand of the person to whom the said narrative and testimony comes, that he should execute this my will to serve Your Highnesses, and make it get into your

45

illustrious hands.

For I, my worthy lords, through certain conversations and discussions which I had with men who are acquainted with cosmography and the terrestrial sphere and the art of navigation and especially with Martin Alonso Pinzón my friend and fellow townsman, who is well versed in regard to things of the ocean, as well as in things which touch upon the war, such as the traffic of merchandise, on May 15th of the year of Our Lord 1481, I departed from my native town of Huelva in my said nao with 16 men of crew all native to that coast, searching, by way of the West in the ocean sea, guided according to the reasonings referred to above and looking here and there for the provinces of the Indies and the Ganges of which the noble Venetian man Marco Polo told in his book which tells of marvelous things which he saw in those areas of the East, where at the end of many days' sailing and without altering course, it was God's will that we should hit upon an island the Indian natives of which call Quisqueya which in their language means Great Land, taking possession of it in the name of Your Highnesses and moreover erecting on an elevated and unobstructed place on the said island a great cross sign of our redemption and of the holy faith which Your Highnesses so zealously defend in all your conquests in the lands of infidels and pagans.

And since in the recounting my narrative more largely comprises the site of the first discovery of the said land, I will now say that according to measurements of the terrestrial globe it is situated just at the farthest end of the ocean to the west with an infinite number of islands of which previously there has been no telling in the books of the cosmographers which treat of the ocean.

And the said island is rich in gold and silver and all commodities which are called spices, and there is a luxurious growth of vegetation so lush that there is no tree there which is not fragrant and fruitful and of great benefit, for none of them lets its leaves fall in all the year, and there is no piece of land which is fruitless. On the contrary all bear fruit, without any of them useless.

And likewise it appears from what came from the tongues of the native Indians of these said islands, that further on in the direction of West is a continent at a considerable distance and difficult to be reached which without doubt is Cipango [Japan] or Cathay [China], whose natives have a color tending toward black, and who for a long time have assaulted and plundered the Indians of the said Quisqueya, who are of a nature very peaceful.

And since all are a people and population living in darkness and blindness of the true faith and are even more blinded by wallowing in so much filth and beastly customs such as cannot be stated, Your Highnesses with your godly hearts and human affections can put a stop to it by providing that the true God be proclaimed to these people, because up to now they do not know it living in places so distant and remote from Christians, by sending to them messengers to bring to them the true Catholic faith, since they are ripe wheat ready for missionaries who will reap it.

Our Lord preserve and promote the persons and estates of Your Highnesses.

Humbly kissing the hands of Your Highnesses your liege,

Alonso Sánchez of Huelva.

The narrative in the handwriting of Alonso Sánchez and with his signature, is on parchment ("pergamino").[3] Several facts seem to indicate that Alonso Sánchez wrote it on his death bed. It seems unlikely that he would have carried a large parchment on his voyage in anticipation of what he would write. João Colom, map maker in association with his uncle Bartolomeu, undoubtedly had parchments in his house on Porto Santo. If Alonso Sánchez had written the manuscript at sea, he presumably would have begun it with his narrative, instead of making the first third of it what it was. Because he put into the first paragraph what he hoped personally to do with the manuscript and that he had instructed one of his crew to do it if he could not, and if neither he nor a member of his crew could do it, he wanted whoever had the manuscript to carry out his intention, we may reasonably assume that he wrote the manuscript while ill and dying in Colom's house, and while he was apprehensive of the probable deaths of the surviving members of his crew.

João Colom was probably the only person in Porto Santo who learned all the facts of the Atlantic crossing, for he may have been the only one there who conversed with the dying captain. The parchment manuscript of Alonso Sánchez was as he requested, carried to Huelva, presumably by a member of the crew. It was addressed to Their Majesties. Since Alonso Sánchez was deceased when the manuscript came to them, his family naturally wished to keep the original with his signature as a momento, a family heirloom. Obeying the behest of Alonso Sánchez, they no doubt sent a copy to the Court of Castile.

Queen Isabel was engrossed with the many immediate problems of the war against the Muslims, and an account of an ocean voyage would at that time have seemed to her of minor or not pressing importance. The long-windedness of the first third of the manuscript would have made her impatient to reading or listening to the reading of the rest of it. She would have filed it away with other documents, and she may have all but forgotten it until, some five years later, she was reminded of it by a project which was then laid before her.

The original document was recently uncovered by Manuel Lopez Flores in the house of a descendant of its writer.[4]

Rumors of the Alonso Sánchez voyage leaked out in the fifteenth century shipping circles. The writer, the Inca, Laso de la Vega, thought the large island Alonso Sánchez had visited on the western side of the Atlantic was the one "now called Santo Domingo." He gave as date for the Alonso Sánchez crossing, "in or about 1484."[5] Vague knowledge of it persisted through the centuries. Because the event was definitely recorded in writing and dated, some historians who knew nothing of crossings by fishermen but accepted the fact of the Alonso Sánchez crossing, expressed the opinion that Alonso Sánchez was the first discoverer of the New World, and should be so credited, with denial to Columbus.[6] Some who have assumed that Columbus stole from it the idea of going west to the Far East, have said that its existence makes Columbus a despicable fraud. In 1924 the opinion was expressed that the big island Alonso Sánchez had visited was Haiti.[7] This is probably correct, since the inhabitants of that large island were not cannibals, but were being raided by cannibals, as were the natives of Haiti, who, as we know, were being frequently attacked by cannibals from the island now called Puerto Rico.

The Alonso Sánchez manuscript was recently published. A photostat copy of it with Spanish text printed, is now available.[8]

Historians of ships of sail tell us topsails first appeared in the 15th century. They will be interested to observe that the drawing of his ship *Atlante,* which Alonso Sánchez placed below his signature, has a topsail.

His manuscript did not clearly state what first gave him the idea of attempting the ocean crossing. His purposes were buried in verbosity and prolixity.

From his knowledge of Atlantic Ocean winds and currents, João Colom assumed, even if Alonso Sánchez did not tell him, that the westbound crossing must have been in the latitude of the Canary Islands.

Signature of Alonso Sánchez of Huelva with his drawing of his ship *Atlante*

The manuscript did not tell how many leagues westward the crossing had been. If that information was not given either by the dying captain or by members of his crew, it was nevertheless obvious to Colom that it had taken less than 40 days. If it had taken more than that, Alonso Sánchez and all his men would have been sick and dying when they reached the islands which Alonso Sánchez called the "Indies". From the fact that the westbound crossing had been successfully accomplished, Colom could make a fairly close estimate of the distance in leagues. This knowledge was startling. The islands of the Indies, at the eastern end of Asia, were within sailing distance from Portugal! It was possible to go west to the East!

Since the people of the islands of the Indies were living in a primitive state of nature, without what Europeans would call decent civilization, but with bestial habits, going naked, and without effective weapons, it was obvious that Christians who came to them with gunpowder and matchlock weapons could set up a strong government for their betterment. If he himself could do that, João Colom would please his wife Felipe.

Knowing as he did the latitudes of prevailing east and west winds and currents in the Atlantic, he knew he would be able to make his homeward crossing of the ocean speedily enough to avoid scurvy.

The more he thought about it, the more clearly he saw what a great opportunity had been opened to him by the voyage of Alonso Sánchez. And he clearly perceived a most effective argument he could use to his advantage. Alonso Sánchez had said that the natives of the Indies were without true religion. João Colom would say that a crossing of the ocean would open the way to carrying Christian salvation to the Far East, to all the pagans. This would in itself be something worth doing. To accomplish it, he would need to have with him enough men to establish him as governor of their large island. He would require more than one ship. He would need at least three ships.

Such a project as he began to envision would require royal backing, since no one except a monarch could establish him in the government of the island. He must therefore have a contract with the king of Portugal. The contract must guarantee him the governorship. He thrilled to the thought of how he might achieve status approaching that which had been denied to his father by the parents of that King Ferdinand of Aragon, who was now obviously planning to seize the throne of Navarre. João Colom was swept by a dream of compensating for what his father should have had. He would ask in his contract with the King of Portugal that his governorship be hereditary, so that his infant son Diego and his heirs forever would inherit it. This he would insist upon.

The possibility of sailing westward to the Far East seemed to him to be a new idea, until he learned that it was not new. Six years earlier, before he himself swam to the shore of Portugal, and while he was active as a privateer, the idea that the Atlantic was not too wide to be crossed had been expressed by a man who also said that on the western side of the Atlantic lay the islands of the Indies. And the old man had given that idea to an acquaintance of his in Portugal. It might be that Alonso Sánchez of Huelva in Spain had gotten the idea from the same source. The idea was in the air.

The idea, so far as records show, was born in the mind of an old man in Italy, in Florence, in an inland city, of all places. Here is how:

Luxury goods from Asia had for centuries been brought on camels overland to the eastern end of the Mediterranean, or by Arab ships through the Red Sea and thence overland to Cairo. Italian ships had carried them to markets in western Europe — silks, drugs, perfumes, jewels, glass, porcelain, and the costly spices, ginger, cinnamon, nutmeg, and cloves.

The capture of Constantinople by the Turks in 1453 had hurt Italian shippers, for there was no more direct contact between Italians and overland carriers of goods from Asia. Turks clamped an excessive tax on all the goods, and everything that passed through Egypt was taxed to one-third of its value. Italian seaport cities suffered greatly. Venice, Genoa and Pisa were forced into cutthroat rivalry, and made disastrous wars on each other. Meanwhile Florence forged ahead of the seaports. She not only had a monopoly of the wool industry, but being inland, was safe from coastal attacks, and so money deposited in her banks had maximum security. In consequence she had eighty banking houses which controlled the business of Europe. Having become the safest and wealthiest city, Florence offered encouragement to every sort of talent. Progressive ideas flourished within her walls.

One of the Florentines was the active-minded Paolo Toscanelli. He was the most advanced thinker of his time in the field of the physical sciences. He was a seeker of reality through research, and was never content with mere theories. He became interested in the information brought home from Asia in the thirteenth century by Marco Polo. While many questioned most of the things Marco Polo told, there was nothing suspect about his telling of the existence of the island country of Japan (Cipangu), which he said was to the east of the coast of China (Cathay, the Kingdom of Kubla Khan). Also, nobody questioned, and it was universally accepted that from the coast of China, Marco Polo had voyaged via the islands of the Indies and all the way to Persia, on which voyage he had conveyed from China some noblemen and a Mongol princess given by Kubla Khan as a bride for the Persian Khan. It was thus held to be a fact that there was a sea passage from the coast of China to India and Persia. To make this passage, the Ptolemy geography showed, one had to turn a cape from the ocean off the coast of China to get into the Indian Ocean. That cape was called Catigara. Ptolemy placed Catigara at 180 degrees east of Cadiz, half-way around the earth from Cadiz, and at 8½ degrees South.

With this sea passage in mind, Toscanelli thought of a way by which ships from western Europe could sail not only to India, but beyond India to China. Through some Portuguese ambassadors, he gave the idea to Prince Henry of Portugal, the idea of sending ships southward along the western coast of Africa to get around the southern end of that continent and so into the Indian Ocean. Prince Henry initiated the Portuguese attempts to carry out Toscanelli's idea, and in so doing was called Prince Henry the Navigator. He sent explorers who pushed down the west African coast and by 1470-71 reached as far as the equator.

Some time after this Toscanelli conceived what seemed to him a better idea. Previously, the only direction to journey from Italy to China had been held to be that which Marco Polo had taken — to the East. But on the surface of a sphere there are other directions from Italy to

China — northward across the Arctic, or southward across the Antarctic, or westward across the Atlantic Ocean. Several years previous to the Alonso Sánchez crossing, Toscanelli expressed the go-west idea to Fernando Martinez, a friend of his in Portugal. Colom now heard of Toscanelli's new idea. He later said that he wrote to Toscanelli, asking his reasons for believing it was possible to sail westward as far as to the Indies across the Atlantic, and that the aged Florentine savant had replied directly to him by sending him a "navigator's chart" of the Atlantic Ocean, and copies of his letters to Martinez which contained these words:

> There is a very short route from here to the Indies by way of the ocean, a route which I estimate to be shorter than that which you seek to find by way of Guinea [African coast]. While the route has never been followed, it is not very far across the ocean.

It is barely possible, but unlikely that Colom received the map and letters directly from Toscanelli, since Toscanelli died in 1482, the year after the Alonso Sánchez voyage. It has been charged that Colom copied the Toscanelli letters to Fernando Martinez and forged the accompanying notes to himself. Whether or not he did this, we can only surmise. We know he treasured those documents for the rest of his life.

It is very likely that the idea of crossing the Atlantic to Asia which motivated the voyage of Alonso Sánchez of Huelva came indirectly from Toscanelli.

Toscanelli gave Fernando Martinez the idea of going west to the East before Colom had it. Colom now saw that Alonso Sánchez had showed that it could be done.

Details of Toscanelli's navigator's chart of the Atlantic were borrowed by Martin Behaim in making his globe. Thus we know that on Toscanelli's chart the ocean appeared to be very narrow. Since the Azores were shown on it, and since the distance from Portugal to the western-most of the Azores was known — about 1200 miles — the distance from Portugal to islands near Cipangu (Japan) on Toscanelli's chart appeared to be no more than about 2500 miles. Obviously, Toscanelli thought it was something less than 3,000 miles from Portugal to Japan.

Behaim's Globe of 1492 shows the Cape of Catigara below the word

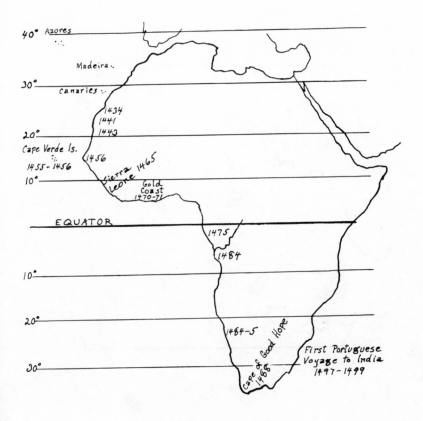

African Coast with dates of discoveries

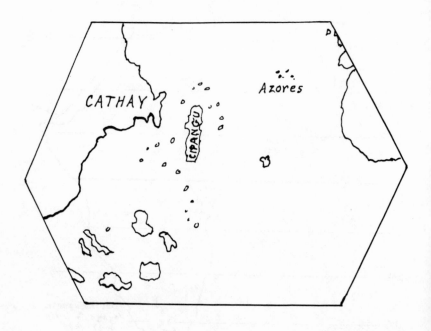

Toscanelli's Map, 1474

"INDIA." Thus, as indicated on the map, the distance from Portugal to Japan (Cipangu) off the coast of China (Cathay) seemed to Colom to be corroborative of what he had heard in Iceland of the distance to a new land the Icelanders called Vinland, with a great island (Newfoundland) off its coast.

❀ ⅍ ❀

Didn't most people in the days of Columbus believe the earth was flat?

No.

The ancients did.

Not the educated. Egyptian priests and Greek astronomers knew it was a sphere.

But in the days of Columbus, weren't sailors afraid of sailing off the edge?

Nonsense! A landsman's concept. Silly to sailors who had observed ship hulls down below the horizon.

How about the clergy?

The Christian Church in the eighth century officially accepted the concept of our planet as a globe.

You think Alonso Sánchez and Colom believed the Far East was just across the Atlantic Ocean?

Absolutely.

Why so sure?

Didn't they want to believe it?

Yes.

Then they did believe it.

How does that follow?

People believe what they want to believe.

Then why write history?

That's the perfect question.

6

GLOBE SHRINKER

Colom had become well acquainted with Portuguese plans and hopes. He knew of the many attempts the Portuguese had made to get around the southern end of Africa. This goal had been persistently pursued by Prince Henry the Navigator until his death in the year in which Joao Colom was born. Perceiving the wealth that would come to them if they succeeded in rounding Africa, but fearful lest other countries beat them to it, the Portuguese had become increasingly secretive as to how far down the west coast of Africa they had been able to explore. Being fearful that Spain or France might take over their project, they had made it illegal to export from Portugal any chart or map. They tried to keep other countries from knowing what they knew.

They were continuing their efforts at exploring, but against seemingly insuperable obstacles. All the way down the west coat of Africa head-winds and a current running northward had stymied their advance. With ships unable to sail effectively into the wind, and not at all against such a strong current, they had for half a century been defeated. It had taken them nine years, from 1475 to 1484, to explore some mere five degrees of latitude in the region of the Congo River. Eventually, they discovered that by sailing far out to the west into the South Atlantic they would have winds and currents to carry them south to the latitude of the southern end of Africa, and then east. After they discovered these South Atlantic currents and prevailing winds, they advanced their ex-plorations southward by 20 degrees of latitude in the one year thereafter. At the time Colom married, their achievements had not yet caught up with their hopes.

One of the most revealing facts in relation to the Portuguese project is that when they finally did sail around into the Indian Ocean, it was without having sighted the coast of Africa, since they rounded the southern end of that continent far to the south of it.

Colom learned all he could of Portuguese intentions. He acquired much information which his uncle Bartolomeo could use in making charts to be offered for sale in the shop in Lisbon.

To Colom's mind, the new idea of sailing west to the East seemed to be preferable to the rounding Africa route. But the Portuguese were not having it. Now confident of finally carrying out the plan of their Prince Henry, they were in no mood to pay attention to the idea of any other route. Colom, with his knowledge of prevailing westward and eastward winds and currents in the Atlantic, thought he saw an opportunity of changing the thinking of the Portuguese. He set himself that task. But no one seemed ready to listen to him when he said that the Atlantic Ocean could be crossed. Everyone said the distance across was too great. Or, same objection, it would take too long to make the crossing.

A fact of absolute and inescapable importance to every mariner was that forty days were the extreme limit for any voyage that did not touch land.

Before the days of refrigeration, food in the hold of a ship in warm latitudes would spoil quickly, and so the distance one could sail in such latitudes without putting into port for fresh provisions was limited by the number of days food on board could be preserved before it rotted. In cold northern latitudes food would remain edible for a much longer time, and this is one reason why Norsemen had frequently succeeded in crossing the North Atlantic. At the latitude of the Mediterranean, as every sailor knew, after forty days, water in the ship's casks would be undrinkable. It would have turned the color of ink and become thick with wriggly creatures. Without fresh vegetables and fruit juices, the necessity of which no one understood, sailors on a voyage of more than six weeks got sick with scurvy and would soon die. Almost everyone, except for a man like Toscanelli, believed the distance westward to China was much too great for any ship to succeed in crossing. And not only the distance. The weather at sea could never be counted on. Being becalmed for a long period could be more fatal than riding through storms.

What the distance across the Atlantic was no one knew. It depended, of course, on the size of the earth — its circumference, The best opinion, that of the most learned, and respected cosmographers, was that the distance across the Atlantic Ocean was at least three times as far as sailors could hope to voyage without putting into port at some island to replenish water and food.

Toscanelli's assertion that the distance across the ocean was "very short" showed his awareness of the adverse opinions of most of his contemporaries. It also showed why he put confidence in Ptolemy, for Ptolemy's estimate of the circumference of the earth was smaller than than that of any other geographer. His estimate was five thousand miles less than that of Alfragano, a thirteenth-century geographer of high-repute, and about six thousand miles less than that of the fifteenth-century Regiomontano, whose estimate many scholars were beginning to prefer. Ptolemy's estimate was 22,500 Roman miles, which were 20,710 English miles. The actual circumference, according to modern science, is 24,902 English miles.

Even with Ptolemy's small estimate, the practical objection to Toscanelli's idea remained. Its opponents said that from Cadiz to Cape Catigara was more than ten thousand miles, and would require a passage by sailing ship of at least three or four months. Only if there were islands less than a month's sailing distance apart from each other, so that a ship could put into port for fresh water and fresh food before every member of her crew had sickened and died, the ship might eventually reach Cathay. Perhaps the island of Cipangu (Japan) would be the one that would serve. From Cathay, of course, the ship could follow the Asian coast to India. This seemed to be the only room for hope. But were there such islands? Would anyone ever find out?

Colom did not have to be laughed at more than once to realize the need for arguments to convince people that the Atlantic Ocean was narrow enough for him to sail across it. He began building his case. One of the wisest remarks ever uttered was made by Julius Ceasar:"Men believe what they hope." This was precisely the way it was with Colom. He hoped the earth was smaller than other men thought, and he began to believe it was as small as he hoped it was. He could not be satisfied with Ptolemy. Ptolemy allowed 62½ Roman miles to a degree, but Colom, by reducing the size of a degree to 56⅔ Roman miles, lopped off two thousand miles from Ptolemy's estimate of the circumference, and thus shrank the globe down to fit his argument. He announced as his estimate of the earth's circumference 20,400 Roman miles, which were 18,777 English miles. With Ptolemy's overextension of Asia eastward, and a bit further overextension in Colom's mind, the distance westward from Portugal to China would be little more than three thousand miles. This distance suited Colom perfectly.

We now see what it meant to him when he recalled that Icelanders had convinced him, as years later he told his son they had, that the distance to the land southwest of Iceland was very likely what they computed it to be, based upon what they asserted were the few days sailing their ancestors had required to reach it. If the earth was as small as Colom said, then the land which the Icelanders had told him about, the land which by both Icelander and Colom estimate was about three thousand miles west of Portugal — that land must be Cathay (China), and the large island which they said was off its coast must be Cipangu (Japan).

To convince people that he could reach Asia by sailing west, Colom, *had* to argue that the Atlantic was no more than about three thousand miles wide. He therefore combed through ancient authors searching for evidence to support his claim that the ocean was only that wide, and he became fond of quoting from Aristotle: "The earth is not only round; it is also not very large." In a book written in the fourth century B.C. by one of Aristotle's followers and entitled *On Marvelous Things Heard,* Colom found a story which in ancient times had gone the rounds of the waterfront in the Mediterranean:

> In the sea outside the Pillars of Hercules they say that an island
> was found by the Carthaginians, a wilderness having wood of all kinds
> and navigable rivers, remarkable for various kinds of fruits, and many
> days' sailing distance away.

The "many days' sailing" had not been too many. It appeared that the Carthaginians who had discovered the island had been residents of Cadiz. Cadiz had been founded by Carthaginians, descendants of whom lived there and still do. Colom heard the "definite tradition among the Carthaginians or Phoenicians of Cadiz" that some of their ancestors at about the time of the Battle of Leutrac (371 B.C.), had crossed the Atlantic Ocean to the land in the West. To Colom, the sailing direction they were said to have followed was significant and corroborative: "The course between the setting sun [the West] and the meridian [direction of the sun at noon]" — or in other words, between West and South. Colom's knowledge of Atlantic currents and prevailing winds had told him that this was the course he would take were he ever to attempt to cross the ocean.

Because he wanted his project to appear unique, "a task to which the powers of mortal man had never hitherto attained," he dismissed ancient reports of Atlantic crossings as "little else than fables." But the stories told by the ancients showed the passage Colom found in Seneca's play *Medea,* and which he began to quote as mystical prophecy of his own project, was a reasonable conclusion based upon what Seneca had heard:

> In years long since there will come a generation for whom the Ocean may
> loosen the chains of conditions, a vast region may be accessible, and a navi-
> gator may discover new worlds, and Thule [Iceland] will no longer be the
> land farthest away.

Now that he was committed to the idea Toscanelli had given him, he wrote again, or said he wrote again, to Toscanelli, who replied: "I note your noble and ardent desire to go to the countries of the Far East by way of the Western Ocean, which is indicated upon the map I sent you."

Colom would use as potent arguments the letters and map which he said Toscanelli had sent him.

He had plenty of time for reading. Some years later he acquired a copy of an Italian translation of Pliny's *Natural History*. Marginal notes in his handwriting dated 1481 and "in hoc anno '88" in a copy he owned of Pierre d'Ailly's *Imago Mundi*, indicate that he had the 1480 edition of this book. From it he quoted: "The length of the land toward the Orient is much greater than Ptolemy admits." Also, "According to the philosophers and Pliny, the ocean which stretches between the extremity of further Spain and the eastern end of India is of no great width. For it is evident that this sea is navigable in a very few days if the wind be fair. From this it follows that the sea is not so great that it can cover three-quarters of the globe as some people believe." In Latin, "Spain" would be "Hispania" which would mean the Hispanic Peninsula and would thus include Portugal.

João Colom met and talked with mariners and merchants who came to Porto Santo. A year or two later he moved to the much larger island, Madeira, where his wife's brother was Captain and Governor. Madeira is 35 miles long and 13 miles wide. On that island he met many merchants and sailors. Among them was one who became his friend, an Italian Merchant from Genoa, who had come to Madeira to buy sugar for a firm in Lisbon. This man was called in Portuguese Cristovão Colom. His name in Italian was Cristoforo Colombo.

News came of the death of Paolo Toscanelli in 1482 at age of 85.

Because of rising prejudice against Jews and converts, João Colom strengthened his position as one who had not only been thoroughly converted, but was with complete sincerity a devout Christian. At Porto Santo the Franciscans had a friary. Franciscans also resided at Funchal, the then capital of Madeira. St. Francis had left a message of love rather than hatred. Everyone knew how he had talked to birds and was kind to the poor. João Colom became a Franciscan tertiary.

Alonso Sánchez of Huelva had applied to the natives of the islands he had visited the term "Indians." From this, João Colom got his great idea, his dream of world-stirring achievement. He began to formulate a project and he called it "The Enterprise of the Indies."

His efforts became unceasingly expanded in attempting to persuade influential people that the distance westward to Cipangu and Cathay was not too great. To answer their objections he had to conjure up a convenient island not too far to the west, where, after reprovisioning, he could from it soon reach the Ganges River of India.

He was an eloquent talker. With firm voice he held attention. When he talked, his listeners were compelled to listen to his every word. He glowed with the enthusiasm of youth, with the conviction that he was right. He was most compelling when he asserted that anyone who did not agree with him was ignorant of the facts. He reminded his listeners that he was a practical seaman of wide experience, and that they were not. Vigorous, constantly alert, he presented his arguments pungently. A recognized aristocrat, he spoke always with a certain elevation, as from above. He communicated the feeling of loftiness which he inwardly possessed and outwardly displayed by stature and facial features. There was in him much of the fanatic, and the fervor of an evangelist. Those who controverted him found him entertaining. He was a great debater. He was always sensational, a passionate salesman of his ideas. Everyone who heard him fell under his spell.

He assembled many reasons, all he could scrape together, for his belief that he could cross the Atlantic to Asia and return to tell about it. He cited various evidences to show that there was land not too far to the West. He said that when he was at Galway, he saw the bodies of a man and a woman washed ashore in two drifting boats. Their corpses showed them flat-faced, different from any Europeans. At Flores in the Azores the bodies of two men had been washed up, "Very broad-faced and differing in aspect from Christians."* He said that Martin Vincente, a Portuguese pilot, told him that four hundred and fifty leagues to the west of Cape St. Vincent he had picked out of the sea a piece of wood of an unknown kind that had been carved by human hands. Pedro Correa, Colom's own brother-in-law, had found a similar piece of wood at Porto Santo. Colom described it as a hollow cane large enough between any two joints to hold four quarts of wine. No such canes grew in Europe.

A one-eyed sailor in the port of Santa Maria in the Azores had told Colom that on a voyage he had made to Ireland he saw land to the west,

---

* Statements made by Columbus are accepted without question by historians, and in this biography need no Source Notes.

which at that time he supposed to be part of Tartary (Asia); that it turned westward; but that foul weather (Bank of Newfoundland fog?) prevented them from approaching it. Also Pedro de Velasco, a Galician, had told Colom that on a voyage to Ireland they sailed so far northwest that they saw land to the west of Ireland.

Colom argued that Portugal should support the Enterprise of the Indies because it would enable Christians in Europe to join forces with the Christians in Asia, so that together they could rescue the Holy Land from the Muslims.

Each additional bit of evidence he collected strengthened his conviction that he was right, for as Aristotle had said: "If a proposition be true, all the facts harmonize with it." He remembered that Aristotle had said: "Greatness of soul must be concerned with one object especially." He concentrated all his thinking on his project. And he quoted further from the *Ethics* his father had translated: "Only a man of inferior quality will pretend to be more than he really is." It suited him well that Aristotle had also said: "Modesty cannot be described as a virtue."

Coupled with determination to be princely like his father, was his strictness in religious matters. He was a devout churchman, but also something of a mystic who would put pen to his innermost consciousness in these words: "Our Lord hath sensibly opened my understanding to the end I may sail from hence to all the Indies." He always placed a Christian cross at the top of each page he wrote, but while his father's religion meant more to him than his mother's, he did not withhold what comfort he could give to Jewish correspondents. Photostat copies of his many surviving letters show that he began some of them with two lightly penciled letters "b" and "h", standing for the Hebrew words "baruch hashem", meaning "Praised be the Lord." These were a greeting with which one Jew religiously greeted another. Thus the evidence is that to help achieve his great ambition, Colom made a profitable use of the two religions.

At the age of 23, he believed he had arguments sufficient to convince the king of Portugal. He would ask for an interview and present his project and ask the king to drop the costly efforts to get around Africa, efforts in which Portugal was wasting time and money. That first idea of Toscanelli, which had become the beautiful dream of Pince Henry the Navigator, should be abandoned forthwith. Colom believed it would be when he told his Majesty of the much shorter route westward to Asia.

Having built up his case with the eagerness of youth, he asked for an interview with King João II. To his surprise, his request was not granted. Nothing daunted, he turned to influential friends and got them to urge the Court to give ear to him. It was thus that he eventually was granted an interview, late in the year 1484.

King João had been on the throne for only three years, but he was far more experienced in political affairs and business matters than Colom realized. During the last years of the reign of his father King Alfonso V, he had administered the kingdom, and had directly supervised the continuing exploration of the coast of Africa. Portugal had wasted energy in a vain attempt to occupy uninhabited desert in Morocco, but she had profited when she had occupied Porto Santo in 1418 and Madeira in 1419. These islands were producing sugar, an important article of trade with the countries of Europe. The Portuguese had sighted the Azores in 1427. By 1445, gold dust and Negro slaves from Africa had made the uncompleted explorations of that continent very profitable. King Alonso V had been so devoted to those explorations that he had been dubbed "the African." Portugal was not living entirely in a dream of the future. She was already enjoying great prosperity. Business in Lisbon was most thriving and promising.

Against these considerations, Colom hoped to persuade King João to relinquish, or at least defer the rounding of Africa in favor of what he believed would be more profitable, a western route to India. He knew he would be swimming against the current. He set himself a tremendous task of persuasion, for it was a period in time when almost everyone clung to the past, held fast to accepted doctrines and age-old notions, frowned on any deviation, and feared new truth. So be it! He would oppose everybody. He would dare assert that all were in error if they did not agree with him.

What nerve Colom must have had!

Self-assurance.

Such audacity, proposing to face a king and contradict the scholars!

Youth versus established authority.

Without opportunity of becoming a scholar, it is obvious he respected books.

Like his father. Prince Carlos was a reader and dreamer. This, combined with the practical business sense of his Uncle Bartolomeo, made João Colom a blend of visionary and man of action.

I've been impressed by the experiences that shaped him.

Tell me how you see them.

First, as a Jew in a Christian majority. Then, as son of a Christian father, a dissident among Jews. Then as privateer fighting against Castile and Aragon. Then what he learned in Iceland and from Alonso Sánchez of land to the west.

His self-selected readings confirmed his opinion.

Do you suppose he was worried lest the Alonso Sánchez voyage become known?

No, because the manuscript of Alonso Sánchez was in Spain.

You mean — ?

If the voyage of Alonso Sánchez became known, Colom would have the better argument. He would play on the Portuguese desire to rival the Spanish.

7

DECISIONS
IN PORTUGAL

Himself a young man, though at least five years older than Colom, King João had shoulders that bore a wise head. He was a master at politics, as a king should be. Perhaps his main quality was caution. He was firm and calculating, and extremely sensitive as to royal power. A model of the successful self-seeking monarch, he had been suspicious of conspiracy until he had firmly established himself. He had done it by using his position of being above the law, and had not only sentenced a rival to execution, but with his own hand and dagger had stabbed to death D. Diego, Duke of Vizeu, the Queen's brother. This he had done in August of 1484, just a few weeks before he granted Colom his interview.

With eagerness and full expectation of convincing the king, Colom presented his project. We have no detailed record of the interview, nothing except that half a century later it was said by João de Parros in *Decades of Asia,* that one of Colom's arguments ran thus: "Since in the time of the Infante D. Henrique the Azores were discovered, so there should be other islands and lands to the westward, since nature could not have made so disorderly a composition of the globe as to give the element of water preponderance over the land, since the earth was destined for human life and the creation of souls."

Very few men in the fifteenth century saw the absurdity of assuming that such a religious fantasy was a fact. It shows us, however that the Gentile-Jew duality in Colom did not hinder him from making use of any theological notion which served his purpose.

It is to be presumed that in the interview with King João he used arguments which we know he used in later years, one of which was that the ocean had been crossed many centuries before. He learned how effective it was to draw evidences from ancient authors. He found what he wanted in Aristotle and quoted from *On Marvelous Things Heard* (Section 84): "In the ocean outside the Pillars of Hercules they say that an island was found by the Carthaginians, a wilderness having trees of all kinds and navigable rivers, remarkable for various kinds of fruits, and many days' sailing distance away." The "many days' sailing" excluded the Madeira and Canary Islands, and the trees and rivers excluded also the Azores and Cape Verde Islands. Of course, Colom pointed out that the "many days' sailing" where not too many for crossing with maintenance of good health, and so the distance was not too far. The story told by Aristotle was retold in the first century by Diodorus of Sicily: "Over against (across from) Africa lies a very great island in the vast ocean, many days' sail westward . . . . The soil there is very fruitful, a great part whereof is mountainous, but much likewise a plain [Mississippi River Valley?] which is the most sweet and pleasant part, for it is watered with several navigable rivers." Claudius Aelianus in the second century A.D. said the discovery was "a definite tradition of the Carthaginians of Gades (Cadiz)." Colom would have wanted to soft-pedal the direction in which the Carthaginians had sailed from Cadiz — "between the setting sun and the meridian." The direction for his project would be his secret until his return from his own crossing unavoidably revealed it.

He made the point that his Enterprise of the Indies would carry knowledge of the Christian Cross to the Indies and open the way to salvation of the souls of all the people of Asia. Thus, if King João supported his project, he would win eternal glory for Portugal and for himself personally. At the same time he dangled before the king the lure of quick enrichment, with repeated mention of gold, silks and spices.

Foreseeing that he must overcome the notion that the distance across the Alantic was too great, he had ready answer that, in spite of what some geographers had given as the circumference of the earth, no geographer had yet set bounds on the distance to which Asia extended eastward. You do not know, he would say, and no one knows, for no geographer, Ptolemy or anyone else, has certain knowledge of the eastward-reaching length of Asia. It was not the ocean that was unknown, but the Far East.

As climax to his arguments and his conclusion, Colom not too modestly stressed his own wide experience in sailing in the Atlantic, and his ability as a navigator, declaring that his knowledge of ocean sailing was unique — that he was the only one who knew how to pilot a ship across the ocean to the nearest island, and that he was willing to make the attempt if the king would agree to his terms. Legendary islands were a plenty. Colom could always conjure up islands when he needed them. He made those islands fabulously attractive. He said he had heard that on the island of Antilia ships' boys had gathered sand — sand which was one-third pure gold! Just listening to Colom one could feel rich.

As for those who might be saying that he could not succeed, they did not know what they were talking about. He said he knew there were islands along the route he proposed to take; islands where he could replenish the ships and save the sailors from falling ill.

He presented his case with the flourish of oratory of which Catalonians were fond, and in which they were proficient.

King João had listened to him attentively. This young man, the king thought, is eager to give us a lesson in geography. He is a big talker and boastful, full of fancy and imagination with his islands. But he makes a deep impression on everyone who gives ear to him. As he looked at Colom, King João could not help admiring the youth's audacity, his princely bearing, his regal air, his voice, his deliberate and weighty manner, his unabashed importunity. Disposed to discounting the young man's enthusiasm, the king realized that this youth was as forceful as he knew himself to be. And this Colom was a sailor and experienced — had sailed extensively in the service of Portugal. But now, his asking for

"island authenticated distance to west 1500 miles"

Andrea Bianco Map, 1448

ships to sail west. There might be something in his project. It was a possibility which must not be overlooked. Of course what he proposed was definitely not wanted, and for good reason; but it was a reason which the king of Portugal was keeping secret. The king knew the ocean had been crossed. Fishermen from Oporto were getting cod from what they said were fishing banks far to the west, to the north of the west. In the secret archives, King João had maps which showed land to the west. One of them by Pedro Vaz Bisgudo showed a large island to the west. Another map in the archives was by Andrea Bianco dated 1448, which told of land to the south of west, land the existence of which the Portuguese had verified, or so the map stated. At the lower edge of the parchment of Bianco's map was the outline of the Brazilian elbow lying to the south of west Cape Verde, and with the inscription: "There is an authenticated island distant to the west 1500 miles." (Bianco, an Italian, gave the distance in Italian miles, and it is 1520 miles from Cape Verde to the Brazilian elbow.) That "authenticated island" was the land which had been sighted by Portuguese ships using winds and currents in the South Atlantic to waft them farther and farther south in hope of reaching the latitude of the southern end of Africa.

Portugal wanted unique possession of the route around Africa. To have it, the ships of all other countries, those of Spain especially, must be denied access to the South Atlantic. The Portuguese must keep secret what they knew, since if it were divulged, the Spanish and the French would take immediate advantage of those helpful winds and currents. This is why Portuguese law strictly forbade exportation from Portugal of any map or chart.

The project of Colom appeared to run counter to Portuguese policy. As King João looked at Colom, he asked himself, Would this young man's proposal lay bare what we are holding secret? Would it permit the stealing from us what we already have discovered? And so he asked Colom: Why have you told us this? What is it you want?

Colom said he wanted His Majesty to seize the opportunity he was offering.

Asked to specify precisely what he wanted, Colom stated his demands: Three good caravels with their supplies and crews provided for a year; and for himself, as reward for giving Portugal a short route to India, recompense which the king surely would admit would be deserved reward for giving Portugal that route. Colom said he must be given a title of nobility, and also the title of Admiral, and be made Governor of any island or land he discovered, his position as such Governor to be for life, and to be hereditary for his descendants to hold forever, and he must be given a reasonable percentage, ten percent of all products and profits made by trade with those islands and lands.

The young man has thought of everything, the king said to himself as he saw the astounded looks of some courtiers and the cynical smiles of others. But what magnificent self-confidence this Colom displays! His demands seem outrageous, fantastic. Yet perhaps not, the king reflected, since all of them except the three caravels are contingent upon his succeeding. But it would be our policy not to want him to succeed. He does not perceive the actual situation, and we do not want him to perceive it. He is a very astute young man, and to keep him from any inkling of the actual situation, we must deal with him shrewdly, not summarily. To do that we must not make an outright rejection of his project, but somehow put him off.

Meanwhile, Colom wondered whether he had sufficiently aroused the king's curiosity and cupidity.

And so King João said that what Colom called his Enterprise of the Indies must be carefully considered, and he ordered that Colom confer about it with Don Diego Ortiz, Bishop of Cueta, and with Master (Mister) Rodrigo, and Master José Vizinho, to whom the king had committed matters of cosmography and discovery. Master Rodrigo was the king's physician, and he and Master José, who was also a physician, were both Jews but converts. Master José had been a pupil of Abraham Zacute, Professor of Mathematics at Salamanca.

The members of the commission well understood that the king was already committed to the plan of finding a route to India around Africa. While they "considered" Colom's project, they were fully aware that the king would not be displeased if they kept Colom waiting. Eventually, as any courtier could have foretold, they reported on his project adversely.

The objection they stated was not their real objection. It was the more obvious one — the distance across the ocean to Asia was too far. Sailors could not survive such a long voyage as would be required. Not only would food and water go foul before a ship could cross the ocean, but the firewood would give out also. On board ship, food was cooked above a fireplace on deck, and there was room on a ship's deck to stack only enough firewood for a month at sea. Besides, on too long a voyage, not only would the sailors get sick, but the hull of a ship, eaten by teredo worms, would leak and the ship would sink. The argument of too great a distance, the commission stated, was the chief objection. It was not superstition. It was not men's fears of imagined sea monsters capable of smashing in a ship's hull; or whirlpools that suck a ship under; or masses of seawood so thick that no ship could plow through or ever draw away; or mermaids who would entice sailors from their duties; or the idea that for men to attempt to penetrate too far into the unknown would be going against the will of God. These notions would get woven in elsewhere as colorful embroidery in the arguments against Colom's project, but the basic objection stated in Lisbon was distance.

Colom's project was not wanted because it was not needed. Portugal was already getting great wealth from African gold dust, Negro slaves, pepper, and elephant tusks. Lisbon had become a rich eity of great luxury. Its people, while not indolent, were in no hurry to begin trade directly with India.

King João was committed to working toward the long-sought route around Africa. A few years later he completed the task. With success crowning his undertakings, it would be the beginning of a great empire for Portugal. For accomplishing it, he would be called "the perfect king."

Every businessman in Lisbon knew, and Colom, if he had been older, would have realized that the idea of a shorter route across the ocean to Asia did not have the appeal he obviously supposed it would. Colom's project was definitely not wanted in Portugal.

But Colom's project had been so impressively presented, King João would keep it in mind. More than that, he felt it advisable to find out if there was any merit in it. To that end, hearing that Fernão Dulmo, a ship captain of Terceira in the Azores, was offering to sail westward at his own expense, King João got Dulmo to agree to look for the island of Antilia, the fabled island of Seven Cities. King João guaranteed Dulmo a donation of anything he might discover, and promised him titles of honor. Then Dulmo took João Estreito of Funchal as his partner, and the two captains agreed that Dulmo would command their combined fleet for the first forty days from Terceira and thereafter Estreito would be in command. They set March 1, 1487 as the date for commencing their voyage. Did they sail? They certainly did not attempt to sail from the Azores, since from there they would have had to buck strong winds from the west. There is no record of their ever having sailed as they planned, but of course the Portuguese would not let anyone hear about it if they did sail.

With ear to waterfront gossip, Coiom soon heard of it, and it seemed to him an outrageous proposal, showing King João to be a perfidious, double-dealing, unconscionable monarch, dead to honor, full of weasel words. He was righteously indignant. He took it as a personal affront. Some of the men in and around the King's court had called him an obstinate fool. What would honest men now call King João? Sailing to the West had been Colom's idea. It was his project, and he had laid it openly before the king. For the king to reject the idea publicly, and then plan privately to send other navigators voyaging secretly to try to carry out his project, was a knavish and dishonorable act. He would never forgive it, never forget it. If he ever could, he would make the King of Portugal regret it.

What could he do? He saw there was no hope in Portugal for his Enterprise of the Indies. But his project must go forward! He would offer it somewhere else, but where? It must be in a country where the ruler was not so sneaky. He thought of England, but that was too far away, and English was a language he did not know. Yet England might do. And there was also France. But the most promising country looked to be the one which was now united and becoming a power. Their Spanish Majesties would welcome an opportunity to get to India ahead of Portugal. In Spain he could speak the language, and put his case in most appealing, terms, and he could instantly catch the full meaning of every phrase of comment, of criticism, of opposition. In Spain he could argue most effectively.

But for him to enter Spain? He could do so only at risk of his life, since he had fought against Castile and Aragon. Yet he had often risked his life in sea battles as a privateer, and for causes which were insignificant compared with the one he now had. But if it were ever known in Spain that he had been a privateer under King René of Anjou allied with Portugal against Castile and Aragon, he would be arrested, tortured, and executed. But the challenge in it! Spain was where that King Ferdinand was sitting on a throne which had rightfully belonged to João Colom's father Prince Carlos of Viana. What a satisfactory turn it would be if he could use King Ferdinand to further his project! And Spain, now the rival of Portugal — that would be where he could give the sharpest strike-back against this double-tongued, dissembling King João.

But could he enter Spain and lay his project before the so-called "Catholic Kings" without anyone knowing what his past had been? How could he do it?

He talked it over with his Uncle Bartolomeo, who agreed with him that there seemed to be no way.

Then he thought of a way. He would assume a new identity. In Madeira he had met a man who became his friend, an Italian, a Genoese merchant who had come to Madeira to buy sugar for a firm in Lisbon. That merchant had the same family name — Colombo, which was Italian for Colón. That Genoese was a few years older than himself, but near enough to his own age. That Colombo, his first name Cristoforo, had told of some of the members of his family still living in or near Genoa. And now, a fact which only a few seamen in the Madeiras knew — that Cristoforo Colombo had lost his life at sea. And so, João Colom said to himself, if I take Cristoforo Colombo's name, I could enter Spain as a Genoese. I will claim to have been born in or near Genoa, but will keep vague about my childhood and boyhood there, and so my actual past will be buried. I will tell everyone that I followed the sea from an early age, in ships of many ports, more than I can recall. I will say that I was a captain of an Italian ship. It should be a perfect cover. Though I cannot speak Italian properly — only a few words in that language — no matter. I will say that from boyhood I was on ships where the sailors spoke other languages. But how explain my having been in that sea battle from which I swam ashore nine years ago? I must keep concealed that I fought for Portugal against Italian ships serving Castile and Aragon, for that was really fighting against Castile and Aragon. How can I? I shall have to muddle the record. I will say that I was serving under the famous Colón the Younger who attacked a fleet of Venetian ships which had rounded Cape St. Vincent coming home from Flanders. That fiction will support my claiming to be Genoese. Genoa and Venice, as everybody knows, have always been rivals and often at war with each other. To thwart any digging into my past, I will make my telling of the story of that sea battle too complicated to be clearly understood by anyone.[1] Yes, I shall say that I am the Italian-born Cristoforo Colombo. My name in Spanish will be Cristóbal Colón. I shall enter Spain with some risk of my life, but the more daring, the safer.

Being young and impatient, he thus made his decision.

To Spain, then, to Portugal's rivals. With God's help, he would some-day get the better of this ungentlemanly King João. And in Spain — the humor of it! He said to himself, I will get an interview with those who are being called "the Catholic Kings." When I do, I will have a good look at my father's half-brother, that usurper King Ferdinand. I will see what kind of man he is. And I will see that Queen Isabel, who is a cousin to her husband, and is my third or fourth cousin.

But the police here in Lisbon will not permit me to leave for Spain. They fear I might tell their Spainish Majesties what I know about the gold mine in Africa, and about Portuguese discoveries and plans for get-ting to India. I shall therefore have to escape from them. They are ex-pecting me to return to my home in Madeira. That is what I shall tell everyone I am going to do. When I disappear from Lisbon, they will here assume that I have returned to Madeira.

He asked his uncle, now "brother" Bartolomeo, to see to it that the small debts he had incurred in Lisbon would be paid.

He skillfully evaded the Lisbon police. With his five-year old son Diego, he went to the harbor shore ostensibly to go aboard a ship which was leaving for Madeira. Under cover of darkness, he slipped aboard a ship leaving for Spain, the captain of which had privately accepted money in advance for taking him and his son as passengers.

❀☙☙☙☙☙☙☙☙☙☙☙☙☙☙☙☙☙☙☙☙☙☙☙☙☙❀

This chapter makes me ask: Aren't you unfair to King João in what you have Colón think of him?

How so?

King João was universally admired. As you say, he was called the per-fect king.

Envied more than respected. It is true that during his reign of fourteen years from 1481 to 1495, the Portuguese rounded Africa, acquired un-paralleled wealth, and gave architectural enrichment to Lisbon, so that today many Portuguese gloat over that period of grandeur.

Well, wasn't the meeting with the King of Portugal a profitable experience for Colón? It must have showed him how to improve in diplomatic approach.

Yes, of course.

But you tell us he thereafter lived a lie in claiming to have been born in Genoa.

Call it a lie if you are morally disposed. It was a deception, but not morally reprehensible. It did not aim to injure anyone. It was the only way he could present his Enterprise of the Indies to the Spanish Court. Since it served his great purpose, do you, my dear reader, feel it belittled his character? Do you condemn him for it?

No. It makes me eager to see how the deception worked.

8

NEW FIRST NAME

It was late summer of 1485 when the ship bearing Colón and his son Diego brought them safely into Spanish waters. She entered the estuary which led to Huelva and Palos. As she rounded the turn into the River Tinto headed for Palos, her passengers saw on the bluff above them the Franciscan Monastery of La Rabída. The conventional story hitherto told with romantic overtones has been that when they stepped off the ship at Palos, Colón, bearing his infant son in his arms, hopefully and wearily trudged the four miles back to that monastery, arrived there dusty and tired, and begged the friar who came to the gate to have mercy and give his son water and bread. It made an appealing scene as the beginning of a great career sensationally achieved against obstacles, picturing Cristóbal Colón as a man who from the day he entered Spain was impoverished, slighted, misunderstood, ridiculed, and compelled to suffer neglect and scorn until with determination, cleverness, and divine aid, he got what he wanted.

We do not know whether he walked the four miles, or was given a ride. Assuming that he did walk, and that he may have carried his five-year old son in his arms at least part of the way, his asking for food at the monastery did not make him a charity case. Religious houses, where there were no hostelries, customarily gave shelter and meals to travelers, but asked them to pay, if they could.

What concerns us is what resulted from his going to La Rabída Monastery. Since he was a Franciscan tertiary, or now became one, there is nothing surprising in his having been made heartily welcome at La Rabída. One or more of the friars there immediately arranged for him to meet some of the top people in Spain.

It was at risk of his life he had entered Spain. His survival depended upon success in maintaining the fiction that his first name was Cristóbal, and that he came from Liguria in Italy, from a family in or near Genoa. Juan Colón, the privateer who had fought against Castile and Aragon would not be seen in him. Hitherto, he had been compelled to resort to subterfuge. Now that he had taken on a necessary cloak of deception, deviousness became compulsory for mere survival. The cover he had chosen was so effective, however, that he remained unmasked, publicly at least, until the day of his death, and four and a half centuries thereafter.

As for his having had a Jewish mother, he had nothing to fear. His awareness that his physique and features gave him the looks of a prince and a Gentile, made him confident that no one would think him a convert, or what the Spanish sneeringly called a Marrano, an insincere convert. His father meant more to him than his mother. In private correspondence with his Uncle Bartolomeo and with his son Diego, he would hold privately to the forms of his mother's religion. But as his father's son and a Franciscan tertiary, he would be as sincere a Christian as any man.

His claim to Genoese origin called for some further deception. Like a spy in enemy territory, he had to watch his tongue. The disguise required duplicity. It is no discredit to him that he falsified his origin. Prevarication was acceptable if directed with due consideration of its effects, and without injury to anyone.

The Christian kingdoms in Spain had been at war against Moorish invaders since 711 A.D. The conflict which had continued for nearly eight hundred years had caused a shortage of materials of every sort throughout the country. All material things commanded higher prices in Spain than anywhere else. Spain desperately needed everything other countries could supply, and thus was the land of greatest opportunity for importers. Merchants from Italy were most hospitably received. Merchants from Bristol in far-off England were also especially welcome.

With all the Christian kingdoms united under Queen Isabel and King Ferdinand, it had become obvious that the centuries-long war against the Muslims would terminate with complete triumph of Christian arms. When it did, Spain would become an effective balance against France, whose power seemed to be a great threat to all her neighbors. Italians naturally wanted Spain to grow strong as a foil to France. Spaniards naturally welcomed Italians most heartily. Thus political events made fortunate for Colón his choice of a new first name and his claiming to be Italian.

We do not know which friar at La Rabída, whether Antonio de Marchene or Fray Juan Perez, was the first to be convinced by Colón's arguments as to the size of the earth — that the circumference of the earth was smaller than the cosmographers had said, and thus made his project feasible. Both friars had imagination enough to grasp the potential value to Spain of a short route to India directly from Spanish ports. At least one of the friars at La Rabída immediately became Colón's supporter and active agent.

Something which has hitherto seemed most remarkable, we now see was inevitable. Only a few days after arriving at La Rabída, Colón was given opportunity to lay his project before the wealthiest man in Spain. With an introduction from Friar Antonio de Marchene, who was custodian of the Franciscan province of Seville, and a scholar of repute as an astrologer, Colón went to Seville to have an interview with Don Enrique de Guzmán, Duke of Medina Sidonia. The interview was in the city which was on the navigable Guadalquiver River and was Spain's principal shipping port. Across the river from Seville was the district called Triana, which had many dockyards, warehouses, and sailors. Trade with foreign countries was centered in Triana.

With the fire of self-knowledge within him, with his consciousness of royal blood, and awareness of royal relationships in Spain, Colón felt his superiority to a mere duke. The duke in this case, after listening to Colón, was ready to promise him the cost of the ships he wanted for his project. But before he got around to acting on the promise, he had a brawl with the Duke of Cadiz, in punishment for which, in spite of his being rich and the Duke of Medina Sidonia, he was summarily ordered to leave Seville.

After the departure of the Duke of Medina Sidonia, Cristóbal Colón was given an interview by Don Luis de la Cerda, a Count who later became Duke of Medina Celi. This nobleman was also owner of a fleet of merchant vessels. Colón presented to him his Enterprise of the Indies and gave his arguments for it. Don Luis was convinced that Colón was right and that the accepted geographers were wrong. He was stirred to such enthusiasm for the project of finding a short route from Spain to Asia, that as a merchant adventurer with an eye to lucrative trade, he immediately offered to furnish Colón with three or four well-equipped caravels, well manned, provisioned for one year, and with a plentiful supply of trading goods. Thus, only a few weeks after Cristóbal Colón arrived in Spain, he was proffered the physical means for carrying out his project.

To the rich nobleman's amazement, Colón flatly refused the offer.

Why? Ships to undertake the expedition were surely what he wanted. Were they not what he had asked? What did he want?

We know what more he wanted. His purpose went far beyond what the Court imagined. The offer of ships was unacceptable. Merely having three or four caravels would not do. What Colón wanted was something no mere count could give. He wanted in Spain what he had demanded of the king of Portugal. As reward for succeeding in his project, he must be given ennoblement. This in Spain was the title of Don. Not only that. It must be an ennoblement which his desendants would forever inherit. Also, he himself must be given the title of "Admiral of the Ocean Sea" which would rank him above all captains of caravels or merchant ships. With the title of "Admiral of the Ocean Sea" he would be like a king in shipping circles and at sea. Because of what he knew himself to be, son of the heir to the throne, he had set his mind on receiving a unique recognition and reward which only a sovereign ruler of a country could bestow. In addition to everything else, and most important to him, he must be given the title of Governor of all islands or mainlands he might discover. On those islands or mainlands he would, as Viceroy, be the effective ruler. His governorship must be like a kingship, hereditary. It must be one which his son Diego and his descendants would forever inherit. Like the title of nobility, his governorship must be hereditary. This he would tenaciously demand.

What he wanted could, in Spain, be granted only by Their Royal Majesties, Queen Isabel and King Ferdinand.

Because of his special knowledge of the Atlantic and his willingness to make a voyage which no one else was offering to undertake, he would not lower his price. He would of course ask for what most people would think were obvious and fitting rewards. He would ask to be given a tenth part of all revenues, metals, and products of every kind which were taken from the islands and mainlands. And this tenth part was to be guaranteed to his descendants in perpetuity. All of his demands put together would seem preposterous, but he would continue to make them. His asking, his demanding was in the style of a prince. As son of an heir to a throne, nothing less would satisfy his ego.

Since his proposal of sailing westward across the Atlantic was based upon knowledge which he was keeping as a precious secret, he would not let anyone know by what route he would sail, lest, as he later told his son Ferdinand, he might be served as he had been by the King of Portugal, and be deprived of his reward.[1]

While to us, who know his parentage, there is no surprise in Cristóbal Colón's rejecting what was to him an unacceptable offer of three ships or four ships, there is a most intriguing surprise raised by his residing later on for two years in the house of the Duke of Medina Celi. The reason for saying this is that the Duke's wife and Cristóbal Colón were closely related. Prince Carlos of Viana had married a noblewoman, Maria de Armendais, and she had borne him a daughter, previous to his going to Majorca. That daughter was called Marie of Aragon and Navarre. The Duke of Medina Celi had married that daughter. With the Duke his patron and supporting him, Cristóbal Colón resided for two years in the home of his half-sister. He of course knew of their relationship. We can only guess as to whether Marie or the Duke knew it. It seems unlikely that they did. We can only surmise as to what Colón's sister thought of the tall, handsome young man who was her half-brother, or what her husband thought of him. We wish we knew whether the in-

Spain and Portugal

vitation to move in with them came from the husband or the wife.

Residing for two years with his sister, a noblewoman, and her husband, a Duke, Cristóbal Colón enjoyed a feeling of beginning to triumph over the circumstances which had defeated his father. Undoubtedly, he was eager to learn from his sister whatever her mother had told her about their father.

❀❊❊❊❊❊❊❊❊❊❊❊❊❊❊❊❊❊❊❊❊❊❊❊❀

Wow! As dramatic a situation as any in Greek tragedy! Colón's being guest in the house of the Duke of Medina Celi without the Duke or his wife knowing that Colón was her brother.

Yes. I was strongly tempted to fictionize it — give imagined conversations between brother and sister.

Somebody someday may put it into a play.

No doubt.

The story of Columbus is terrific drama.

At every turn. He was never static.

You have implied that his entering Spain, which compelled duplicity, had an effect upon his character.

It did.

How?

With awareness that he was risking his life, he not only firmed his demands but became relentless and deliberately defiant of the man he had most reason to hate.

Who was that?

You will see in the next chapter.

9

ISABEL

The Prior of La Rabída Friary had the privilege of private audience
with Queen Isabel.* He or some other Franciscan informed her of
Colon's project, and advised her to give the young man a hearing. She
agreed to do so. Colón promptly went to Cordova to meet with both
Queen Isabel and King Ferdinand, but when he arrived in that city on
January 20th, 1486, their Majesties had left for Madrid. Late in April,
they returned to Cordova, and resumed residence in the Alcazar Palace.
About the 1st of May, Colón was admitted to their presence. Their
Majesties gave him respectful attention, and heard his arguments for his
Enterprise of the Indies.

It was no discouragement to Colón when the Queen said she would have to submit his project to advisors. From his experience with the King of Portugal he expected this, the more since he understood that all resources of the royal treasury were being employed in prosecution of the war against the Muslims.

Queen Isabel had been more deeply impressed than King Ferdinand had been. She immediately planned to see Colón again, and her doing this raised the highest hopes in him. It was only eight months after he had landed in Spain. The Queen and he were in rapport.

* The Queen's name, erroneously spelled in the encyclopedias and in many other places, was never "Isabella." "Isabel" is the Spanish for "Elizabeth," and just as neither of the Queen Elizabeths of England has been called "Elizabetha," the name of the Queen of Leon and Castile had only three syllables, Isabel. Ferdinand Colón, in his biography of his father, spells the Queen's name "Isabel," as do all Spaniards.

They felt a sort of harmony. "Surely," says Samuel Eliot Morison in *Admiral of the Ocean Sea,* "some mark of mutual comprehension and understanding passed between them when Colón was first presented in the audience chamber."[1] We know, as Morison did not, why Colón and Queen Isabel felt an affinity. She, his aunt by marriage, was a third or fourth cousin. They had the same royal blood in their veins. Though we give feminine intuition due credit, that was not all. The Queen was emotionally moved when she saw Colón, not only by his physical appearance, but by the ugly facts of her marriage. That marriage had been forced upon her. As princess, daughter of King Juan II of Castile and of Isabel of Portugal, Isabel was for political reasons affianced to Prince Ferdinand of Aragon, although she and he were within forbidden degrees of cousinship. They were married in Valladolid on October 19th, 1469, when she was eighteen and he seventeen. Previous to their marriage, Ferdinand had begotten an illegitimate son, Don Alfonso, born in 1469, at almost the same time as the marriage. When King, Ferdinand made this son the Archbishop of Zaragoza.[2] Ferdinand's marriage to Isabel did not deter him from begetting bastards in almost every year thereafter. Isabel had cordial reason to dislike her husband. He disgusted her. She hated him. She could never forget that in her early girlhood she had expected to marry Prince Carlos of Viana. In retrospect, Prince Carlos was a challenge to her loveless marriage. Whether or not she knew that Cristóbal Colón was the son of Prince Carlos, his face and figure brought to her memories of Prince Carlos.

Her husband was in no way physically attractive. Portraits of him painted from life by two different artists agree in telling us how he looked. Though strongly built, he was far from handsome. He was of medium height, with a pale, unhealthy face. He had a serious look that showed no warmth of heart. The only impressive feature in his appearance was a pair of staring eyes, clear and firm, but displaying malevolence and lack of compassion. He had a small but full-lipped mouth. Taken all together, his facial features were too small for his large and inelegant head. He exuded selfishness. He was calculating and secretive, and became infamous for those qualities.

He was capable of the most obscene cruelty. At an audience at Barcelona, a man struck at him with a dagger. The blow was deflected by a gold chain. Ferdinand knocked the would-be assassin down. Then he had the man's offending hand cut off. Then he had his feet cut off. Then he had his eyes gouged out. Then he had his heart cut out. Not satisfied with his butchery, he ordered people to stone what remained of the corpse. After they had stoned it, he had the remains burned and reduced to dust.

Instinctively, as well as for conscious reasons, Colón had no illusion as to King Ferdinand's character, and of course never trusted him. Neither did Isabel. In the first five years of their marriage, the breach between husband and wife had widened. Her seizing the throne of Castile by having herself hastily proclaimed queen, so enraged King Ferdinand that he wanted separation or divorce. She, knowing him better than he knew himself, won his acquiescence by offering a lure. She proposed to give him power of attorney with which, she assured him, he could act for her, as though he were indeed King of Castile. He swallowed the bait, but she held the reins. She saw to it that the power of attorney meant nothing, and he never was allowed to act for her or exercise any power infringing upon her own. She outdid Ferdinand in political shrewdness. She did not interfere with his governing of his kingdoms, but she never let him dictate to her as to her ruling of hers. The only real cooperation between them was in their fighting the Muslims and in eventually uniting all Spain, for which reason they deservedly came to be called "the Catholic Kings."

That term gave the impression that they as rulers were closely knit together. While they cooperated fully in their prosecution of their religious war, they were in no sense ever a congenial couple. The disparity between them was too great. Felipe Fernandez-Armesto in *Ferdinand and Isabella* (a splendid dual biography though it has the misspelling of the Queen's name) says: "Ferdinand was by nature a philanderer," his "disposition little given to love."[3] Isabel tried to hedge his pleasures and wean him from paramours. In this she failed. She never found any happiness in her marriage. As wife and mother, her life had been pitiful and tragic. She had borne four children to Ferdinand, three who had died, and a daughter, Juana, who was declared insane.

Armesto says: "Isabella was capable of flirtation."[4] While he assumes that she was a faithful wife, though "surrounded by the sexually permissive," he says that she "had favorites."[5] The implication seems to be that she had love affairs. Samuel Eliot Morison says of Queen Isabel: "This man Colombo or Colón appealed not only to her reason, but her instincts."[6] Morison gives a physical description of her. She was a strikingly handsome woman "with regular features, a fresh, clear complexion, blue eyes and auburn hair."[7] As did most royal persons, she showed in her face her Viking ancestry. She was gracious, dignified and tactful. Like Colón, she was temperate in her habits of eating and drinking. She and Colón were of the same physical type, very similar in character. Both of them were proud, sensitive, and passionate. Like him, she had great physical vigor. She frequently made long, arduous and quick trips, arriving unexpectedly on horseback to inspect affairs in many places in her kingdoms of Leon and Castile. She had great daring. Though she was sweetly feminine, she was tied into what was no true marriage — a union which had begun in defiance of church law of consanguinity, and which had been continuously violated by King Ferdinand's love affairs. King Ferdinand's reaction to his wife was inevitably affected by hers to him.

We know King Ferdinand's attitude toward Colón, and Colón's reaction to that attitude. The son of Colón, many years later in his biography of his father said the Queen had always favored him, but King Ferdinand had always seemed "cold and unfriendly" toward him and his affairs. It was indeed so. Colón knew that this King Ferdinand, his uncle, was on his way to getting possession of the throne of Navarre, and thus to Colón he represented all those who had denied that throne to its

Queen Isabel and Columbus portriats on postage stamp
First U.S.A. stamp showing a portrait of a woman

rightful heir, Prince Carlos of Viana. Colón had such a strong reason to hate the king that it may have been impossible for him to conceal his antipathy. There was always a coldness between King Ferdinand and Cristóbal Colón. In return for the way his father had been mistreated and thwarted, Colón had within him a strong impulse to spite King Ferdinand, and do anything he could against the king without injury to himself. And he was a young man who dared.

Are we warranted in entertaining a suspicion? Is there ground for making an obvious assumption? The facts are persuasive, and indeed, most extraordinary. Queen Isabel, in giving a private audience to Christóbal Colón, gave herself an opportunity and met with a temptation. She was thirty-six years of age, at the height of her powers as a woman, meeting a young man of twenty-six, at the height of his powers as a man. He had an imperious personality like hers. He knew that he and she were distant cousins, and that he like her was of royal blood. Of that, she may have been convinced by his stature and hair and eye color He was a princely romantic. She was an abused wife. She instinctively

91

desired to requite her husband for all he had made her suffer. With this young man of her own type, she could to her own satisfaction settle the score.

She placed Cristóbal Colón in the charge of her comptroller of finances, Alonso de Quintameilla, who put him up in his house in Cordova. Queen Isabel saw to it that beginning on July 3rd, 1487, monthly payments were made to Colón until the middle of 1488.

Colón's son Ferdinand was born in mid or late summer of 1488. It was given out by Colón that Beatriz de Harana, was his son Ferdinand's mother. She was the daughter of Pedro de Torquemada, who was distantly related to the Inquisitor of Spain. Her mother was Maria de Trasierra. Her parents had grown vegetables and grapes and had made wine for the Cordova market. In their time and place classed as peasants, we today think of such a family as members of a rising middle class. Beatriz became an orphan in her early years, and was taken to Cordova to live in the home of Rodrigo, her first cousin. Rodrigo was "a man of culture."[8] Beatriz had learned to read and write. She was 23 years old in 1488. Since there was general acceptance of what was given out publicly that the handsome Cristóbal Colón had had a love affair with her, we assume she was attractive and very likely beautiful. She was of good stock and intelligent. She seems to have been a natural and perfect choice for foster parent of an infant. If she or her brother Pedro, or her cousin Rodrigo, or Rodrigo's son Diego ever thought to make question of the baby's parentage, they said nothing about it because of the favoritism extended to them by Colón through the years, in his making Diego Marshall of his fleet in 1492, and in giving Pedro, the brother of Beatriz, command of a caravel in 1498. Colón maintained cordial relationship with the de Haranas, and his descendants did also.

King Ferdinand was preoccupied with his diplomatic scheming, ambitious war making, and his paramours. If it were announced to him that a baby born to Queen Isabel had died at birth, it would be to him just another of her failures to give him a healthy male heir. She, who had such valid reasons for detesting her husband, would not have wanted him to rejoice in thinking he had sired a healthy and normal boy. She would have had such a baby not his son smuggled out of the palace and placed in the hands of a capable foster mother.

Seventeen years later, in his Last Will, Colón made a bequest and an extraordinary statement. It was addressed to his son Don Diego, as Executor of his estate:

> "I order Don Diego, that he should keep recommended Beatriz Enriquez, the mother of Don Ferdinand, my son, that he should give her enough to live on honestly, as a person to whom I am grateful, and this I say to relieve my conscience, which weighs on me.
>
> "The reason of it is not the kind to be divulged here.
>
> "Given the 25th of August, 1505, in Segovia."[9]

Why the mystery? What could it be that was "not the kind to be divulged?" Cristóbal Colón had no hesitancy in telling the world that he was the father of Ferdinand, that he had not married Beatriz de Harana, and that his conscience troubled him. Why then did he not marry her? Samuel Eliot Morison says the reason "may easily be inferred. It was not to his advantage," since it would have been "an unsuitable match for an admiral and viceroy."[10] This opinion is neutralized by the fact that for the first five years after son Ferdinand was born, Colón was not an admiral and viceroy. This opinion is also negated by the associations Colón openly maintained with members of the de Harana family and asked his heirs to maintain. He held the relatives of Beatriz as his respected friends, from the time he first knew Diego de Harana and had met with him with men of learning, and he kept the male relatives of Beatriz close to him and among his most trusted officers. None of them ever displayed resentment at his having befouled the name or reputation of Beatriz, and this was their attitude from five years before Colón became famous. He was never averse to having his name associated with hers, and he repeatedly declared that she was the mother of his son. He left Ferdinand in her care until the boy was old enough to go with him on his last voyage. If all that troubled his conscience was his not having married Beatriz, all he needed do to clear his conscience was to marry her and make his son legitimate. Why then did he not clear his conscience? It was most probably because marriage to Beatriz de Harana would not have done it, for the reason that she was not the mother of his son Ferdinand, and he was naturally never willing to disavow to himself the love he had shared with Queen Isabel. It seems likely that the members of the de Harana family must have known the behind-the-scenes story. What else kept them from demanding that he marry Beatriz? And since King Ferdinand had not given Queen Isabel a male heir, Colón may have harbored a dream of a change in the situation at the Spanish Court which might make his son Ferdinand's royal parentage politically important.

If it is as the evidence indicates, Queen Isabel had done no injury to her husband, but had found considerable satisfaction in spiting him. Does belief that Ferdinand Colón was her son injure her reputation? We, in the twentieth century, think not. It makes her the more interesting. In her day bishops and princes of the church openly paraded their mistresses, as Morison remarks. Bastards were common in and around royal courts. If Queen Isabel had an extra-marital love affair, it would in retrospect have been on her conscience. Her becoming pious to the point of extreme fanaticism may have been a reaction to such an affair, if not precisely a cover up. Something heightened her religiosity, and intensified her determination to please God by putting horrible pressure on Jews who were professing Christians, but were suspected of not being completely sincere. A troubled conscience may have been a factor in her pushing for the Inquisition.

❁❈❈❈❈❈❈❈❈❈❈❈❈❈❈❈❈❈❈❈❈❈❈❈❈❁

Have you had no wish to save Queen Isabel's reputation?
Why should I?
Like Ceasar's wife, a queen should be above suspicion.
Like the empresses in Rome? Like the queens in Constantinople? Like Queen Catherine the Great in Russia?
Yes, I know. But take the queens of Scotland —
Scotland! The first queen of the Steward line (later called Stewart or Stuart) on her death bed confessed that the Crown Prince was not the son of the king.
So there was only one genuine Stuart king?
Only the first — never another.
History gets turned inside out!
It has to be, no matter what it does to reputations.

10

CONTRACT AND CREDENTIALS

There may have been a touch of irony in Cristóbal Colón's choice of name for his illegitimate son, Ferdinand. The naming of the infant may have been suggested by the Queen. In the mind of Colón, knowing how his grandfather, King Juan, had withheld the throne of Navarre from Prince Carlos and had assured it to his second son, Ferdinand, the name Ferdinand represented illegitimacy. This thought may have been a further reason why Colón would never make his son legitimate.

Queen Isabel's confessor was Fray Hernando de Talavera, Prior of a monastery near Valladolid. He later became Archbishop of Granada. In 1486 the Queen had appointed him to head the commission which would examine Colón's project. Colón understood clearly that his project, if approved, would have to be deferred until the war against the Muslims had been won. In 1488 the Queen's comptroller of finances introduced Colón to Don Pedro Gonzales de Mendoza, Archbishop of Toledo, Grand Cardinal of Spain, and first minister of the crown of Castile. Late in life, when Colón sought to awaken public sympathy for himself, he spoke of the years 1488 to 1491 as a period of intolerable waiting and heartless treatment, when he had to battle against prejudice and deliberate delay, a time during which he said he had been insulted, maligned, ridiculed, and repeatedly put off with vague promises. While any man who attempts to climb above everyone else will encounter unfairness, the complaint voiced by Colón was greatly exaggerted. In major part, it was contrary to fact. He was not shabbily treated during those six years, for during those years he was supported financially by the Court at the Queen's orders, or by money sent to him by her directly, although all funds were desperately needed for the war. He had some private income from his partnership with his Uncle Bartolomeo in making and selling maps and charts, and he visited with an increasing number of well-to-do friends, who entertained him frequently. His son said of this period in his biography of his father: "As he was a person of amiable character and pleasing conversation, he there gained the friendship of men who became his warmest advocates and who were in the best position to urge his cause upon the Sovereigns."

The commission appointed to examine his project met at Salamanca in the College of St. Stephen. The Court went to Salamanca for Christmas of 1486, and so Queen Isabel and Colón were both there at the same time.

The commission held long discussions, some with the young man in person, and some behind his back. The discussions always turned on how far it was from Spain westward to Asia. When the professors showed that they thought Cristóbal Colón was a vain, highly imaginative and obstinate theorist, he deftly reminded them that he was a practical navigator of wide experience, and that they did not know anything about the Atlantic Ocean. He insisted that anyone who knew anything about the ocean would agree that his project was practical. The professors described him as "expert, eloquent, and very boastful." To call the professors at Salamanca prejudiced would be as unfair as it would be to say that their reasoned objections discouraged Colón. A man who never tires of arguing has a strong reserve of patience. Knowing the Queen's attitude toward the project, the commissioners, none of whom would accept the narrow width of the ocean, postponed making their report.

Queen Isabel had Colón come to Malaga to witness with her the surrender of that seaport by the Muslims, on August 18th, 1487.

Colón wished to confer with his business partner in Lisbon. Fearing he might be thrown into jail in Portugal for having summarily left that country while owing money to his creditors, he wrote in 1488 to King João requesting a guarantee of non-arrest. By this time, Bartolomeo had paid the debts. King João replied with a most cordial invitation, calling himself Colón's "especial friend," and assuring him the protection he requested. Colón had not changed his opinion of King João's character, and he understood the reasons for the ingratiating phrases in the king's letter. One of the reasons was that Dulmo and Estreito, after sailing some hundreds of miles to the West, returned to report that they had failed to find any island or land. A far more potent reason was that Bartolomeu Dias, who had sailed from Lisbon in August of 1487 with two caravels and a supply ship to attempt to reach the southern end of Africa, was long overdue. King João was now ready to flirt with the idea that maybe Colón's previously rejected Enterprise of the Indies might be worth reconsidering.

Colón arrived in Lisbon in the late autumn of 1488. We do not know what conferences King João and he had. Whatever negotiations there may have been, they were abruptly broken off by one of the most dramatic events in Portuguese history, the triumphant return to Lisbon Harbor of Bartolomeu Dias. He had been unheard from for sixteen months, but now, amid the wildest acclaim, he reported that in the first four months of his voyage with winds often against him, he had reached farther than any Portuguese had yet — to about 26½° South on the coast of Africa. There at Christmas time, when he saw the wind rising and threatening a dangerous blow, he had sailed out westward with his two caravels, and had been caught in a gale which blew him southward out of sight of land. For nearly a month he saw no land even though he sailed for a great distance to the east to regain sight of the continent. Then he changed direction and sailed northward, and with the sighting of land to the north of him, he guessed where he was — in the Indian Ocean. He sailed back westward close to shore for 200 miles and confirmed his guess that he had without knowing it rounded the southern end of Africa. With the culmination of more than fifty years of Portuguese attempts to do what Dias had accomplished, it was announced in Lisbon that the cape which Bartolomeu Dias had rounded, was to be called The Cape of Good Hope. Everyone in Portugal was jubilant over what Dias had done, except Colón, who was the only man in Lisbon who was not happy over it.

There could no longer be any doubt that Portuguese ships would soon be sailing directly from Lisbon to Asia, establishing trading posts in India and maybe also in China. And they would be transporting precious products of the rich Far East directly to Lisbon wharves, and cheaply, undercutting the costs of carrying such goods on camels or in ships to Egypt, plus the freight charges on Italian ships in the Mediterranean. Everyone now foresaw that Lisbon would become the most important marketplace in Europe. King João was now no longer interested in Colón's project. What Colón now hoped to do was to get to India before the Portuguese did. He was confident that his would be a much a shorter route. But from now on it would be a race between him and them. He naturally supposed they would be immediately sending ships via the Indian Ocean, and he therefore was eager to have his project receive authorization from some royal court without delay. Any royal court would do.

He could not wait for favorable action by the Spanish Court who were putting every coin they had into their war. The success of Bartolomeu Dias might bring an immediate contract from a monarch in another country. In haste, he arranged for his "brother" Bartolomeo to go to England to present his project to King Henry VII, and if the King of England did not quickly accept the project, then Bartolomeo was to present it to the King of France.

Colón realized that Spaniards would be jealous of this promise of a rosy future for Portugal, and indeed they were, for it seemed to them that a just God should not have given such a reward to Portugal, but more justly should have given it to Spain as deserved recompense to Spanish Christians for their sufferings during centuries of holy war against the infidel Muslims. Although Colón knew why there would be delay in getting his project acepted by the Court of Spain, he would, while his uncle was in England and France, himself continue asking for and hoping for a favorable response from the Examining Commission Queen Isabel had appointed. The accomplishment of Dias and the glorious prospects for Portugal might speed the Commission's decision.

Like everyone else, Colón supposed the Portuguese would quickly be using the route opened to them by Dias. But King João continued to experience political and financial difficulties which compelled postponement of his providing ships for the first expedition by way of the Cape of Good Hope to India. In spite of their eagerness for that first expedition, the Portuguese were unbelievably slow in preparing it. Incredible as it may seem, they delayed the sailing for nine years. Colón returned to Spain in 1489. He continued to advance his arguments, sustained by belief that Queen Isabel would grant his terms even if he could not persuade the members of the royal commission. Attempting to change the geographical opinions of scholars, he had a constant battle on his hands. For four years he continued to look for more arguments to support his argument. He found them in several books, which he annotated. Presumably for part of the time he was in Cordoba, where Beatriz was bringing up his son Ferdinand. He visited La Rabída to keep in touch with his son Diego. To him at that monastery, on May 12th of 1489, the sovereigns (which in this instance meant Queen Isabel) sent him an open letter by which all officials in Castile were ordered to give Cristóbal Colón, who has to come to our court," food and lodging on his journey there. "Why the sovereigns wished to see Colón at this juncture we do not know," says Samuel Eliot Morison.[1] With what we now know, however, the reason seems obvious. Queen Isabel wanted to show off among her Castile and Leon followers a handsome man whose face and figure were superior to her husband's. She foresaw a forthcoming important event which would merit utmost display. It was the surrender of Baza, a strong Muslim defensive post which capitulated on December 4th, 1489. This is implied by Morison's saying that after the Baza surrender, Colón was "again turned out to grass."[3]

The Muslims now clearly saw the end of their last kingdom in Spain. The father of their King Boabdil had foreseen what would make it inevitable, for an anecdote is told of his demonstrating to his entourage how the Christians would capture Granada. He put a gold platter in the middle of a large carpet, and asked his courtiers to seize the platter without stepping on the carpet. No one could see how to do it. He then rolled the carpet and lifted the platter, explaining that their last stronghold, Granada, would be compelled to surrender after the Catholic Kings had seized all the seaports like Baza, through which Granada could obtain essential supplies. Queen Isabel and Ferdinand were rolling up the carpet.

Bartolomeo Colón, meanwhile, had for more than a year been in England trying to convince King Henry VII that the Colón concept of geography was correct. Having failed to persuade that king, Bartolomeo went to France. Though he failed to persuade King Charles VIII, he remained for three years at Fontainbleu as a retainer of Anne de Beaujeu, the sister of the king.

In 1490 when Queen Isabel and King Ferdinand were not campaigning, their court was for part of the time in Seville, while Cristóbal Colón was residing there with the Duke of Medina Celi.

It was after four years of debate and deliberate postponement that the Examining Commission which had met at Salamanca presented its report. As expected, it was adverse, with the same objection which it had raised at the beginning of its deliberations — the ocean between Spain and Asia was too broad. While Queen Isabel officially received the report, she did not agree with the findings, and Colón knew that she did not. She must have given him to understand that, after the conclusion of the war, his Enterprise of the Indies would again be reconsidered. Such at least is to be assumed, since in 1491 he went to Palos and there talked with its leading ship owner, the man of whom Alonso Sánchez of Huelva had written: "I . . . consulted especially with Martín Alonso Pinzón my friend and fellow townsman."[2] Martín Alonso Pinzón was undoubtedly fully informed as to the 1481 voyage of Alonso Sánchez. Colón, ten years later, had no difficulty in persuading Pinzón that he should be thinking of ships, and of getting men to serve as their crews on the voyage which Colón confidently expected to get royal sanction to undertake.

Colón spent the summer of 1491 at La Rabída. Because he there talked openly about leaving Spain for France, it has been supposed that he was actually planning such a move. There is no evidence for this assumption. His talk was motivated. He wanted to create the impression that he was contemplating departure. He wanted the court to hear of it, and the court did. It caused Fray Juan Perez, head of the La Rabída friary, to write to the Queen, urging that she do what she could to persuade Colón to remain in Spain. She was at that time at Santa Fé, the fortified camp in the neighborhood of Granada. She immediately wrote a letter in reply, and had it carried speedily by special messenger to La Rabída, urging Fray Perez to tell Colón that he would soon be asked to come to court. Fray Perez hastened to Santa Fé and reported to her that

Colón would stay in Castile, and would come to her when asked, but he wanted money for new clothing to appear properly at court, and would need a mule on which to make the journey. Since Granada with its hill-top palace was under siege, it was now obviously only a question of time when that last stronghold of the Muslims would be starved into surren-der. Queen Isabel wanted Colón, as he well knew she would, to appear distinctively dressed at the coming victory celebration. Just as she had sent him extra money for him to come appropriately dressed to witness the surrender of Malaga, and again had sent him money to come appro-priately dressed to witness the surrender of Baza, she now sent him 20,000 maravedis. She knew how his tall and handsome figure would make an impression at the coming event, and she was not adverse at having with her on the coming great occasion, a man who looked more regal than anyone else.

That autumn he appeared before her. He remained close to her in the army headquarters at Santa Fé, and when Granada ceased resistance on January 2nd, he marched in with her and the victorious soldiers, and witnessed the historic scene. He saw the Moorish King Boabdil come out of the gate of Alhambra Palace, and kneel, and kiss the hands of King Ferdinand and Queen Isabel. He saw the red and gold banner of their Catholic Majesties raised on the palace towers. This was the greatest day and greatest year in Spanish history, marking as it did the end of a strug-gle of Christian arms against infidels — the end of a war that had lasted for 781 years. It would therefore be the year Spaniards would forever remember.

It meant unity for Spain, for all the kingdoms of the country were now under one rule, under Queen Isabel of Leon and Castile, and King Ferdinand of Aragon, who had also as his, Navarre, Catalonia, the Balearic Isles, and a kingdom in Italy. Spain would never forget 1492.

The ending of the war brought many problems of readjustment. Span-ish energies were now released for peaceful enterprises. Spain did not immediately become a great power among the nations, but Colón firmly believed that he could make it the leading country of Europe. Sharing with him that belief, Queen Isabel disregarded the findings of the Exam-ining Commission and submitted the Colón project to the Royal Coun-cil. She wanted Colón to succeed in finding for Spain the short route to India. She foresaw how his doing it would bring him honors, and would give Spain an opportunity of forging ahead of Portugal. She wanted

Colón to win credit for doing it. She would stand for his project against all opposition.

Before the end of January, the Royal Council flatly rejected Colón's project, and declared that his demands of titles, a viceroy governorship, and financial rewards were inordinate and outrageously exorbitant. They said the opinionated navigator was asking far too much.

Colón, holding to his dream of achieving regal status, was playing for the highest stakes. Knowing himself to be an aristocrat, and son of a prince, with royal blood in his veins, he demanded that success in carrying out his Project of the Indies be rewarded by his being given a title of nobility and a governorship that would be hereditary, for his heirs to hold forever. He would not yield on any of his stipulations. He knew that if he yielded in the slightest, he would appear less than certain as to the possibility of succeeding in his Enterprise, and he therefore continued to insist that he was offering Spain a unique opportunity and a fair bargain — reasonable terms in return for so great a thing as a short route to India, which would bring Spain wealth above that of any other country in Europe. He either guessed that Queen Isabel would reject the thinking of the Royal Council, or she may have privately assured him that she would. But he realized, or she told him, that she must be given a valid excuse for disregarding the Council, and in giving her that excuse he showed consummate skill. He gave the impression that he had lost patience with the Spanish Court, and had made up his mind to leave Spain for France, and give to France the opportunity which Spain was blindly rejecting. He announced that he was packing up and departing from Spain. Ostentatiously, he left Santa Fé. He went, however, a very short distance. A mere four miles away, he put up for the night at a roadside inn. There he confidently waited for what he foresaw would happen. He knew that Luis de Santangel, Keeper of the Privy Purse, believed that Spain must not let slip her one chance of getting to India ahead of the Portuguese.

Santangel, probably by prearrangement with Colón and presumably also with the Queen, hastily went to Queen Isabel to urge her to recall Colón. Santangel said that, while the terms Colón was demanding appeared preposterous, what he was asking would not be too high a price to pay if he should open a Spanish route to India. On the other hand, if he should fail to find the route, or should lose his life in the attempt, the terms would not have to be met.

Santangel's urging was not needed in the way he thought it was. The Queen listened to him and gave the impression that he had changed her mind. She immediately cut through all the red tape, and made an extraordinary gesture, which not only showed her full confidence in Colón, but revealed her feminine trust in him, for she offered to pawn her jewels to pay for the needed ships, and for the sailors' wages. A woman will offer to give up her jewels only where her heart is involved.

Santangel told her that Colón's project would cost her nothing, and that he himself, as he did, would advance the Queen's share of the costs. Colón, Santangel said, since he was backed by friends with means, would himself bear one-eighth of the expense of fitting out one ship.

Seeing now no alternative, the Spanish Court agreed to all of Colón's demands. Lawmen got busy preparing the wording of the various documents that would commit their Majesties to the project.

First was the contract between King Ferdinand and Queen Isabel on the one hand, and Cristóbal Colón on the other. This was formally signed on April 17th. It was called the "Capitulations," since it was a listing of the rewards to be granted to the navigator. This contract granted to him the title Don Cristóbal de Colón "for what he hath discovered." The past tense made his ennoblement conditional, to take effect on the day he came to land in the West. The Capitulations made him "Viceroy and Governor-General over all such mainlands and islands as he shall discover or take possession of." They guaranteed him "a tenth of all gold, silver, pearls, gems, spices and other saleable articles produced or obtained by trade and mining, free of all taxes." They gave him "the option of paying one-eighth of the expenses of any ship sailing to these new possessions, and taking one-eighth of the profits."

The sovereigns and Colón obviously assumed that the inhabitants of the islands off the coast of China would be unprepared to resist Christians with muskets, and would be in need of enlightened governing. The Catholic Kings and Colón thought in terms of war — the use of force backed by divine sanction. Unlike Alonso Sánchez who had gone to the islands on his own, as it were, Colón was going as accredited representative of royalty, with the authority of royalty, and as such he would formally take possession of islands and govern them as Viceroy of their Spanish Majesties.

In another contract called the "Titulo" signed on April 30th, Colón was addressed as plain Cristóbal Colón. The Titulo said:

> After you have discovered and taken possession of the said islands and mainland, or any of them, you shall be our Admiral and Viceroy and Governor-General therein, and shall be empowered thenceforward to call and entitle yourself Don Cristóbal Colón, and your heirs and successors forever may be so entitled, and enjoy the office of Admiral of the Ocean Sea."

Becoming Viceroy and Governor-General, Colón would immediately rule over inhabitants of islands or mainland far removed from the court of any monarch like the Great Khan of China. But the lawmen saw another contingency.

Of course in meeting with and dealing with established monarchs, proper diplomatic amenities must be observed, and so Colón was given credentials. One was a passport inscribed in Latin, the language which all educated people on earth could read, or should be able to read, and it ran thus:

> We herewith send the nobleman Christophorus Colón with three armed caravels across the Ocean Sea toward the regions of India for certain reasons and purposes.

The other was a letter of introduction in three copies — the blank spaces to be filled in with the name and title of any ruler Colón should encounter:

> To the most serene prince
> our very dear friend, we, Ferdinand and Isabel, King and Queen of Castile, Aragon, Leon, etc., give greetings and wishes of good fortune. We have happily learned of your deep respect and high regard for us and our country and of your great desire to be fully informed as to our triumphs. Therefore we have decided to send to you with these letters, our noble captain Christophorus Colón, who will tell you of our good health and prosperity.
> I the King   I the Queen

❋ ⋩⋩⋩⋩⋩⋩⋩⋩⋩⋩⋩⋩⋩⋩⋩⋩⋩⋩⋩⋩⋩⋩⋩⋩⋩ ❋

You have showed that Queen Isabel broke the impasse. Do you think when King Ferdinand signed the Contract and Credentials with her, he was in full agreement with her?

Of course.

Maybe he just came along for the ride?

No. While she did not let him have any voice in affairs of her kingdoms, Colón's project concerned Aragon as much as Castile.

You have said he disliked Colón.

He did, most cordially.

In 1492 King Ferdinand was forty years of age, and Colón was thirty-two. He may have hated him.

They hated each other. But King Ferdinand would welcome Colón's succeeding.

Do you suppose he may have thought to himself, If this much too handsome young man loses his life in his venture, it may be just as well?

I don't think so. The King saw as clearly as anyone what it would mean to Spain to have a short route to India.

11

ENTERPRISE
OF THE INDIES

The young man, who had imposed his will on the Spanish monarchs, now had the agreeable and engrossing task of preparing ships for his expedition. On May 12th he left Granada for Palos, in which tiny port he was well acquainted with the leading shipowners and captains. His negotiations with them were speeded, and simplified, by a penalty which had been placed on the port for some infraction of law. Palos was required to furnish use of two caravels for a year, at no cost to their Majesties. The royal order to that effect had been signed on the same day with the Credentials, and was carried to Palos by Cristóbal Colón. There is therefore a strong suspicion that it was at the wily suggestion of Colón, and undoubtedly with the hearty agreement of King Ferdinand, and their Majesties deliberately caught the people of Palos in some misdemeanor, in order to save the Crown from having to pay for the two ships. Colón called the mayor of Palos and the councillors of the town to a meeting on May 23rd, at which the royal order was read to them. Here are the pertinent sentences from it:

> Ferdinand and Isabel, by the grace of God King and Queen of Castile, Leon, Aragon, Sicily, etc. etc., to you Diego Rodriguez Prieto and all the other inhabitants of the town of Palos, greeting and grace.
>
> Know ye that whereas for certain things done and committed by you to our disservice you were condemned and obligated by our Council to provide us for a twelve month with two equipped caravels at your own proper charge and expense .... And whereas we have commanded Cristóbal Colón to go with three armed caravels as our Captain of the same, toward certain regions of the Ocean Sea, to perform certain things for our service, and we desire that he take with him.the said two caravels with which you are thus required to serve us; therefore we command ... you have all ready and prepared two caravels, as you are required by virtue of the said sentence, to depart with the said Cristóbal Colón whither we have commanded him to go ... and we have commanded him to give you advance pay for four months for the people who are to sail aboard the said caravels at the rate to be paid to the other people who are to be in the said ... caravels.[1]

One sees in this the fine hand of a man who knew the perfect blending of compulsion and compensation to get the ships and sailors for a voyage to an unspecified destination. There was of course much resentment in Palos against Colón. Many complaints were openly voiced that his voyage would be a vain effort — would fail to find islands. Opposition based upon this argument might have delayed preparations for much more than three months, if it had not been for an old sea dog in Palos, Pedro Vasquez. Forty years before, Vasquez had sailed with a captain from Madeira, Diego Teive, who had crossed the weed-strewn Sargasso Sea, and had gone northward to Ireland, and then southward and eastward, and had discovered Flores and Corvo, the westernmost islands of the Azores. Known and respected by his neighbors for having made this large swing out and around in the Atlantic, and now asserting positively that Colón could and would find the islands he sought, Vasquez silenced most of the skeptics.

In a little over two months, Colón had three ships conditioned, provisioned, and manned. Getting crew members was eased by an announcement that all civil and criminal charges would be dropped in the case of any man who sailed with him. He got ninety men as crew and officers. He himself paid one-eighth of the cost of the expedition, the money for that purpose advanced by friends, such as the Duke of Medina Celi.

Queen Isabel had lent ear to the growing demand that Jews who did not become sincere Christians be expelled from Spain. It seems that King Ferdinand hesitated to go along with her in this, and if so, it is one fact to his credit. She may have believed that if she persecuted unconverted Jews, God would more readily forgive all her sins. Since she supported the Spanish Inquisition, we should look at the origin of that horror.

Early Christians in the first three centuries were thrown to the lions by Roman Emperors. In natural reaction, St. Augustine (354-430) permitted the persecution of heretics. The Vandals, who were Arian Christians, persecuted orthodox Christians for 105 years until they were crushed by the orthodox in 534 A.D. The orthodox reacted not only by preserving "vandal" as a word of execration, but by instituting a wholesale persecution of all heretics by fines, imprisonment, confiscation of property, exile, hanging, and burning at the stake. This un-Christlike activity continued popular for more than a thousand years. The most regrettable thing about it was what it did to Christianity. It set doctrine and belief above love for one's fellow human beings. It created a spiritual vacuum into which, only a few decades after it began, the spiritual teachings of Muhammad naturally flowed. In 1478, Pope Sixtus IV granted to Spanish kings the right to appoint persecuting inquisitors. In October of 1483, Queen Isabel and King Ferdinand made Tomas de Torquemada the Inquisitor General. Eventually, in Spain there were 100,000 trials of suspected Jews, and 2,000 executions. Their Majesties knew that several officials in the royal administration were converts, but these were shrewd, politically minded and efficient and respected servants of the Crown, and so there was no reason to question their sincerity.

The ships of the Colón Enterprise left Palos on the day when unconverted Jews were expelled from Spain. That fact has raised question as to whether Colón's choosing that day to sail was more than mere coincidence. Knowing him as we do, it is a safe assumption that he sailed as soon as his ships were ready, and with consideration only of wind and depth of tidal water down the Tinto River into Saltes River and so to sea. The Christian side of him, his father's side, dominated him. Having for a good reason become a Franciscan tertiary, and feeling himself a Christian prince, he would not have felt overwhelmingly distressed by the exiling of Jews unwilling to conform. He had looked out for himself. Let others look out for themselves.

School children can tell the names of his ships, or think they can; but they know them mistakenly, for the name of one of them was *Santa Clara*. It was in respect for her popular master-owner, Juan Niño, that the *Santa Clara* was called *Niña*. Samuel Eliot Morison expresses regret that no one knows what the *Pinta*, the so-called *Niña*, and the *Santa Maria* looked like.[2] After which he devotes twenty pages to an attempt to reconstruct their appearance so that we can visualize them. For students of seafaring, this is instructive. But this is where enthusiasm for shipping draws Morison off course. Biography is concerned with motivations, impulses, desires, and their effects upon character and actions. The names of Colón's three ships have no biographical value. What difference would it make if their names had been *Seahorse, Coca,* and *Bingo?*

As for those who raised question as to the size of the ships in which Colón and his men sailed successfully in the Atlantic, we today hear of crossings of that ocean even in hurricane season in sailboats less than thirty feet in length, and of crossings not in hurricane season in boats of twelve feet, eleven feet, and ten feet, etc. The ships of Colon's crossing were in order of seventy feet in length. The *Pinta* and the *Niña* were about 80 tons each, and the *Santa Maria* was about 100 tons.

Children have been taught to think of Colón as a man who had more courage than any other man who ever lived, a super-courage in facing unknown perils. They have been told he was the only navigator of his day who dared sail far to the West in the Atalntic. This notion of him was conceived by landsmen. Many sailors had been accustomed to making annual trading voyages betwen the Mediterranean and northern countries of Europe, and some to Iceland. There was some trade with Greenland. It is true that Colón did what he did against a background of ignorance and fear. Perils there were, but no more than in other fields. There was a risk in doing anything. Colón insisted that he knew how to conquer the ocean. His courage was obvious. What needs to be emphasized was the tower of strength within him. His self-assurance exuded confidence. He subdued fears in others. He knew prevailing winds and currents, and had a close estimate as to the ocean's width. His personal power was sustained by meditation and prayer, and by his conviction that he was in close and constant touch with God.

From the coast of Spain Colón set his course for the Canary Islands. News of his preparations had gone the rounds of seaport talk. The Portuguese, suspecting that he intended something different from what he had announced, had a fleet of several armed vessels at the southern side of the Canaries to prevent his going into the South Atlantic. In the Canaries, he got the *Niña* altered so that she was square-rigged like the *Pinta* and *Santa Maria*. While at Gomera, he met the ruler of that island, Dona Beatriz de Peraza. She had been born Beatriz de Bobadilla. She was a beauty who in her girlhood had been a maid of honor to Queen Isabel. King Ferdinand had eyes for her, and she had borne a child to him. At the time Colón met her, she was a widow and under thirty years of age. He was entertained by her in her residence from September 2nd to 6th. They fell in love, illustrating the adage, "A sailor has a wife in every port."

On September 8th, Colón with his three ships sailed out of sight of land, headed west from the Canaries. Martín Alonso Pinzón was in command of the *Pinta,* and his brother Francisco Martín was her Master. A younger brother, Vincente Yanes Pinzón was in command of *Niña*. On the flagship *Santa Maria*, Colón was in command of the expedition. Juan de la Cosa, a different man from the map-maker of that name, was her Master, and Peralonso Niño, her Pilot.

Keeping the three ships in sight of each other in the daylight hours was no problem, for the *Santa Maria* was a slower sailer than the smaller ships, and so with shortened sails they could keep position behind and in sight of her. At night they might outsail her, and so a torch at the stern of the *Santa Maria,* enabled them to keep in consort. Colón's orders to them were transmitted by the number of flashes of torch.

On the foremost sails of each ship, the ensign of Castile and Leon, a green cross with a crown on each arm, one over an F for Ferdinand and the other with a Y for Ysabel, gave Colón assurance that he was backed by royal authority against any disagreement or criticism from any of the captains and pilots. No one else except his Uncle Bartolomeo would ever know how this voyage he was making would recompense him for what his father had been denied. With considerable self-satisfaction, he looked up and saw the sails being steadily filled. They were bowling along day and night at close to 4 knots. The prevailing wind, what we now call the Northeast Trade Wind, was what he had known he would have from the Canaries, and it was what he welcomed. The stronger and steadier it was the more he rejoiced. But the wind so favorable to his purpose raised a fear in everyone else. The captains, pilots and common sailors could not see how they could ever sail back to Spain if they continued with such wind westward. They knew that only by constant tacking could they make any progress against such wind. It would be slow progress. Unless they turned back at once they would soon be so far out that they would never again see home. They feared they would perish for lack of water and food, or would die of scurvy.

Colón knew how he would get home. It would be at a different latitude, where, as he knew, there were prevailing winds from the west. But he held this knowledge secret, and would not divulge it to anyone until it was unavoidably revealed by his returning to Spain.

He had foreseen the reactions of the officers and men when they found they were being blown steadily westward. He knew they were wondering how they could persuade him to turn back before it was too late, as they supposed, for them to save their lives. He sensed that they might threaten him, and so he kept two logs, one for his eyes only, and the other to lessen their apprehension. In the log he showed them, he entered a lesser distance traversed each day than that he had privately computed. His eagerness to cover distance caused him to over-compute.

His voyage out of sight of land was 3100 nautical miles, sailed in 34 days. The best twenty-four hours' sailing was about 182 miles, a speed of over seven knots.

On one occasion when officers and men, all but four of whom were Spaniards, threatened his life if he did not desist sailing west, he sharply replied that if they killed him, they would all hang when they got home. He had the law of the sea with him as well as the backing of Their Royal Majesties. Being forcefully reminded of the situation, they ceased threatening him, though they continued to mutter against him.

He has been called the best navigator of his time. He was certainly the most open-minded. Mariners had assumed that Polaris, the North Star, was precisely at the true North and that the compass would always point to it. On his crossing of the Atlantic in that year 1492, he observed that the compass no longer pointed to Polaris and each night pointed farther to the west of it. By mid-September, it was pointing six degrees to the west. Seeking an explanation of this, he concluded that Polaris is not precisely at the North, but rotates as do all the stars, though in a very small circle around the Pole. So far as we know, he was the first to make this discovery. His conclusion, however, did not explain the swing of as much as six degrees from the North. Neither Colón or anybody else in his day understood magnetic variation, and did not yet know that the North Magnetic Pole is located some 900 miles away from the True North Pole though which all the geographic meridians pass.

When the Master and Pilot of *Santa Maria* saw that the compass no longer pointed at Polaris, they were terrified. They despaired. Colón sensed he must somehow ease their fears. How could he? Always resourceful, he found a way to beat the compass. He remembered how in his privateering he had reacted to fears of the crew of his ship when they were near Sardinia, and how he had secretly changed the point of the compass, so that they sailed in a direction for which they lacked courage, to a position off Cape Carthage. He now did the same thing. He told the Master and Pilot that just before dawn they would find the compass pointing to the True North. That night he secretly tampered with the compass, shifted it around so that it would point to the North Star, and thus he set at rest the fears of officers and crew.

On September 22nd, a brief stiff blow came from the west, and he wrote in his Journal of the voyage: "This contrary wind was of much use to me" since the men were "thinking no winds blew for returning to Spain." And again he wrote: "Very useful to me was the high sea."

The officers and men of all three ships became resigned to looking for the land he told them they would soon find. Eagerness to sight some island caused hope to rise in them as sight of seaweed, and a flight of migrating birds, and clouds at the horizon which they mistook for islands.

At the commencement of the voyage Colón had given orders for night sailing. But he had also told the Captains and pilots of the three ships that they were not to do any night sailing after they had sailed a distance to the west which he specified. From what he had learned in Reykjavik of a land to the southwest of Iceland, and from what he knew of the voyage of Alonso Sánchez of Huelva, and from what he believed to be the distance from the Canary Islands to Cipangu (Japan), he was convinced that night sailing would not be safe after they had gone 700 leagues. The greatest peril at sea was being caught on the windward side of land. With a following wind, and in the darkness of night they might approach too closely to waves breaking on a rocky coast, and thus be wrecked. Colón's estimate of his actual crossing from the Canaries was 1090 leagues, or 3466 nautical miles. At the time he gave orders to cease night sailing, his computation of width of ocean seemed to be correct, for they saw in the water a green branch that was bearing a flower. Land could not be far. Then they saw a cane floating, and various man-shaped wooden objects. Knowing they were near land, Colón was imprudent in giving orders to resume night sailing on the evening of October 11th, when a gale was blowing them at about nine knots. But he had been pressured by having promised to change course for home if they did not sight land within three days. At 10 p.m. that evening he thought he saw a waving light ahead, and so did one of the crew on the *Santa Maria.* The light may have been imagined. It may have been on an islanders' fishing boat. When the moon rose at 2 p.m., *Pinta* was in the lead, and her lookout, Rodrigo de Triana clearly sighted land. A signal shot was fired from the *Pinta,* and everyone saw an island six miles ahead.

Luckily it was not too large an island and they were able to clear its southern end and get to the leeward side of it.

After daylight, when they landed, Cristóbal Colón made as big a show as he could in planting a cross, and in taking possession of the island with unfurling of the royal banners, and formal proclamation of that island's now belonging to their Spanish Majesties; and the moment that was done, he had everyone hail him as Don Cristóbal de Colón and as Admiral and Governor and Viceroy, and had them all swear to obey him as such.

One thing you should have done in this chapter.

What?

Tell on what island Colón first landed. Did'nt he name it San Salvador?

He did.

Well then, — Don't just shrug your shoulders. Readers want to know what island it was.

All we know is it was an island northeast of Cuba.

Isn't it generally understood that it was not the one now called San Salvador, but was Watling Island?

That is what Samuel Eliot Morison swallowed.

But Watling Island is of the size Colón said, and it was what he described — a large lake in its interior, and a point of cliff at its northern end almost separate, which could easily be made an island and would be a good site for a fort.

Yes, but several islands in the area are similar in size, with interior lake and broken cliff, Dr. Robert H. Fuson, of the Department of Geography at the University of South Florida at Tampa, has argued that the sailing directions to other islands as given by Colon, with assumption that those directions are as he wrote them, simply do not fit with Watling Island, or other islands near it. Professor Fuson shows that an island of the Caicos group about 200 miles southeast of Watling may be the one on which Colon landed on October 12th.

So it is an open question?

Yes. Whatever island, Colon believed it was in the Indies.

12

LARGER THAN NAVARRE

The people of the islands which Colón believed to be the Indies seemed to him to be existing without restraint of law in that state of nature of which ancient philosophers and poets had enthused. Their unashamed nudity suggested the original condition of man, before sin entered. To Colón, as to most of the Spaniards, they were people from whom gold could be obtained by trade, honest bargaining, or if necessary, by force. On the second day after landing, Colón observed and wrote of these Indians that they were "unskilled in war . . . . With fifty men they could all be compelled to do all that we wished . . . . They would obey without opposition every order given to them." A few days later he was saying: "Ten men could put to flight ten thousand of them

. . . . These people can all easily be made Christians, since they have no religion, and do not worship idols." He thus put into words what was to be the compulsion which Europeans would press upon primitive people.

The discovery of hammocks in which one slept in mid-air with a most comfortable sensation helped create the impression that life in the Indies was idyllic, except for the ugly fact soon learned that the people of these charming islands lived in daily terror of "Caribs" who were cannibals, and frequently raided them to capture boys and girls to be eaten. On an island near to the one on which he first landed, a party sent out by Colón to look for water visited several houses, looking for more than water. They no doubt found women in the houses. Colón, being a strong and lusty young man, was both shocked and fascinated at seeing out in the open for the first time in his life what was never seen in Spain, naked men and women without a stitch of clothing. And beautiful naked girls. They did not seem to be at all embarrassed by their complete nudity, but were obviously fascinated by the white male strangers who had not come to kill or eat them. Whatever dalliance there was, and there seemed to be no limit to it, Colón held to his purpose. He wrote in his journal: "In any case I am determined to go to the mainland, and to the city of Quinsay, and to present your Highness' letters to the Grand Khan." For this reason he took on board native guides. Illiterate islanders the world over have been able to draw surprisingly accurate maps of islands neighboring their own, from direct knowledge acquired through travel between the islands. Colón wrote in his Journal of seeing a dug-out canoe 70 feet in length, capable of carrying 150 people. Although his native guides and he could not understand each others' language, they showed him that he was far from a very large land. They said the name of this was Colba or Cuba. To Cuba he went, thinking it might be Cipangu (Japan), but when he saw the nudity of its inhabitants, he concluded it was not Japan.

A year later in a letter to Gabriel Sánchez, Treasurer of the King, he wrote of Cuba: "I found it to be so large, without any apparent end, that I believed it was not an island, but a continent, a province of Cathay."[1] It suited him to believe Cuba was part of the continent of Asia, even though he wrote in the same letter to Gabriel Sánchez: "Meanwhile, I learned from some Indians I had seized at this place, that this country was really an island."[2] But the belief that Cuba was part of the continent was so essential to his Contract that two years later he changed his mind about it, as we shall see.

Near the eastern end of Cuba's north shore, he took sight of a star which he mistakingly assumed was Polaris. In consequence of this error, he set his latitude at twenty degrees north of where he really was. From this he concluded in 1492 that Cuba must be the mainland of Asia.

The naked girls were exotic and an irresistible lure. The Spaniards were also much taken with tobacco. They described it as a firebrand held in hand with burning herbs in it, and from which one drank the smoke. The men with Colón failed to perceive that smoking by the Indians was a meaningful or a religious ceremony. An Indian did not smoke just for his own pleasure. After one puff, or a couple of puffs, he passed the firebrand to another man in a gesture of friendship.

Europeans made smoking a personal habit.

Some of the Indians wore rings, arm bands, and necklaces of gold. The Spaniards soon got possession of these by giving in exchange brightly colored beads. But where did the natives get their gold? The question was not immediately answered, since the Indians did not at first understand what the white men were eager to know. The Spaniards assumed that the metal came from a mine. Where was the mine? Martín Alonzo Pinzón, resentful at having been compelled to provide Colón with his ship the *Pinta,* was eager to go on his way and be the first to reach the gold mine. The moment he understood from the Indians that most of their gold came from an island to the east of Cuba called "Bohio," he summarily departed for that island without asking the Admiral's permission, or telling in which direction he was going. It was an incipient gold rush, and of course, mutiny.

Colón, who had ruthlessly kidnapped five young men, seven women and three boys, was looking for the source of the gold. When he learned that its principal source was on an island to the east, he sailed on December 6th from the eastern end of Cuba, and crossing fifty miles of water, landed on the island which he at first called Johanna. He followed its north coast eastward.

He recorded his impressions in writing that this island had the beauty of Spain and mountains comparable with the grandeur of the Spanish sierras. He found "resemblance to the land of Spain though much superior." On December 9th he named this island (now Haiti) the Spanish Island — Española. Into his journal, which would be read by their Majesties, he repeatedly expressed ardent Christian orthodoxy. He said of the natives over whom he would be Governor, "your Majesties can convert them, as you have destroyed those who would not confess to the Father, Son, and Holy Ghost."

With delight close to ecstacy he entered harbors and thrilled to the beauty of the trees and rivers. He planned cities and forts. His imagination soared, for the size of the island exalted him. This island, he made comparison, "is larger than England and Scotland together . . . . The distance around Española is greater than all Spain from Colonia to Fontarabia."[3] He congratulated himself with the thought of what a great thing it would be to be governor of so large an island. Believing that God had chosen him to accomplish what he had done, he told himself that he deserved such a reward, "for God is wont to listen to his servants who love his precepts, even in impossibilities, as has happened to me in the present instance, who have accomplished what human strength has hitherto never attained."[4]

On December 12th he took formal possession of Española at a place where he intended to establish his headquarters as Governor of all the Indies. In his journal he at once began to express gubernatorial policy: "Your Highnesses will command a city and a fort to be built." You "ought not permit any foreigner to set foot there." "Send learned men who will ascertain the truth of all."

When he heard what the natives of Española called the man-eating men they feared, he concluded from their word that the "cannibals" were "Khan" people, subjects of the Great "Khan."

A young and lovely naked girl was brought aboard the *Santa Maria*. He gave her food and "other wants," and sent her off fully clothed. He believed that she thought him to be the leader of "men from Heaven." Everything in Española seemed to be near to heavenly. He acquired parrots of blue, red, green, purple, and yellow plumage. He noted that some of the girls in Española were "almost as white" as girls in Spain. The land was "fertile and beautiful, better than the plains of Cordova." In Española, the "mockingbirds sang like the nightingales of Spain." The ships were daily visited by many naked "most handsome men and women" who were "without any shame." Española was "a terrestrial paradise."

Keeping most of his thoughts above the nudity, he named capes, harbors and rivers from the days in the church calendar on which he came to them. Seeking the source of the gold, he believed he was getting near to the gold mine. When he heard the natives call the central area of their great island "Cibao," he assumed they were mispronouncing "Cipangu." Everything seemed to be shaping to perfection when he learned that the natives got their gold from Cibao.

Confident that he was about to achieve everything he wanted, he felt he could relax. Sailing along near the coast he retired on Christmas Eve, leaving the officer of the watch in charge of the sailing. That officer soon lay down to sleep, leaving the steering to the helmsman. The helmsman left the steering to the ship's boy. Just after midnight the *Santa Maria.* touched a coral reef and slid up on it. The boy shouted. Colón immediately ordered launching of the ship's boat to be rowed with as many oars as possible to draw the ship back off the reef, but the officer of the watch fearing consequences to himself, cowardly took the boat and had himself rowed to the *Niña.* The captain of the *Niña* promptly sent him back to the *Santa Maria,* but by then it was too late, for each swell had lifted *Santa Maria* farther on to the reef, and the coral had already cut through her hull. All Christmas Day Colón kept the crew busy taking the food and equipment and everything of value out of the wreck. The shock of losing his flagship was however soon relieved by belief that the wreck had been divinely purposed, when he learned from the natives that from the bay where the wreck occurred, there was a direct route inland to the gold-bearing area.

Since the *Niña* could not carry more than the number of men in her own crew plus the Indians Colón had with him to be taken to Spain as showpieces, he was compelled to leave about as many men on shore as had been in *Santa Maria.* This gave him the opportunity to choose who were the most efficient men to sail home with him, and to part company from some he had found to be not reliable, like the officer of the watch, Juan de la Cosa, whose negligence had caused the wreck. He ordered the building of a fort, using timber from *Santa Maria.* He named the bay and the fortified settlement La Navidad (Nativity) — Christmas Day. He left in the fort 39 men, in the charge of one he thoroughly trusted, his friend Diego de Harana, cousin of Beatriz de Harana.

While the fort was being built, natives brought word that another ship, obviously the *Pinta,* was somewhere along the coast to the east of them. At about the same time, the men on the *Pinta* heard from the natives of the wreck of the *Santa Maria.* Colon had intended to sail directly home from La Navidad, but he preferred to have two ships in company for the homeward ocean crossing, and so on January 4th he sailed away from La Navidad to the eastward along the coast, looking for the *Pinta*. Two days later he met that ship sailing westward.

The old experienced sea captain, Martín Alonso Pinzón, very well knew that he had violated maritime law in deserting the Admiral Colón. It seems obvious that he would not have to come to the meeting if he had not heard of the wreck, for the charges against him would be unanswerable if Colón sailing home with only one ship were lost at sea. The excuses he gave to the man who was now Admiral, for having separated from the flagship, were dishonest and invalid, but the Admiral swallowed his anger, and did not condescend to dispute with him.

Colón held his temper and reserved judgement. He made it appear that he accepted Pinzon's excuse and bore him no ill will. But when he got back to Spain, he would have the old man punished for disobeying their Majesties who had ordered that Pinzon's ship serve the purposes of the Enterprise of the Indies. Pinzon would regret having gone off on his own as he did. It had been desertion. The old man ought to be clapped in irons as an object lesson. But he was a capable captain and his help might be needed in the homeward crossing. In Spain, charges against him would make a perfect case of mutiny, and would show everyone that the Admiral of the Ocean Sea was not a man to be trifled with. What most deeply disturbed the Admiral now was that Pinzon had visited the mid-island region, the gold-bearing Cibao. It was more than presumable that Pinzon and his crew had obtained much more gold than they had admitted to having found. He could order a search of the *Pinta* immediately, but that would antagonize everyone on the *Pinta,* and he wanted cooperation for the return winter crossing which he knew would be rougher than the western crossing had been. At Palos, he would have the *Pinta* searched for gold, before he would permit any of her crew to go ashore.

On January 16th the two ships sailed away from Española, with the Admiral setting their course for Spain.

We can safely assume that we know what must have been his emotions and thoughts as he began his homeward crossing. He now had everything he had demamded. He had become a nobleman, and Admiral of the Ocean Sea, and Viceroy and Governor of islands. He believed he would be a supremely capable and good governor, since he was giving thought to the nature of the people who would be under his authority. He wanted the inhabitants under his governing to cease to be naked

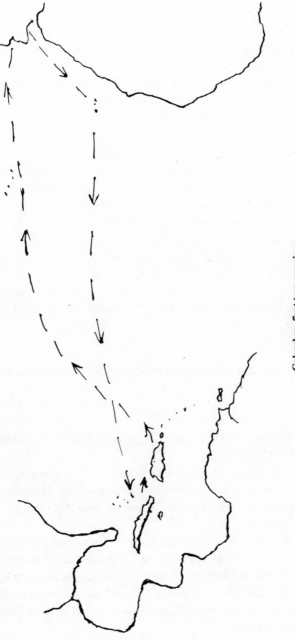

Columbus, first two crossings

men and women running around shamelessly, and lacking the character and stability which religion and Spanish customs would bring to them. He would have them wear clothes. He would have them taught to be obedient to law. He would change their habit of living. He perceived no great problem in all that.

His governorship gave him the deepest satisfaction. As he saw the mountains of Española disappearing below the horizon, he congratulated himself on having obtained what he had dreamed of ever since that day in his boyhood, when he had been told who his father had been. Knowing that he could not reveal himself as a prince of royal blood, he had gone about realizing his dream in the only possible way open to him. He had shaped everything to give himself power like that of a ruler. And now he had it — what would compensate for what his father had failed to get. His contract, as he had insisted it must be, gave him title as Perpetual Viceroy and Governor. Its being hereditary made it like a kingship. Whatever kings there might be on the mainland of Asia in Cathay and India, on Española there was as yet no single overlord. As Viceroy and Governor of Española, he would have everything he wanted. He would build his island into a kingdom, his kingdom.

❀ ⁂ ❀

So it was gold that made Colón prefer Española to all the other islands in the Caribbean.

Not only gold. The natives there were comparatively peace-loving, not war-like Caribs. They were not cannibals. The beauty of the island rivalled the best in Spain. Above all, Española met his ambition.

How so?

Because it was larger than Navarre. It was more than seven times the size of Navarre. It was larger than all of Aragon and Navarre put together. In becoming its governor, Colón would wield power which had been denied to his father. He would take personal satisfaction in avenging his father against the scheming Queen Juana who had stolen a throne for her son, King Ferdinand.

13

FAME

For six months sailors in Palos and Cadiz and Seville had been saying that if Cristóbal Colón was lucky he might find some islands. If he did, he might manage to get from island to island as far as to the Indies. Learned men were saying that only by lucky island hopping could he sail the several months it would take him to get all the way to Asia. Since it would take him another several months to return, he would not be heard from until a full year had passed. The chances were he would never be heard from. Everyone agreed that their Majesties had taken on an improbable gamble with Colón. All along the waterfront, men who knew the sea were sure he had been lost, and the extortionate terms of his Contract would never be fulfilled.

By the end of January, reports from Portugal and the west coast of Spain were that there had never been known a winter to set in with such great ocean storms. The more surprising was it therefore when there came a rumor that one of Colón's three ships, the *Pinta,* had entered a port on the Spanish coast just north of Portugal. Her captain, Martín Alonso Pinzón, it was definitely reported, had sent word post speed across Spain to their Majesties in Barcelona that Colón had been lost at sea in a terrible tempest. Nevertheless, there had been an important discovery. Pinzón asked permission to come to court at once to tell their Majesties all about it. Pinzón saw himself as the great man who had won the honors. He thought he would receive credit for having added islands of the Indies to their Majesties' possessions.

To his surprise, their Majesties immediately replied that they would not give audience to him, the captain of one ship. They would give audience to Colón, the commander of the whole expedition. Old Pinzón was hit hard by this rebuff.

On the heels of the word from Pinzón had come definite news that the smallest of Colón's three ships, the *Niña,* on March 4th, had been driven by a storm toward the Portuguese coast. She would have been wrecked, if her captain had not been able to steer into the mouth of the Tagus River and into the harbor of Lisbon. And following that, it was learned that the captain on the *Niña* was Cristóbal Colón.

The next word from Lisbon was that Colón had succeeded in reaching the Indies! This news spread like wildfire, not only in Spain but on to other countries. It was reported that King João of Portugal had received Colón with courtesy. He had actualy permitted him to sit down in the royal presence! The people of Portugal had been no less generous. In churches throughout their land, they had given thanks to the Lord that now missionaries could be sent directly to China and India to convert all the rest of the world to the true religion. Many of the Portuguese appeared to have rejoiced sincerely that God had given to Christian kings, the sovereigns of Spain, such a great opportunity to convert souls and further the religion of Christ. Religious fervor for the moment surmounted national rivalry. Hearing how it was, Spaniards swelled with pride.

Everyone eagerly awaited Colón's return to Spain. On March 15th he sailed the *Niña* up the Tinto River and dropped anchor in Palos Harbor. Just after her, and with the same tide, came in the *Pinta.* But when the

Pinta dropped anchor in Palos Harbor, Martín Alonso Pinzón was not on board. Why not? Everyone in Palos began asking: Where was he? Then they learned that, while the *Pinta* was coming up the river, Pinzón had himself rowed ashore in the ship's boat, and had gone into his house.

If they asked Colón, who was quick to insist that they call him Don Colón and Admiral, why Captain Pinzón had avoided coming into the harbor to enjoy the hearty reception they would have given him, the Admiral probably refused to answer, or may have said merely that Captain Pinzón had his reasons, and always did what he thought it wise to do. It was soon learned that the old man had taken to his bed and had died.

From the men on the *Niña* everyone in Palos heard of the fearful storms they had endured for many days and nights when they were wet and cold, with nothing hot to eat or drink. They all showed the physical effects of what they had suffered, and the admiral most of all. The Admiral would not tell them what course he had followed on the homeward voyage, for the latitude of both crossings, westward and eastward, was his secret. It was what he had discovered years before, when he had sailed on Portuguese ships, and the details of it would be only for the ears of their Majesties. He did tell them what all his crew vividly remembered, their losing sight of the *Pinta*, and their battle to keep afloat for three days without sleep just before they got into the lee of Santa Maria, the southernmost of the Azores. They had desperately needed water, wood, and provisions, but the governor of that island assumed that they had trespassed into waters claimed by Portugal. He thought they had sailed around Africa to India, in defiance of the treaty Portugal had compelled Spain to accept. When half of the crew of the *Niña* went ashore to a church to give thanks to God as they had vowed to do for having let them survive the storm, the governor had arrested them. The governor did not believe that Don Colón was Admiral of the Ocean Sea under the laws of Castile, and laughed at him until one of his own officers inspected the Contract and Credentials, and told the governor he would be starting a war with their Spanish Majesties if he did not release the men he had arrested. With everyone back on the *Niña*, they were glad to get away from the Azores and the Portuguese.

Why then, the Admiral was asked, since the Portuguese were so ready to suspect you, why did you go into Lisbon Harbor? He told them why. He had no choice. He had congratulated himself on being free of the

Portuguese, but then came a great tempest, the worst he had ever experienced. Thinking that the *Niña* and all on board would be lost, he wrote a brief account of his findings of the islands of the Indies, and put it in a barrel, which was then sealed and cast into the sea. He hoped it might be washed ashore somewhere. (It never was). He had been constantly cold and wet and without sleep for several days and nights. He suffered agonizing pains in his legs, and was crippled almost to being unable to walk. His hair was turning white. The storm seemed endless. They were being driven helpless. Suddenly he saw land directly ahead, and expected they would in a few moments be dashed to pieces. But by God's good mercy, he recognized from a contour of the land, that it was the coast of Portugal close to the Tagus River. He was able to save the *Niña* by steering into that river, and so into Lisbon Harbor.

The authorities in Lisbon suspected that he had been around Africa. Bartolomeu Dias, who had found the Cape of Good Hope, came on a warship to the *Niña* intending to take Colón and his men prisoners. He and Colón had met years before, and when he was shown the Contract and Credentials, he was persuaded that Don Colón had found for Spain the short route to India. Recognizing Don Colón as now Admiral, he ordered a celebration, and sent a message to King João to inform him of what he believed the Admiral had accomplished.

King João invited him to meet with him in a monastery where he happened to be staying, about thirty leagues from Lisbon. The Admiral felt almost too ill to make the journey of two days on a mule, but he went, taking with him to show the king some Indians, parrots, and gold ornaments from Española. The king received him with courtesy, but could not quite conceal his displeasure at what the Admiral said he had accomplished. He implied that the islands of the Indies might be in a region claimed by Portugal, and he asked several questions trying to find out precisely where they were. The Admiral avoided answering the questions by calling attention to the parrots and saying that nobody in Portugal or Spain had ever seen their like. From his not answering the king's questions directly, he sensed that the king's advisors wanted him to be killed, and he cleverly caught them mentally off base as it were, by asking for some beans. The king and his courtiers could not imagine what for, until the beans were brought and one of the Indians laid them out on the floor to make an outline of the islands in the Indies. Then King João realized fully what he had lost by not accepting Colón's Enterprise of the Indies years before, and he gave the Admiral a message to carry to their Spanish Majesties.

On his return toward Lisbon, the Admiral met the Queen in a castle and gave her a brief account of the Indies without beans. He then put up for the night at an inn. But by that time King João had obviously listened to his advisors who had changed his mind and had suggested a way to dispose of the problem presented by the finding of the Indies. The king sent to the inn a proposal that the Admiral travel overland across Portugal to Castile on mules with an escort of soldiers.

The Admiral was suspicious of the king's motive. He feared that if he submitted to a soldier escort he might never reach Spain, but could be slain en route, with no witnesses to tell what had happened to him. The king's proposal was obviously purposed to separate him from the *Niña* on which he had his Journal giving the details of the course he had sailed from the Canaries, and his proofs of his finding the Indies — information which Portugal would retain and withhold from their Spanish Majesties. If he let the king do that, even if the soldiers escorted him safely to Castile, his Contract with their Majesties would be unfulfilled, and he might lose his titles and governorship. Fearing that he might be forced to do what the king wanted, he quickly left the inn and traveled through the night to Lisbon, got on board the *Niña,* raised sail at 8 A.M., and unceremoniously departed from Lisbon Harbor and the Tagus River.

The sailors from the *Niña* and *Pinta* were asked endless questions by their friends and neighbors in Palos. They told all they knew. They knew the number of days they had sailed from the Canary Islands to the first island upon which they had landed in the Indies. But the precise distance they had sailed westward, and the compass direction by which they had sailed — these things were known only by Don Colón. He talked as freely as the sailors about everything else, or almost everything else. He was keenly aware that every word he uttered would be carried ahead of him to their Majesties in Barcelona, and that is how he wanted it to be.

On March 31st, he went to Seville, where everyone was prepared to pay honor to the man who had found for Spain a short route to India. Word had gone the rounds that he was now to be called Don Cristóbal Colón and Admiral of the Ocean Sea. To him the city of Seville gave a hero's tumultuous welcome. In the parade through the streets, the Admiral displayed his proofs that he had reached the Indies: colorful parrots, six copper-skinned natives of the Indies, samples of cotton from the Indies, curious weapons, strange plants, and some gold ornaments. The Admiral, with unbending dignity, with a wave of his hand, acknowledged the plaudits of the populace. The spectators, looking at Don Colón as he rode by, said to each other, Portugal is welcome to her long route around Africa to India, if she ever uses it. We have the quick short route! The Indies are only one month's sail west of the Canary Islands! Don Colón had been right, and everyone else wrong! No huge block of land such as the continent of Africa was encountered by Colón! His route was a clear straight ocean crossing, only a third as far as the Portuguese will have to sail! It is like a miracle! God has sensationally rewarded Spain for the blood and suffering of centuries of holy Christian war against the Muslims. The Admiral Colón's short route to the Far East — which he has proved is really not far — will make Spain the richest and most powerful country on earth.

All parts of Spain were now united. Spaniards everywhere rejoiced at the glorious prospects. Aragonese, Castilians, Galicians, Catalonians, Navarrese, Andalusians were all now loyal subjects of their Majesties. Don Colón's discovery of the short route would enable Spain to triumph over Portugal in all the markets. The products of China and India and the Spice Islands were so accessible, practically at Spain's doorstep. Those who were envious could if they wished call Spain's route the back door to Asia. It was more properly the front door.

A frenzied eruption of shipbuilding began in Seville even before Don Colón set out to meet their Majesties in Barcelona.

While the Admiral was making preparations for the journey across Spain he was asked many questions. One of the questions most frequently asked was: "Is there much gold in the Indies?" He replied that the natives wore many gold ornaments around their necks and arms and ankles, and were simple-minded people who could be kept in subjection. It would be, he said, "easy to convert them to the Christian religion, and make them work for us." He said the natives ate strange foods, and he described one of their foods as "brown earth, powdered and then kneaded." He did not give the native name for this, which we now call chocolate. He told of wild cotton, sweet potatoes, tobacco, and Indian corn. He said the islands he had visited were, he estimated, perhaps nearer to the Ganges River in India than to the capital city of China — only two or three days' sail from the Ganges, and that was why he called the islanders "Indians," people of the Indies. They lived in a very warm climate and went completely naked.

Naked? his hearers exclaimed.

Both men and women, and without shame, he told them. His reply was profoundly shocking to Christians. But what could one expect of uncivilized heathen? The nudity must have been something to see. The sailors must have had a time with the naked girls.

The Don's every word fascinated the people of Seville. A realist as a navigator, he was charmingly disposed to superstition and romantically credulous in regard to people and lands which he had not seen. Having coasted only a portion of the eastern end of Cuba on its north side, he said of its western province: "There the people are born with tails." His hearers were highly entertained with such tales.

He said that native Indians, naked Indians, told him of a land not far from them which they called "Canniba." He cited this as showing the Indians ignorant as to correct names of countries. He said the inhabitants of Canniba, who were called "Cannibals," were people who belonged to the Great Khan, and so the proper spelling would be "Khannibals." He said also that Cuba and Khan were variations of the same name.

Asked why he had not brought home his largest ship, the *Santa Maria,* he did not directly answer, but cleverly skirted the fact of her being a wreck and total loss. He did this by saying of the men in the fort in Española: "I left them one caravel, and a man with knowledge of shipbuilding, so that they could build others."

The Admiral was now the most famous man in all Europe. Publicity brought inevitable question of his antecedents. Everyone wanted to know all about him. Where born? In what year? Who were his parents?

Acutely conscious of the shock it would be to Spaniards who were applauding the severities of the Inquisition if they learned that the man who had become Admiral of Castile was the son of a Jewess, he gave vague answers to personal questions. Cristoforo Colombo, whose name he bore, had left Genoa more than 25 years before. A Domenico of the Colombo family in Genoa had been the father of three sons, the eldest, Cristoforo. The other two sons had been Bartolomeo and Giacomo. This Bartolomeo had left home in early youth, without the family in Genoa knowing whether he was alive or dead. This fitted nicely, for it meant that his uncle Bartolomeo could safely come to Spain and pose as his Italian brother. The Admiral therefore sent to Fontainebleau in France to his uncle Bartolomeo to come to him and be known by everyone as his brother. But the adoption of the first name of a man born in or near Genoa compelled adoption of the whole Genoese family. The Domenico Colombo of that family had a brother Antonio who also had three sons. These sons were living and their names were Matteo, Amigeto, and Giovanni. They would believe the Admiral was their cousin, whom they had not seen since childhood, and could not recognize. The Admiral wrote to these three brothers suggesting that if they who were his cousins, wished to choose one of them to come to him, he would receive him and give him employment. The three chose to send the youngest, Giovanni. His name in Spanish was Diego. When Diego arrived and met the Admiral, he was readily accepted as the Admiral's younger brother. And so the Admiral's cover was made secure. In the year of 1493, Bartolomeo Colón was about 43 years of age, the Admiral was 33, and Diego was 25.[1] The considerable difference of years between Bartolomeo and Cristóbal Colón was not apparent, for the Admiral had already been aged by many sleepless nights and days, by arthritis, and by his hair turning white. He actually looked older than his uncle. Since the Genoese family record showed that their Cristoforo was born in 1451 or 1452, that became accepted as his date of birth, and the cover-up was complete.

On April 7th, a letter came to the Admiral in Seville from the sovereigns in Barcelona, written on March 30th. Post mail was carried across Spain at about 100 miles a day. Their Majesties' letter said that their realm had received so much advantage from what the Admiral had accomplished that they wanted him to make no delay about coming to them. It also told him that they wanted him to plan to return that same year to the Indies.

He now felt that he had everything as he wanted it. He got himself new clothes for his reception at Court as nobleman and Admiral. With six Indians and some parrots, etc., he traveled on mule via Cordova, Murcia, Valencia, and Tarragona. Immense crowds turned out along roads and in city streets to see him come riding through. He reached Barcelona before April 20th. There, most of the population and all the Court, came out of the city to meet him on the road. We can imagine the satisfaction he felt at making a formal entry to the city to which his father Prince of Viana had made formal entry with wild acclaim 32 years before. In the royal reception in the palace, he was given unprecedented honor. The two monarchs rose to their feet when he knelt to kiss their hands. Queen Isabel gave him a seat at her right hand.

He was in Barcelona for five or six weeks of glory. On May 20th their Majesties gave him a patent for a coat-of-arms under the laws of Castile. It showed a gold castle on a green background in the upper right corner (left as you looked at it), and a purple lion on a white field in the upper left; and gold islands in waves below the castle, and five anchors below the lion. We do not know whether the number five was selected because he had brought three ships to anchor in the Indies, and two to anchor when he got home. It may be noted that Castile and Leon were of Queen Isabel's Castile, and not of King Ferdinand's Aragon.

On May 28th all his titles and terms of his Contract were formally confirmed:

> We confirm to you and your children, descendants and successors now and forever, the offices of Admiral, Viceroy, Governor of the said islands and mainland that you have found and discovered, and of the other islands and mainland that shall by you or your industry be found and discovered henceforth in the region of the Indies.

Also confirmed was his "right to appoint and remove all judges and other officials in the Indies." All who sailed in the ocean were to obey him.

This confirmation was not merely for him. Their Majesties needed him as Admiral and Viceroy Governor in order to secure their title to the Indies with Portugal and the Holy Sea. Pope Alexander VI was a Spaniard, and he confirmed that the islands of the Indies belonged to Spain, by virtue of Colón's discovery. But Portugal claimed everything west of Africa, and spoke of or hinted of a mainland to the south. Portugal was insisting that everything south of 30° North and west of 38° West was hers.

King João either knew or believed that fifty years prior to Colón's achievment Portuguese ships had sighted, far to the west, land to which Portugal therefore had a first claim. In any case he demanded legal protection for the route around Africa, which he insisted would entail a Portuguese monopoly on sailing into the South Atlantic. He threatened war if he did not get it. He sent an urgent message to Pope Alexander VI, and let their Spanish Majesties know that he had sent it. He asked that the unexplored parts of the world be peacefully divided between Portugal and Spain. The pope accepted Don Colón's suggestion that the dividing line between what belonged to Portugal and what belonged to Spain be set at one hundred leagues west of the Azores. Early in May of 1493, the pope assigned all lands west of that line to Spain, and to Portugal all east of it, which would safely include all the coast of Africa. As we shall see, Portugal in 1494 insisted that Spain sign the Treaty of Tordesillas, which established the Line of Demarcation much further west. Since this Tordesillas line gave eastern Brazil to Portugal, historians ever since have suspected that the Portuguese already knew of the existence and approximate location of the Brazilian elbow.

As nobleman, Admiral and Governor, Don Colón needed a formal signature. He invented one for himself:

.S.

S.A.S

X M Y

: Xīo F E R E N S ./

The bottom line of the signature is obvious — Christoferense in a Greek-Latin mix. No one knows with certainty the significance of the seven letters in the top three lines. There have been rather convincing explanations of Christian significance, and also a convincing explanation of Jewish significance. This biography accepts both. It behooved a nobleman to have his secrets. Don Cristóbal Colón with a superior smile may have declined to explain his signature to anyone.

Formally invested with his titles, the Don rode beside the king as a grandee of Spain. He congratulated himself on being Governor of islands whose combined area was maybe as large as all of Spain. What if those islands were inhabited by naked ignorant people? No matter. He would change them. And with his ownership of ten percent of all the gold, pearls, and profits from trade with the Indies, incalculable riches would be his. Basking in the royal favor, he gloated over those who had called his project impracticable.

It was soon announced with universal joy, that the six Indians he had brought to Barcelona, had been converted to Christianity. Their baptism was made a public event. Missionary fervor spread everywhere, with all men talking of gold, trade, soul saving, and stark-naked girls.

There came at the same time to Barcelona the venereal disease called syphilis, which we now know was indigenous among the Caribbean islanders and hitherto unknown in Europe. A doctor in Barcelona noted its appearance in Barcelona in 1493. The disease may have been brought across the Atlantic by the six Indians. From Spain, it spread rapidly throughout Europe.

Since ships of Spain could sail effectively only with a fair or following wind, mariners observed that Don Colón had not only found a westward route to Asia but also an eastward return route. Merchants were saying that the return route was if anything the more important, since it would be by that route that heavily laden ships would be bringing home cargoes of gold and precious goods. Sea pilots pointed out that Don Colón had sailed home at the latitude of the Azores and Lisbon.

Thus his great secret was out — the latitudes where winds made two-way crossings of the Atlantic feasible. He had opened the ocean. Though landsmen did not appreciate this, mariners saw it as a unique discovery. The Admiral himself beautifully expressed it: "I gave the keys of those mighty chains of the ocean which were closed with such mighty chains." He used the word "chains" in this watery connection because it had been so used by Seneca in the mystical prophecy in *Medea.*

In line with Don Colón's discovery, Queen Isabel, only one month after he came to Barcelona, ordered monthly sailings across the Atlantic in both directions. How modern it sounds! It is indeed Colón's unbrakeable link with all subsequent centuries.

In June 1493, the Admiral, with his newly acquired "brother" Diego and five converted Indians, traveled from Barcelona through Madrid and Toledo to Seville. There the merchants were feverishly preparing to handle the expected flow of trade with China and India. Don Juan de Fonseca, Archbishop of Seville, was in charge of organizing an immense expedition to the Indies. Everyone believed that all those who were lucky enough to be permitted to participate, would soon come home rich.

Don Cristóbal Colón flattered himself that he had succeeded in achieving his private dream. He had used their Majesties for his purpose. He had realized his ambition to become a Governor. He no doubt believed he had practically achieved for himself a kingdom. In course of time he might become the recognized ruler of Española and all the neighboring islands. One of his heirs might someday be recognized as an independent sovereign. He felt sure that what he had accomplished would have made his father proud of him. He knew he was envied by everyone. Feeling envied, he believed he had everything shaped to his wishes. Those who had been skeptical and had sneered at his Enterprise of the Indies were now admitting he was right and they had been wrong. They were clamoring to sail with him. Many young noblemen were begging to be given passage on the ships being prepared for him.

The Admiral did not realize what was happening to him — what happens to anyone who gets tremendous publicity. He was rousing expectations which he would be asked to fulfill, and which he could not fulfill. He did not foresee that if any slightest one of those expectations was not fufilled, he would be blamed, and no one else. He was a builder of triumph — and disaster. He saw no consequences. People did not question the divine right of kings. He did not foresee how they would question him.

He did not realize that he was like a bird closing himself in his own cage. He saw himself as Viceroy and Governor issuing orders which would be unquestionably obeyed. He did not realize the truth expressed by Jesus that he who would be master of all must be the servant of all. Like all men who win fame, he would have to pay the price. He did not foresee what price.

❀ ❊❊❊❊❊❊❊❊❊❊❊❊❊❊❊❊❊❊❊❊❊❊❊ ❀

You seem to depreciate Columbus.

How so?

You imply that he was inevitably doomed to failure.

So he was.

But his achievement was brilliant. No man with merely an idea ever changed the world so much as he did.

I quite agree. But he was a winner already defeated.

People want him as a hero. You seem to decry him.

I think not. Knowing himself son of a prince, he dreamt of having the power of a king; but not wearing a crown, he could not compel obedience.

What you say brings up the question: Do great events shape great men, or do great men shape great events?

I think the answer to that is that men and events interract.

Until 1493 Columbus shaped events. After 1493, events shaped him.

14

MAINLAND

On his return from Barcelona, the Admiral had visited with the Duke of Medina Celi, and from him and other wealthy friends, received financial backing, which enabled him to take up his one-eighth share of the cost of equipping the seventeen ships being readied for him by Bishop Fonseca. The Court was paying seven-eighths of the cost, and so only through the Admiral could anyone other than Their Majesties invest in the expedition. In Seville, there were three months of feverish preparations. The experience Colón had when he sailed from Lisbon with supplies for the Portuguese Mine, gave him a more practical concept than Bishop Fonseca had of what would be most necessary and useful in Española. The ship chandlers had never been so busy. The Admiral bargained for the ship's stores, tools for mining and for agriculture, seeds for planting crops, food for six months, horses and some other domestic animals, breastplates and helmets, weapons, crossbows and muskets. No one argued against the need for military force, since nobody believed that the natives of the Indies would obey as readily as the Admiral had been saying they would. Transactions were many and varied. Not all the purchased materials were as specified. The Admiral thought he had bought good wine casks, but those which were delivered to him leaked. He purchased spendid horses, which were put out in a meadow to graze until the day of sailing, and then it was discovered that worthless nags had been substituted for some of them. In a quarrel with a salesman who had cheated, the Admiral became so enraged that he knocked the man down on deck and kicked him as he lay prone.

The quality and character of many of the 1200 to 1500 men the Bishop selected to go on the expedition were not to the Admiral's liking. Some of them were soldiers brutalized by years of war. Spanish aurthorities were glad to get rid of them by shipping them out of the country.

The Admiral insisted upon taking with him five body servants, though Bishop Fonseca thought five were too many. The Admiral, of course, took with him none of the Pinzón family. He had with him on the *Niña* a map-maker who had the same name as that of the man who had been responsible for the wreck of the *Santa Maria* — Juan de la Cosa. He appointed his "brother" Diego Colón as ship's officer. His uncle Bartolomeo did not arrive from France in time to go with him.

When the seventeen ships raised sail at Cadiz on September 25th, the Admiral's sons were there to see him off — Diego, who was then thirteen, and Ferdinand at age of five.

Everyone on the ships was fired with the expectation of getting rich quickly. Nobody foresaw the hell they would bring to the natives of Española. Everyone believed the natives of the islands would bless them for bringing to them the joy of salvation, since Bishop Fonseca had placed on the ships a dozen missionary priests.

The Admiral set course for the Canaries. He arrived at those islands on October 5th to take on water, wood and provisions. At Gomera, he renewed his intimacy with the ruler of the island, Doña Beatriz de Peraza. With her he spent nearly a week. She was a person who did whatever she wanted to do. Later, she hanged a man for questioning her chastity.

On October 13th, the fleet sailed out of sight of land. Except for a brief rain squall, they had perfect weather for the crossing. On November 3rd they sighted the island of Dominica. At the third island they came to, Guadaloupe, the sailors took on board the ships twelve native naked girls of ages 15 and 16, and two boys.

It has often been said that the Admiral on this voyage discovered the islands which he named: Dominica, Mariagalante, Guadaloupe, Montserrat, Antigua, San Martin, Santa Cruz, San Jorge, the Virgin Islands, and San Juan Bautista (now Puerto Rico) while en route to Española. Since the Indian guides with him had made for him a map of those islands, and had directed his course to them from Dominica on, we must avoid such glib use of the word "discovered," or revise our meaning of the word. The Indians guided the Admiral to the eastern end of the north shore of their native Española. By the time he reached there, more than 300 men of the expedition were seriously ill, and more were falling sick everyday. Being eager to find out how the men he had left in the fort at La Navidad were faring, the Admiral sailed westward along the island's north coast with wind and current speeding him. He went 170 miles in two days. He turned into the bay near where the *Santa Maria,* had been wrecked, looking for the fort. There was no fort to be seen. It had been burned to the ground. He soon learned from the natives what had happened. The thirty-nine men at the fort had quarreled. Most of them had left the fort and had gone inland to Cibao to pick up gold and girls. The natives, outraged by the beastly behavior of the white men, had, under the leadership of their chief Caonobó, massacred them. Then Caonobó had led his followers in a surprise attack upon the fort. There were only ten men in it, and they were living each with five women apiece.

The hundreds of Spaniards now with the Admiral were outraged, and even if he had wanted to, he could not have restrained them from taking bloody revenge on the natives thereabouts.

Wanting to dissociate himself from the site of shipwreck and massacre, he sailed back eastward along the north shore, but in this he attempted almost the impossible, for strong headwinds and opposing current slowed his advance, so that it took him twenty-five days to sail thirty-two miles. Trying to make up for lost time, he hastily chose a site for a trading post, which he named Isabela. He later discovered that the place had no adequate supply of fresh water near it, and no good harbor. It had one advantage, however, since from it there was an easy and quick access to the central area of the island. Three days after landing at Isabela, he sent a large party in to the gold-bearing Cibão, and in a few days they got from the natives, or picked up, 30,000 ducats' worth of gold nuggets. Meanwhile at Isabela, the Admiral could not get enough men to plow and plant crops. The two hundred young gentlemen thought any kind of manual labor was beneath them, and would not lift a finger to help. The cavalrymen would carry out assignments on horseback, but when not on their horses, would not do work. Many men had fallen ill from eating unfamiliar food. Many were stricken with malaria. Syphilis was rife. There was general disillusionment with the Admiral's much touted Indies. Everyone was now blaming him for everything that was going wrong. Fearing that if they had weapons in their hands they might kill him, he had the weapons from the other ships put on board the flagship.

A month after he had placed his settlement at Isabela, he sent twelve of the ships home to Spain, carrying several hundred men and his urgent request that Bishop Fonseca quickly send food to the colony. With the number of trouble-makers greatly reduced by illness, death, and departure for home, the Admiral led a party inland near to the center of the gold-bearing region, built a fort in which he left fifty men, and returned with two thousand castellanos worth of gold which had been officially and openly collected. Half as much again had been secretly pocketed by some of the men, and for this, the Admiral punished them by whipping, and in some cases by slitting of ears or noses. Back at Isabela, many more had died. The gentlemen there simply would not do any work, and almost everyone wanted to return to Spain. To avoid the menace of open conflict, the Admiral talked of the easy gold pickings in Cibão, and persuaded the potential trouble-makers that they would all very soon get rich if they went there. He thus got 400 men to go to join the fifty already at the fort in the interior. In doing this he thought he was acting like a governor, but he was being manipulated by circumstances beyond his control. He was trying to solve his problems by refusing to face them. He had bitten off more than he could chew.

With the challange to his authority greatly reduced, he felt he could safely leave Española in the hands of his orother Diego Colón and four others to govern the island in his absence, and he sailed away with three ships to establish one of the essential terms of his Contract, the finding of the mainland of Asia. He would make it a fact that he had found it.

He believed that the inhabitants of the eastern end of Cuba were un-enlightened people who did not know how to pronounce correct-ly the name of their own country. Their land was what Europeans knew as "Kubla," the Kingdom of Kubla Khan. Those uneducated natives along its shores had mispronounced it "Cuba." In spite of what they thought, their mis-called Cuba was part of the continent of Asia. He himself would now determine that it was part of the continent. In April, with 60 men in three of the smaller ships, he sailed to the eastern end of Cuba and westward along its south shore, with the avowed pur-pose of proving that Cuba was mainland. As a side issue, he did some coasting of the island of Jamaica.

His Journal of this perversely motivated voyage is a record of a re-markable feat of navigational skill among islands and across bays and shoals, with vivid and accurate descriptions of islands, mountains, and in one place, the sea extraordinarily colored by bottom sands and re-flections from cliffs, showing blue, white, green and black in one patch. He ceased exploration of the south shore of Cuba fifty miles from its west-ern end; for there he took the turn of the coast to the south to be proof of what he believed, that Cuba was a peninsula of the continent extend-ing out toward the Indies. He there chose to announce what he wanted to believe.

Since one of his guides had said that he had heard from a native that Cuba was an island, the Admiral decided that such thinking must not be allowed. He had his secretary prepare as an official record that no one on board had ever heard of an island of such great length running from east to west; that Cuba was part of the continent of Asia; that further along to the west there were now more civilized people; that Cuba was mainland. It had to be. Any doubt of his having reached Asia must be dispelled. Such doubt would jeopardize his Contract with their Majes-ties. His titles, his governorship, and his ten percent of everything were to be, as his Contract expressly stated, his rewards for having opened a route to Asia. He had to have reached Asia, and he was determined that everyone should believe what he wanted them to believe. And so, on July 12th, he had his secretary draw up a document which he compelled every officer, sailor and boy on his three ships to accept. What he re-quired them to sign was a notarized declaration that Cuba was not an is-land but mainland.They must never say that it was an island.They must agree with him that it was part of the continent of Asia. He announced

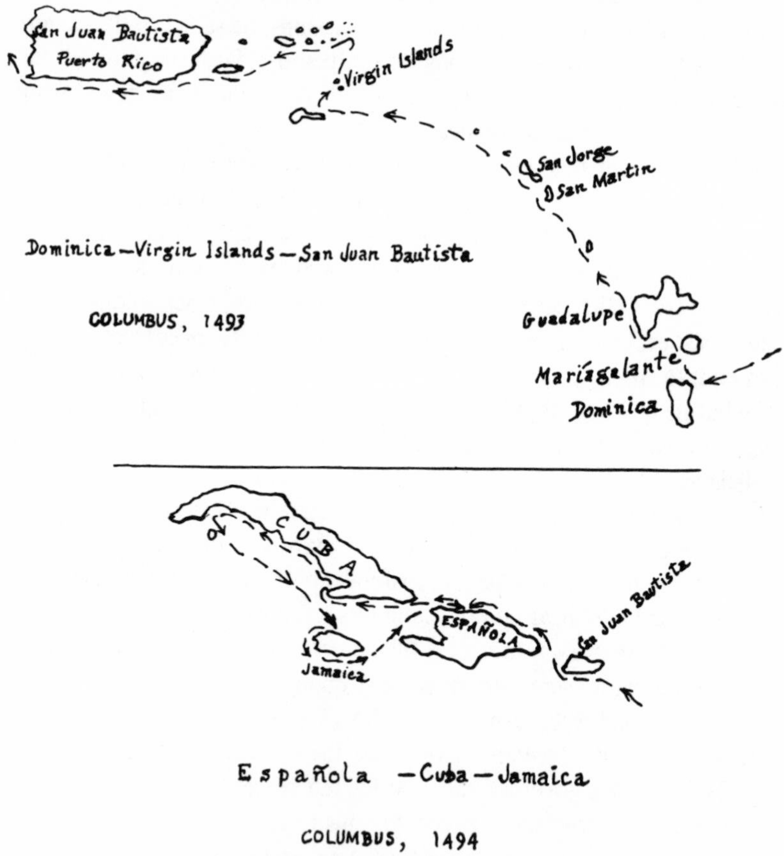

San Juan Bautista
Puerto Rico

Virgin Islands

San Jorge
San Martin

Guadalupe

Mariagalante

Dominica

Dominica — Virgin Islands — San Juan Bautista

COLUMBUS, 1493

CUBA

ESPAÑOLA

San Juan Bautista

Jamaica

Española — Cuba — Jamaica

COLUMBUS, 1494

Columbus, 2nd voyage

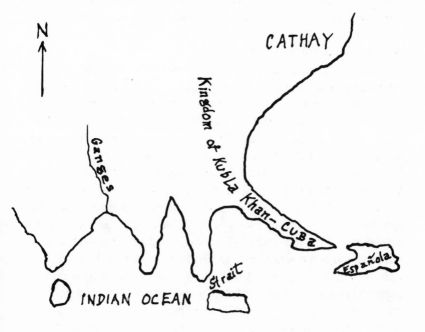

The Admiral Colón's mental picture of Cuba

that "if any should contradict him at any time, there should be imposed upon him in behalf of the Admiral a fine of one thousand maravedis for each occasion, and that his tongue should be slit; and if he were the ship's boy or a person of such degree, he should be prepared for this penalty by receiving a hundred lashes."

To give further support to his claim of having opened a route to Asia, the Admiral embraced another coincidence in names. When the natives of Cuba told him the western part of their country was called "Magon," he declared that it was that part of southern China which Marco Polo had said was called "Mangi." He now began to think that Puerto Rico was Cipangu (Japan), and that the gold-bearing region of Española called Cibao (Sibao), was Sheba, the fabulous land of the Queen of Sheba, where King Solomon got his gold.

While the Admiral had been making Cuba into mainland, reports of his findings had dismayed the Portuguese, who now revealed some knowledge of, or belief in, the existence of extensive land to the West which was not China or India. They did this by threatening war if Spain did not agree to a cancellation of the papal bull which on May 4, 1493, had divided in half the unknown regions of the world, giving to Portugal everything east of a meridian line 100 leagues west of the Azores or Cape Verde Islands, and to Spain everything west of that line. And so, on June 7, 1494, five days before the Admiral was threatening to slit tongues, the Portuguese pressured Spain into signing the Treaty of Tordesillas, by which the Line of Demarcation between the possessions of Portugal and Spain was moved to 370 leagues west of the Cape Verde Islands. Before the year was out, the Portuguese were congratulating themselves that they had succeeded in making a timely move, for secret informers let them know that fishermen pursuing their trade from Bristol had reported to King Henry VII the existence of a continent to the west of England.

In this chapter called MAINLAND, the Admiral has almost everything around him go contrary to what he wants.

He sure does.

He must have become slightly unbalanced.

No.

But that statement he forced the men to sign?

It was logical, to make his governorship secure.

And his treatment of gold stealers — slitting of tongues and noses?

In his day common legal penalties.

Then he was not a cruel man?

No more than King João and King Ferdinand, as records show.

But his demanding that everyone say Cuba was not an island! He knew he had not proved it.

It was what he had to say he believed, to make others believe it.

Do you think he himself really believed it?

I don't know. What do you think?

15

GOLD

Though he insisted that Cuba was not an island, the Admiral had no objection to proving that Jamaica was one. He sailed around it. From it, beating to windward to Española and sailing along Española's south shore for 350 miles against wind and waves and current, called for constant alertness, and he went without sleep for several days. Teredo worms had riddled the hulls of his three caravels, and only by constant pumping were they kept afloat.

The people of Española, who were called Tainos, were preyed upon frequently by the Caribs of Puerto Rico. The Caribs were cannibals, and the Admiral was determined to put a stop to cannibal raids. He did so effectively by sailing to Puerto Rico and destroying the Carib longboats.

Wanting to show quick profits from his Indies, he seized many Caribs who would bring high prices in the slave market in Seville.

But strain, worry, pain from arthritis, and fever brought delirium. The Admiral fell into a coma. On the return of the caravels to Española, he recovered consciousness, but for a long time he was confined to bed.

On September 28th, 1494, Bartolomeo Colón arrived with three ships from Spain. Nephew and uncle had not seen each other for five years, not since they had been together in Lisbon. The Admiral gave Bartolomeo, now called his "brother," the title of El Adelantado — The Leader.

Those who have not known Bartolomeo's family background, his Majorcan origin, his having been owner of ships, and one of the leaders of the revolt in his native island, have described him as having little originality, and no mysticism such as Cristóbal Colón frequently evinced. They have known, of course, that Bartolomeo was a map maker. He was a good linguist, as is to be inferred from his having resided for years in each of four countries. He spoke Spanish, Portuguese, English, and French. He had a commanding presence, good judgement, and a decisive mind. He was vigorous in everything he undertook to accomplish, He was always a loyal supporter of his famous nephew "brother."

He brought to the Admiral a letter from their Majesties which reflected what was being said throughout Spain about the Admiral and his Indians.

It should have been obvious to the Admiral, with the Adelantado at his side, that the reaction of their Majesties to the glowing reports he had sent them as Governor of the islands, and to the bitter criticism from his detractors, were now of necessity being shaped in the light of the new political relationship between them and Portugal.

While the Admiral and Bartolomeo were by nature optimistic, conditions in Española had become horrible and irretrievably destructive to the natives. The Spaniards, many of them ill with various diseases, had crossed the ocean to collect gold, not to work. They refused to bend their backs to plow or plant. In consequence there was a food shortage. To save themselves from starving, they forced the natives to work for them. They were also taking food from the natives, stealing everything of value, and forcing their often impossible demands by whippings. With uncurbed licentiousness, they seized wives,daughters and boys to serve their lust. Don Diego Colón, acting chief while the Admiral was away, had been unable to prevent the atrocities. With the vile behavior of white men having exemplified the character of those who called themselves Christians, the missionary priests did not convert a single native in Española until three years had passed.

Many of the colonists were on the verge of revolt against the Admiral. Some of them seized the three caravels Don Bartolomeo had brought, and sailed home. With them went an Irish Friar, Bernardo Boyle (Biul in Spanish), who went to talk to their Majesties, and throughout Spain preached that Cristóbal Colón was a humbug. He did all he could to hurt the Admiral's standing. He quoted the natives of Española as saying that Don Colón and his men on his first voyage were not the first white men they had seen, and that others had come among them a few years before.

This was damaging to Spanish expectations of acquiring a short route to India. The deception of Cristóbal Colón in giving out that he was from Genoa was known to the royal treasurer, but he shrewdly refrained from making that knowledge public.[1]

Four caravels that came to Española in the autumn of 1494 brought a request from their Majesties that the Admiral come home if he could conveniently do so. Fearing that their Majesties might turn against him if he did not show immediate profits, he seized 1500 natives to be sold at the slave markets in Spain. Two things can here be said for him. His judgement may have been warped by his illness; and in starting the West Indian slave trade he was engaging in what was a widely accepted activity in his time. He had the best 500 of the 1500 packed into four caravels under the captaincy of Don Diego Colón. Most of them died before the caravels reached Spain. Not having ships to carry any more to market, and knowing that others could be picked up when wanted, the Admiral announced that any Christian could take as many as he pleased of those who remained, and he was thus relieved of about 600. Nobody wanted the 400 leftovers, and they were told to leave. As they ran away, some of the soldiers practiced shooting them like animals being hunted. One cannot conceive of an atrocity which was not committed by the lawless Spaniards in Española.

The natives of that island attempted to drive all the white men into the sea. A battle was fought, the Spaniards using twenty horsemen and twenty dogs, for they had discovered that a vicious dog could be worth ten men against natives.

In June of 1495, a hurricane destroyed most of the ships at Española.

Although the *Niña* survived the storm, the Admiral postponed sailing home. From May of 1495, he and Don Bartolomeo Colón were busy "pacifying" the island, and by March of 1496, had completely crushed native resistance.

Gold gathering by the Spaniards in Española was fiendish. The Admiral's son Ferdinand in his biography of his father, described the inhumane procedure:

> Each one went where he willed among the Indians, stealing their property and wives and inflicting so many injuries upon them that the Indians resolved to avenge themselves on any that they found alone or in small groups .... The Admiral found the island in a pitiable state, with most of the Christians committing innumerable outrages for which they were mortally hated by the Indians, who refused to obey them.[2]
>
> They reduced the Indians to such obedience and tranquility that they all promised to pay tribute every three months, as follows: In the Cibáo, where the gold came from, every person of fourteen years of age or upward was to pay a large hawk's bell of measure of gold dust; all others were each to pay twenty-five pounds of cotton. Whenever an Indian delivered his tribute, he was to receive a brass or copper token which he must wear about his neck as proof that he had made his payment. Any Indian without such a token was to be punished.[3]

The punishment was death. If the Indian went into hiding or fled, he was hunted with hounds and killed. The inhabitants of whole villages were tortured and executed if those who had fled were not caught.

When it was realized that the amount of gold they were demanding of each native male every three months was too large, it was not mercy but a calculated decision agreed to by the Admiral, which reduced the amount to half a hawk's bell. The reduced tribute was also impossible.

It would be unfair to censure the Admiral for failure to maintain or restore order and decency in Española. For several years, no one could. On the other hand, we must repudiate eloquent callousness that could compose such a sentence as this: "If Columbus was a failure as a colonial administrator, it was partly because his conception of a colony transcended the desires of his followers to impart, and the capacity of natives to receive, the instititions and culture of Renaissance Europe."[4] Culture? Has it ever been possible to save primitive people from disaster forced upon them by civilization?

The thirst of Europeans for gold, and their notion that Christians had an innate right to mastery over any people who are not Christians, had atrocious consequences. The Indian population of Española, when the Admiral first arrived, has been estimated at more than two hundred thousand. One hundred thousand of them were killed in the three years, 1494-1496. By 1508, only 60,000 were living. Thirty-five years after that, their numbers had been reduced to less than five hundred. Nine hundred and ninety-eight out of every thousand Indians had been exterminated or carried away into slavery. Queen Isabel had expressed righteous indignation when the Admiral sent shiploads of West Indian slaves to Seville, for she piously disapproved of enslaving people she hoped to see converted.

We cannot state precisely what was the present-day purchasing power of the Admiral's ten percent of gold shipments to Spain. He became a rich man, and in later years an extremely rich man. In addition to other products of the island, ten percent of everything his — his establishment of the West Indies slave trade enriched the coffers of all participants.

Word was being passed in Spain that the Admiral was hopelessly incapable as Govenor. It was realized that most of the colonists in Española were clamoring to return home, and that only a lucky few were collecting sizeable quantities of gold, of which the useless Admiral was taking his ten percent. Their Majesties were beginning to realize that if the Admiral were to be retained in his governing of all lands to the West and ownership of a tenth of all their products and all trade with those lands, he would become the richest man in all the world. They regretted having given him a contract that was so rewarding. They had bestowed on him what was practically a monopoly. And now the businessmen of Spain wanted navigation to the West to be thrown open to all Spaniards who could afford to build ships.

Bishop Fonseca was already offering pardons to lawbreakers who would consent to go to the Admiral's colony. Their Majesties now wanted to know precisely what was happening in Española, and they sent Juan Aguada with four caravels to investigate and report. Aguada arrived in October of 1495 and soon collected voluminous testimony against the Admiral. While the Admiral could by dire punishments discipline sailors on a ship, he could not control the thousands of men on land. This inability was obvious to everyone, and he himself now feared he might lose his Governorship. The seat of government, Isabela, was in a wrong location, and a new capital was established on the south side of the island, and given the name Santo Domingo.

In March of 1496, the Admiral sailed for Spain with two ships, the *Niña* and the *India*. He put in at Guadaloupe for provisions on April 9th, and left there April 20th. In June, he dropped anchor at Cadiz.

He had often held forth the lure of gold, and he had declared that the most essential thing in human life is gold. Knowing that he was being criticized in Spain for having lured everyone with promises of quick wealth which were not being fulfilled except for Their Majesties and himself, the now wealthy Admiral wanted to combat the adverse reports which had gone home ahead of him. He thought of a way to create the impression that he was both humble and poor. He stepped ashore at Cadiz on June 11th of 1496 "dressed in the robes of the color of the ancient habit of the brothers of St. Francis, made also like a habit and wearing the cord of St. Francis."[5] As a Franciscan tertiary, he had a right to wear the garb, but in this instance his wearing it was fakery, an attempt to appear as one pledged to poverty and humility.

❉⚬⚬⚬⚬⚬⚬⚬⚬⚬⚬⚬⚬⚬⚬⚬⚬⚬⚬⚬⚬⚬⚬⚬⚬❉

His gold getting! — How rich did Columbus become?
Ask a more searching question.
What?
How spiritually poor did he become?
You mean he was one of those Spaniards who were the most brutal of all people?
That is what the English say. But the English treated Indians just as heartlessly. All Christian conquerors in the New World were cruel. They stole every acre of land from Indians, unless you think buying Manhattan Island for twenty-four dollars was not stealing.
That's how people with superior weapons have always behaved.
Yes, as Mark Twain observed. Since humans are the only animals who deliberately kill others of their own species, Mark Twain said human beings are the lowest form of animal life.
But civilizaton against savages? — Survival of the fittest?
If you think having a phrase to describe it makes it sweet.

16

EXCUSES

The Admiral was received at Court with a great show of cordiality, and he again effectively displayed parrots, Indians, and gold nuggets. But doubts were expressed as to the correctness of the geography which he had shaped to the way he wanted it. No one could deny that he had indeed visited large islands. In the face of increasing questions being thrown at him, he insisted that those islands were not far from the mouth of the Ganges River.

The Spanish Court was disturbed at knowing that kings of other countries were pushing to reach India, and it began to look as though they might succeed before the Admiral did. English merchants in Spain when the Admiral returned from his first voyage, had persuaded an Italian ship captain, Giovanni Caboto, a citizen of Venice who was in that year 1493 in Spain, to leave Spain and take service under King Henry VII of England. The English were calling him John Cabot. In 1494 fishermen from Bristol had reported discovery of "a mainland to the West." A continent to the west of England! That might be China. And now in 1497 it was reliably reported that King Henry VII had sent John Cabot to find out what it was, and Cabot had brought back news of his finding a coastline extending from the latitude of England for a tremendous distance toward the southwest, a coastline which he said was "part of Asia." It was also reliably reported that Cabot preceived that along that conveniently directioned coastline ships could take on fresh water and food and firewood when needed, and could thus continue regardless of distance. Cabot announced that he planned to follow that southwest line of coast the next year to below the latitude where the Admiral Colón had found the Indies, and by so doing he expected to sail to a longitude far to the west of the farthest west the Admiral Colón had reached, and thus the English would beat the Spanish in getting to India.*

In spite of the continuing adverse reports from Española, and the opposition of many at Court, Don Cristóbal Colón in the spring of 1497 succeeded in persuading Queen Isabel and King Ferdinand to reaffirm his titles and his right to one-tenth of all products. The fact that this reaffirming was necessary shows the undercurrent of criticism flowing against him and speaks volumes as to the doubts that were rising.

The Admiral's geographical claims were increasingly under question. If he had reached Asia, as he claimed, why had no one yet found the great cities of Cathay which Marco Polo had visited? Where were the spices and jewels? Peter Martyr, an Italian in Spain, suggested that the Admiral had found islands lying near the Malay Peninsula. The Archdeacon of Seville said the Admiral should not have called his islands "the Indies." The Admiral's reply was that the islands were "the eastern un-

---

* With his well-conceived purpose, John Cabot sailed from Bristol in 1498. He was lost at sea. Later, King Henry VII sent Cabot's son Sebastion, who explored the southwest-tending coastline, from what we call Labrador to what is now Maryland.

known lands of Asia, and he had given them the name of the nearest country, calling them West Indies." He did not tell anyone, except his son Ferdinand, to whom he said it privately, that knowing how all men dreamed of the riches and wealth of India, he had used the name "Indies" to win the support of their Catholic Majesties. He knew their Majesties better than he knew the islands.

While making feverish preparations to handle the expected trade with Asia, merchants throughout Spain wanted immediate answers to questions they persisted in asking: "Where, in relation to the newly discovered islands, are the fabulously wealthy seaports of China and India? The Admiral answered glibly, but could not convey assurance that he knew. He could not stop the questioning. Evermore insistently he was asked: From your Española, how many leagues is it to those cities? What are the precise sailing routes from Española to those cities? As with clouds gathering, these questions hit the Admiral like a hurricane.

The Admiral was being judged in the light not only of what the English were doing but what the Portuguese were doing, for the news from Lisbon brought by seaport gossip was even more upsetting. In July of 1497 a Portuguese fleet of three large cargoes had set out for India under Vasco da Gama. Obviously, the Portuguese expected he would get around Africa. Would he succeed? He might. The Spanish Court feared the Portuguese might reach India before the Admiral did. If they did, what then? Were they to let the Portuguese get ahead of them? The Admiral was now told he must look for and find India immediately. In his next sailing, he should not return directly to Española to resume his governorship duties until after he had explored in the right direction. Spain must learn the direct route to India, to keep ahead of the Portuguese.

To speed acquisition of this vital information, the merchants of Seville and businessmen everywhere in Spain urged their Majesties to issue orders to the Admiral to make his third expedition one of exploration to the southward from where he had previously been, for it was being said that from the islands of the Indies the sea passage into the Indian Ocean must be further to the South. It was reported that King Manoel of Portugal had said there was "land to the South."

To the Admiral the questioning as to directions and distance was not only embarrassing but dangerous, because it exposed his ignorance. Doubts as to his having reached Asia must not be allowed to spread, because if they did, it might invalidate his Contract. His governorship and his percentages were guaranteed by his having opened a direct short route to India. Why were they demanding that he do further exploring? He had already given proof. Let others seek out the passages to the seaports of Cathay and India. He well understood that he could not expect to be governor over those cities or kingdoms. He could be governor only in islands and parts of the mainland which were far enough from the seats of government of Cathay and India, in places where those governments were obviously not operating. Conscious of and fearful of the implications that would be drawn if he did not explore in a new direction, he nevertheless could not evade the pressure being placed upon him. Or could he? Before he sailed, he would declare that exploration to the South was now his purpose, but he would look for valid reasons to break off from explorations as soon as he could. In response to the questions being heaped upon him, he began to talk of the exploring he was planning to do. He told everyone "that he intended this time to sail more southward." He said he would find out how correct was the idea of the idea of the former King João of Portugal "who said that to the south there was mainland." Apparently it was because they knew of this southern land that the Portuguese had insisted upon having the Line of Demarcation shifted to 370 leagues west of the Cape Verde Islands. Queen Isabel now sent a letter to the Admiral asking him to go south for greater profits. Her asking amounted, of course, to a direct order. But the idea of not going directly to his Española troubled him. On a mainland, if there were one to the South, he might not be able to take governorship. He did not want to be too far away from the islands where he was governor. Nevertheless, the Admiral now said he would go more to the South "with the intention of discovering new land beyond that already discovered."

Exploring was not an attractive motive. No Spaniards wanted to go exploring. They wanted the promise of wealth. They wanted to share in gold getting. The Admiral had upped his intake by obtaining from their Majesties an understanding that, at no cost to him in providing six ships, he would receive one-eighth of the profits from the voyage. Beyond basic pay, sailors were being offered nothing but vague promises. To get men to man the ships, pardon was issued to all prisoners who would go, except those who were in jail for heresy, first degree murder, treason, arson, counterfeiting and sodomy.

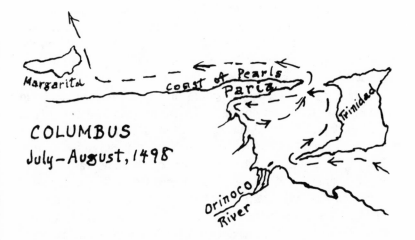

Third voyage of Columbus

On May 30th, 1498 the Admiral raised sail and set course for the Canaries. He put in at Gomera, but this time Beatriz de Peraza did not entertain him. Their romance was dead. We can surmise a probable cause of its demise. She now had another lover, or the Admiral's physical appearance or physical condition no longer made him attractive to her.

From near the Cape Verde Islands, the Admiral sent directly to Española three of the ships loaded with food and supplies. His crossing out of sight of land was from July 4th or 5th to July 31st, on which day a man in the crow's nest sighted three peaks. This sighting gave the name Trinity to the island, upon which the Admiral landed the next day.

He sailed along the south shore of Trinidad for several days, getting fresh water, firewood, and provisions. On August 4th he sailed across a gulf, which the Indians said was called Paria. On August 5th, on the north side of the gulf, he set foot on what he thought was another island, and which he named *Isla Santa* ("Holy Island").

On August 14th, word was brought to him on the *Niña,* that not far to the south were four river channels. He said to himself, that report of four channels will do for all the exploring they expect of me. In this decision not to explore further to the south, he made the most serious mistake of his life. Contrary to the view many have held, he was never primarily a geographical discoverer. He explored land only when circumstances compelled it as a step toward what he considered more rewarding. His heart was not in discovering, but in getting gold and quick profits, and in establishing his hereditary governorship. Since he had been asked by their Majesties to do some more exploring, he knew he would be charged with violating orders and would certainly be criticized for not continuing land hunting to the South. Therefore, keenly aware of how the Spanish Court would react to the reading of his Journal, he set down in his Journal all the excuses he could think of for not doing what he had said, with tongue in cheek, he greatly desired to do.

> Since supplies he was carrying for the people in Española were deteriorating he did not wait to discover more lands . . . . When he left Spain, he had not told the seamen that he was sailing with the intention of making discoveries, for if he had, they would have demanded more pay. The seamen were now weary. Also, the ships, one of one hundred tons and another of seventy, were too large for exploration.

He omitted mentioning his third ship, which was small enough to enter tiny coves and rivers. Knowing he would be criticized for what he failed to do, he repeatedly mentioned what he had done. He wrote that from his findings of the islands of the Indies their Majesties would gain more though they had paid less than the Portuguese had spent in establishing their route to India. He said those islands were an *otre mondo* ("other world"), which he had given to their Majesties, and now, like an artful courtier, he wrote: "I desire that your Highnesses may be the greatest lords in the world." He added that their acquisition of the islands would be a great triumph for Christianity.

He terminated his southward exploring and left the Gulf of Paria with a swift current that poured out to the northward. The sea water was almost fresh, only a trifle brackish like the river at Seville. He did not recognize the current and brackishness as evidence of nearness to the mouth of a huge river (the Orinoco), until after he had left the gulf, thinking again about the volume of fresh water, he could not account for it as coming from a very large river, "unless this be a continent. I believe this to be a very large mainland, which until today has been unknown."

Does this not justify calling him the discoverer of America? But no. Two days later he discarded this geography, and expressed an idea which suited him better. He wrote that the land around the Gulf of Paria was the Terrestrial Paradise, the Garden of Eden, at the easternmost end of Asia; and in support of this he quoted from a book:

> The Lord God planted a garden eastward in Eden . . . . at the farthest
> point of the Far East, where the sun rose on the day of creation. A river
> with four mouths waters the garden.

From what his sailors had reported of four river channels he now deduced that the swiftness of the current of fresh muddy water was made not by the size of the land but by its high elevation, and to support this notion, he wrote for their Majesties to read:

> I have come to a new conclusion respecting the earth: namely, that it is
> not round, as they describe, but of the form of a pear, which is very round
> except where the stalk grows, at which part it is most prominent.

Thus the Gulf of Paria was at the stem of the pear; and he further explained the region to which he had turned his back:

> The globe at this point has a hump on it like a woman's breast, and the sweet water is running downhill.

The idea that the Garden of Eden was elevated and closer to heaven than any other part of the earth's surface would be acceptable to religious persons whether Jewish or Christian. It gave the Admiral two unanswerable excuses for not exploring to the South: the Holy Scriptures said that God would never permit any descendant of sinful Adam and Eve to enter the Garden of Eden, and it was obvious to everyone that ships could not sail uphill.

Having named the shore north and west of the Gulf of Paria the Coast of Pearls, because the natives in the gulf said it was along that coast they got their large pearls, the Admiral turned his back on exploration, and sailed away from his unique opportunity of making the most stupendous discovery — the discovery with which he was mistakenly credited centuries later. He had to believe, or say that he believed, that the land to the south was an island. If a continent, it would upset his Indies theory. He had previously made a continent out of an island (Cuba). Now he had to make an island out of a continent, and did it by placing the eastern end of Asia where he wanted it.

Eager to return to gold getting in Española, he steered toward continued ignorance and confusion.

The earth with a hump like a woman's breast! The earth shaped like a pear! Did their Majesties accept such silly excuses?

No.

Did anybody?

Of course. Most people did.

But so absurd!

No more absurd than belief in U.F.O's. and proof of life after death will appear a hundred years from now.

Do you suppose Columbus himself believed the earth was pear-shaped?

Who can say?

He was literate.

Yes, what they called a "Latin scholar," which meant a reader of books, since many books were in Latin.

His saying he could'nt sail uphill was no excuse for not sailing along the coast to the South. The ocean is level except for the rise and fall of tide.

We laugh at his excuses, but they made a sorry mess of his career.

How so?

They destroyed his highest hopes. They ruined him, as we shall see. In making those exuses he defeated himself.

17

SEARCH FOR INDIA

When their Majesties learned that the Admiral had failed to explore to the South, as he had been asked to do and as he had said he would do, they ordered Bishop Fonseca to find someone to send to the West who could and would explore and thus ascertain the geographical facts so urgently wanted. Since this was what was now of greatest interest to businessmen, Fonseca turned to businessmen in Seville. They were practically unanimous in suggesting that the man known to them as Américo the Florentine, an Italian born in Florence as Amerigo Vespucci, was the best man qualified for the task. From early youth, Américo had been interested in maps and cosmography. Everyone had full confidence in him. His firmness of character promised perseverence to the end in whatever he set out to do. As representative of a branch of the Medici Family, and as leading ship chandler after the death of Berardi, he had the highest reputation for probity. No one knew better than he what materials and supplies would be useful on a long voyage. He was 44 years of age, robust and strong, a natural leader.

Thus it was that the Admiral in Española received news that on May 18th of 1499, Américo the Florentine had sailed with the purpose of finding the waterway by which Marco Polo had voyaged from China to India. A map in the Atlas of Ptolemy showed that to get from the coast of China into the Indian Ocean one must sail through a strait and around a cape called Catigara. The map showed Catigara at the end of a long peninsula extending to more than eight degrees south of the equator. The Admiral no doubt said to himself, if my friend Américo turns that cape and gets through that strait, their Majesties will see that I have given Spain a short route to India, and all those ignorant fools who have been opposing and slandering me will be silenced.

In command of the two ships their Majesties had provided for him, Américo made his Atlantic crossing in consort with ships under Alonso de Hojeda. They made their landfall at about four degrees North Latitude, but there parted company, for Hojeda, with the map maker Juan de la Cosa as one of his pilots, turned northward toward the Coast of Pearls, the enticing name of which drew him like a magnet. Américo turned southward.[1]

Américo believed he was somewhere on the coast of Asia, not far from the Cape of Catigara, which he expected soon to turn. He had made his landfall about the 27th of June. Either on June 27th or a day later, as he went south, he was sailing along the coast of Brazil, and was thus the first of record to reach the coast of that great country.[2]

On July 2nd he entered a great gulf, and soon discovered it was the mouth of a river of incredible size. It was so wide it was like an inland sea. Only after he had sailed far into it could he see the forest on both sides of him at once, where it was only sixteen miles wide. This greatest of all rivers flowed out of the land from west to east. He discovered also another immense river, which flowed from south to north, and was twelve miles wide. He ascended one of these rivers for seventy miles. We can only surmise which of the two it was, the Amazon or the Pará. The estuary of the Amazon is 150 miles wide, and its principal channel narrows to sixteen miles about sixty miles inland. The mouth of the Pará, forty miles wide, narrows to twelve miles about 140 miles inland. Whichever it was which Américo ascended for another seventy miles, he was the first discoverer of both.

The Admiral, with his mystical religosity, was able to believe that the Gulf of Paria was near "the Terrestrial Paradise." Américo, having a very different type of mind, with strict realism, wrote of the Amazon region: "The trees were so beautiful and so fragrant, that we thought we were in a terrestrial paradise."[3]

Américo explored the coast for more than 1300 miles to the southeast, until he estimated he was six or more degrees south of the equator. He was actually at about five degrees South. He felt sure he was getting near to the Cape of Catigara. His disappointment was intense when the ships "encountered an ocean current which ran from southeast to northwest, and was so great, and ran so furiously . . . that when it struck our bows, we could not make any headway, even though we had a brisk fair wind."[4] The current which prevented his turning the Brazilian Elbow was the Equatorial Current, the major portion of which sweeps to the northwest into the Caribbean, and helps to form the Gulf Stream.

Américo's ships were compelled to turn their bows to the northwest. They touched shore again on August 4th at a cape which they named for the saint of that day in the church calendar, Saint Dominic.[5] That cape is at the northern tip of Brazil, close to their original landfall. Having explored as far as he could in one direction, Américo would now explore as far as he could in the other direction — to the north and west.

For the sake of future navigators, he had begun to map what he could see of the southern heavens. "Very desirous of being the author who should identify the polar star of the other hemisphere, I lost many a night's sleep in contemplation of the motion of the stars around the South Pole, in order to record which of them had the least motion and was nearest to the Pole."[6] He was unable to accomplish this purpose on this voyage because he had not been far enough south. "I did not observe any star that had less than ten degrees of motion around the Pole . . . . If God grants me life and health, I hope to return to that hemisphere, and not come home without identifying the Pole."[7]

From Cape St. Dominic, aided by the current, he sailed 700 miles in almost one week. With 22 men he went ashore on Trinidad, and accepted the invitation of the natives to visit one of their villages, and eat breakfast with them. Their hosts had no dietary inhibitions. They were cannibals. Américo wrote of them: "They do not eat one another among themselves, but they sail in what they call canoes, and with these canoes they drag their prey from the islands or mainland, from tribes which are their enemies . . . . They are people of affable comprehension and of beautiful physique . . . . They are religious people."[8]

Américo's interest in the social life of cannibals was incomprehensible to Europeans, who read of it five years later. It was felt that he had confessed the most scandalous behavior. He, a Christian, a civilized man, sitting down to breakfast with man-eaters! Though the bill-of-fare at the first meal of the day was not human, it was revolting that he had sat at a table with cannibals! Something must be wrong with him! Few in his day understood what he meant in saying that cannibals were "religious." He meant of course that with them the eating of human flesh was a religious practice. He would have been excommunicated, and perhaps burned at the stake by the Inquisition, if he had explained the motivation of cannibals, their desire to acquire the heroism of a strong warrior by eating his flesh and drinking his blood. The Church would not have tolerated the suggestion that in the Mass it celebrated the same motivation — that it held what was in essence a cannibalistic concept in its doctrine that in the Eucharist the bread and wine are changed into the body and blood of Jesus, by eating and drinking which, Christians may acquire the strength and spirit of Jesus. Heretics were saying that Holy Communion was merely a ceremonial remembrance of the Last Supper Jesus had with his disciples. Europeans were not yet ready for an inquiring mind like Américo's.

Americo wrote: "The natives gave us some small pearls and eleven large ones, and told us by sign language that if we would wait for several days they would go fishing and bring us many. Not caring to delay, we departed."[9] Most Europeans thought it incredible that Américo did not take advantage of this offer. How could any man be so eager to continue exploring that he would not remain for a few days to acquire many pearls? Only a fool would scorn wealth. An historian, who wanted his readers to think Américo's exploring was motivated by a mean desire to steal credit from Admiral Colón, quite unintentionally paid Américo the highest compliment: "Americo Vespúcio did not bring home many pearls, and failing to imitate properly the acts of the Admiral, his desire to push on for discovery was greater than for the acquisition of riches."[10] No one

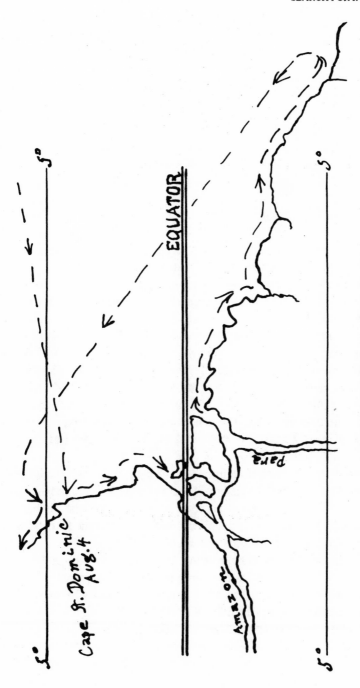

EQUATOR

Cape St. Dominic
Aug. 4

Amazon

Pará

Américo's landfall to his farthest east in 1499

has ever more clearly delineated the choice a scientist must make, or has more tellingly stated the contrast between the Admiral Don Colón and Américo the Florentine.

From the Gulf of Paria, Américo explored the coast westward for hundreds of miles. He landed on Curacao, which he called "Island of Giants" because on that island he met natives who were head and shoulders taller than any of the men with him. From Curacao, he went to another island, Aruba, and wrote: "We entered a harbor where we found a town built over the water like a Venice; there were about twenty large houses after the fashion of huts based upon very thick piles."[11]

On the western side of Aruba, near its southern end, is the site Américo described. Tidal water there flows into and out of a large lagoon, like the one in which Venice lies. It is recognized today as an ideal site for fishing. A long pier there stands on piles.

Américo gave the site its name — "Like a Venice" — in Italian — "Venecuela." This name he invented got transposed into Spanish — Venezuela. The people of Venezuela have reason to give the same recognition to the man who coined the name of their country, as do those citizens of another nation, who give recognition to Thomas Paine for coining "United States of America." Credits get transposed. Columbus was the first European of record on the coast of Venezuela (in the Gulf of Paria in 1498), which country was named from Américo's description a year later. Américo was the first European of record on the coast of Colombia, (at his farthest west in 1499), which country was named in honor of Columbus.

From Aruba, Américo returned to the mainland coast, and entered a gulf, (Maracaibo) which he hoped was the strait into the Indian Ocean, but he found it was not a strait, for it terminated in a lake. He named it Golfo de Vericida. With hope recurrent, he approached a cape which he called C. de Espera ("Cape of Expectation.")

After rounding the cape, he came to what he called Cape de la Vela ("Cape of Watching Without Sleep"), because on that cape he stayed up all night for several nights, for a very good reason which will be explained in the chapter called CLOCK IN THE SKY.

From Cape de la Vela, his farthest west, Américo sailed directly north to Española. In his story of his voyage, he said that his reason for doing so was that "he and his men judged the ships to be unseaworthy, be-

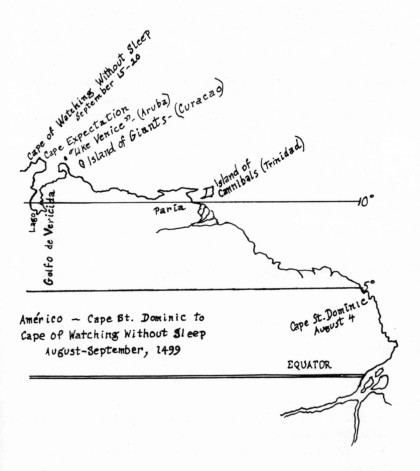

Cape St. Dominic to Américo's farthest west

cause they leaked endlessly, and they could hardly reduce the water with two pumps going constantly. The men were worn down with fatigue and hardship, and the provisions were growing short. Since we found ourselves, according to the reckoning of the pilots opposite and within one hundred and twenty leagues of an island which they call Española, discovered by the Admiral Colón six years before, we determined to proceed to it, and since it was inhabited by Christians, to repair our ships there."[12]

While his ships were being reconditioned at Santo Domingo in Española, he undoubtedly visited with the Admiral, and told him of the immense land he had coasted. When his ships had been made ready, he sailed to the north, and found many islands (the Bahamas). He returned to Spain in June of 1500.

❊ӠӠӠӠӠӠӠӠӠӠӠӠӠӠӠӠӠӠӠӠӠӠӠ❊

Do you suppose the Admiral was, in any way, disturbed by what Américo had discovered?

Not at all. At least, not by anything Américo had yet learned.

You imply that something he later learned did disturb the Admiral.

All I have said thus far is that what Américo announced in 1500 in no way contradicted the Admiral's claim that he had opened a direct route to India.

Are you hinting that investigation would take a new direction?

Of course, as you will see.

18

SHACKLES

When the Admiral sailed away from the Coast of Pearls, how did he know, as his steering showed he did know, in which compass direction to sail to Española? An admirer of his, who let his enthusiasm run away with his judgement, says the Admiral "had kept such accurate dead-reckoning that he knew the correct course for Hispaniola . . . . He had that mysterious knowledge, partly intuitive, partly based on accumulated observation and experience, which had enabled so many unletterd mariners in days of sail to 'smell their way' safely around the seven seas."[1]

More sensibly, let us look at the facts. In this steering, the Admiral was undoubtedly piloted by Caribbean natives, who had traveled long distances in canoes, knew directions from one island to another, and drew remarkably accurate maps, if not on paper, by laying out of beans. From near the island of Margarita, where the Admiral started the sailing, the east-west spread of Española spans 25 degrees of compass. Therefore, the Admiral's fetching up on its coast was not a triumph of intuition, or mystical knowledge, or sailor's sensitivity. Actually, the current carried him 175 miles to the west of where he had intended to land.

He came eventually to a lucky meeting with his "brother" Bartolomeo, a meeting which saved him from immediate disaster, for Bartolomeo gave him timely warning that throughout Española colonists were fighting each other. Much of the island was in the hands of rebels. Francisco Roldán was leading a bloody revolt against the Colóns. The Admiral would have a long hard struggle to reestablish effective control. Being governor involved much more than making a legal division of gold and other valuable products appropriated from unwilling natives.

As it happened, the Admiral was allowed less than a year to show what he could do. With mind on profits, he decided that against the express wishes of Queen Isabel, he would continue the slave trade under pretext that only prisoners of war were being sent to the slave market in Spain.

In October of that year 1499, the Admiral sent two ship loads to Spain, and with them, a request that Bishop Fonseca provide him with good colonists. By that he meant men who were willing to work and would obey him. He could enforce obedience at sea, where he had the backing of maritime law. On land, in spite of the prestige as Viceroy of Their Majesties, he was not an effective commander. Men who defied him ran away to join with Roldán. He therefore made another request to Bishop Fonseca that a learned judge be sent to relieve him of the burden of holding court to try law breakers. He also asked for an astute councillor to help him decide what actions would be best for him to take. In Spain these requests appeared to be a damaging admission of inability to govern. They made authorities feel that the Admiral was responsible for all that had gone wrong in Española. They blamed him for the fact that hundreds of men on the island were ill with syphilis.

Because of what were being called his "delusions," their Majesties saw it as their duty to restore peace and order in the island, even if it meant repudiation of Don Cristóbal Colón's Contract. And so, they selected a

tough fighter, Fransisco de Bobadilla, and empowered him to do whatever needed to be done. Bobadilla sailed from Cadiz in July of 1500.

That summer, Don Bartolomeo Colón, profiting from his experience
as one of the leaders of the revolt in Majorca nearly thirty years before,
had been successful in an encounter with some of the rebels, and had
sent a report which gave great satisfaction to his "brother," the Governor. Don Cristóbal Colón had appointed his friend Miguel Ballester to
be castle governor of the fortress of Conception a few miles to the northwest of Santa Domingo. He counted on Miguel Ballester to save Santo
Domingo from enemy attack. With the aid of Bartolomeo, and the not
always effective support of his other "brother" Don Diego Colón, the
Admiral was striving to make his governorship secure in spite of all set-
backs. His property in Seville and his share of the gold as it occasionally
arrived there, was being competently handled by his capable son Diego,
now twenty years of age. In Santo Domingo he had seen the completion
of the citadel, and now the governor's house, which though small was
sufficiently imposing. And he took pride in the jail which he had recently enlarged to hold all those convicted of theft, murder and rebellion. He
felt confident that when the officials in Spain learned of the stability of
the peace he and Don Bartolomeo Colón had begun to establish by sub-
duing almost all of the rebels, their Majesties would no longer criticize
but would cooperate fully, and would see to it that every ship coming to
Santo Domingo brought not only food, materials, furniture, and equipment of all kinds, but colonists who were willing to work. And on those
ships returning to Spain, he, the Governor, would send home all the
idlers. The success he and Don Bartolomeo had in putting down rebellion in Española would compel all the scoffers to recognize that he had
indeed founded a governorship worthy to be hereditary like a kingship.

Congratulaing himself on what seemed to promise the ending of his
most difficult problems, the Admiral went off to tend to some matters
outside of Santo Domingo, leaving Don Diego Colón in charge. This was
the situation on August 23rd of 1500 when Don Francisco de Bobadilla
arrived. On his ocean crossing Bobadilla had been giving thought as to
how best to carry out his orders. He knew, as every one at Court knew,
that their Majesties had lost patience with the Admiral and wished they
could cancel his Contract. He surmised that King Ferdinand would be
pleased if he could somehow dispose of the troublesome Don Cristóbal
Colón. What I should do, Bobadilla thought to himself, is try to find a

way to provoke the Admiral into a show of resistance to royal authority. As his ships sailed into the harbor, he saw the bodies of seven men hanging on the gallows. Someone on shore told him they had been rebels, and that Don Diego Colón had five others in the jail, who would be executed the next day. This gave Bobadilla the opportunity he was looking for, and he demanded summarily that Don Diego Colón release to him the five prisoners who were in jail. Don Diego, standing on his dignity as brother of the Governor, refused; whereupon Bobadilla arrested him, ordered him put in irons, seized the citadel, the Governor's house, and the jail. He sent a messenger to carry word of his arrival to the Admiral, and ask the Admiral to return at once to Santo Domingo. The Admiral, happy in his belief that he had gained effective control of his entire island, was eager to welcome the newly arrived colonists, and he came quickly without having heard of how Bobadilla had dealt with Don Diego. The moment they met, Bobadilla, without any show of courtesy or respect, told him to give ear to what he was about to hear.

Before the days of newspapers and modern news media, any important political decision had to be declared at a public meeting dramatized with as many witnesses as possible, so that it would be immediately and widely established as fact. We can well imagine the scene that now ensued between the Admiral and Don Bobadilla and what they said to each other.

The Admiral, rejoicing that Bobadilla's coming with so many fresh troops would dissuade any who might be thinking of rebellion, pointed to the jail in which he said he already had some malefactors who had been caught, and had cells waiting for more. Bobadilla flatly said he had brought from their Majesties a special order, which his lieutenant would read aloud for all to hear. It was brief and terse. Until their Majesties were satisfied that the revolt was crushed and conditions throughout Española had been restored to what they should be, Don Francisco de Bobadilla would give voice to the wishes of their Majesties, and Don Cristóbal Colón must take orders from him.

It was a profound shock to the Admiral. Here in Española where he was the Viceroy of their Majesties, the one to give orders, must he now take orders from someone else? Bobadilla had made it so publicly embarrassing that the Admiral felt he could not yield. If he asserted that he was the governor of the island, and the one to give orders on the island, he would be rudely told that their Majesties had changed their minds.

As for his contract, an essential part of it had been cancelled. Bobadilla gave him only a moment in which to say he would agree to take orders, but the Admiral did not say it. His attitude was obvious. It showed in his eyes and the set of his mouth. Bobadilla, having foreseen the outcome of the public meeting, gestured to his lieutenant, who barked an order to the soldiers, and they laid rough hands on the Admiral, and put manacles on his wrists and fetters on his ankles. If the Admiral protested that Bobadilla could not or must not do this to him, he was rudely told it was being done, and the soldiers would have had a loud laugh.

This was a most dramatic ending of a dream of greatness. In an instant, the Admiral had fallen from almost kingly preeminence to prison and disgrace. It hit him where it hurt most. He could not believe it at first, or that it happened to him. He felt he was a victim of foul deception. Their Majesties not only wanted him to cease to be Governor, but wanted him jailed. Only by making him appear to be a criminal, and treating him as one, could they pose as honest rulers who had not cheated him, their faithful servant. Why had their Majesties done this terrible thing to him who had done so much for them? Were their Majesties no better than thieves? Is this what Queen Isabel wants? No. Not she. This must be the doing of that usurper King Ferdinand.

The Adelantado, Don Bartolomeo Colón, did not have enough soldiers to attempt combat with the many Bobadilla had brought. Upon his jailed nephew's advice, he surrendered to Bobadilla, who immediately put him in irons on board a ship.[2] Bobadilla then gathered complaints against the Colón's, on the basis of which he had all three of them sentenced to be shipped home for trial. After two months of imprisonment in Santo Domingo, the shackled Don Cristóbal Colón was put on board a ship to be carried ignominiously to Spain.

However, as soon as the ship cleared the island, the captain offered to strike off the irons. Though suffering discomfort and intense humiliation, the Admiral refused to let him do it. He foresaw the favorable publicity he would win if he landed in Spain wearing the irons. He, the Admiral of the Ocean Sea and Viceroy of their Majesties, and Governor of Española and all the islands of the Indies, shackled like a convict, although he had not been accused of any crime! His wearing irons would stir the hearts of all beholders and rouse public sympathy. It would put their Majesties to shame. Wearing irons would make everyone see the perfidy of their Majesties and how they had violated his

177

Contract. He would wear the irons until public sentiment pressured their Majesties into ordering their removal. It would be a conflict of wills. And so in Seville, he wore the irons from near the end of October until December 12th, on which date the order came from Court that they be stricken off.

Freed of the irons, he immediately set out for the Court. Furious at having his power as Governor snatched from him, and having been subjected to humiliation and physical suffering, his purpose was now to persuade their Majesties to rectify the injustice by keeping their promises and holding strictly to the terms of their Contract with him.

He arrived at the Court about a week before Christmas, but it was not until after the New Year's festivities that he was permitted to meet their Majesties. The formal hearing was embarrassing to them, as he wanted it to be. Queen Isabel consoled him as well as she could. She assured him that she and King Ferdinand had not ordered Bobadilla to put him in jail and shackle him with irons. Bobadilla's doing those things had been without their permission and beyond their intentions. They had no wish to deprive him of his Governorship, but reports from Española had shown the necessity of giving Bobadilla power to restore peace throughout the island. They now were confident that they would soon hear that peace had been restored. The Admiral should be patient. Yes, Bobadilla had exceeded their instructions. The King and the Queen were agreed upon that.

The best the Admiral could get from them was that they were reconsidering the whole matter.

❁❄❄❄❄❄❄❄❄❄❄❄❄❄❄❄❄❄❄❄❄❄❄❄❄❄❄❄❄❄❄❄❄❁

I used to think the story of Columbus was so popular because everyone believed he had discovered America.

And now you don't?

I now see it was because of what happened to him — so many sensational incidents.

Yes. His story is perhaps the most dramatic of any human being.

What a downfall! A princely Governor all of a sudden shackled and clapped into jail!

It has meaning for us.

How so?

What Cristóbal Colón did not perceive — that his downfall was the consequence of his own shortcomings.

One feels sorry for him.

More than sorry for him. — Fearful for ourselves. — His tragedy shows how selfish dreams and one's own inadequacy invite disaster and make it inevitable.

19

CLOCK
IN THE SKY

When Américo went to Court to report on his voyage, their Majesties wanted to know if he had found passage into the Indian Ocean. They were disappointed that he had not, but he had something to tell them which brought a new political situation which required immediate attention.

He told their Majesties that he had explored thousands of miles of continuous coastline, and that much of that land belonged to Spain, while some of it unquestionably belonged to Portugal. According to his estimate, he said the Line of Demarcation would run through a great gulf at the mouth of two immense rivers, but he could not say positively until he had checked with sky watchers in Toledo. Their Majesties wanted facts, and he explained to them that only after he had compared the Toledo sky watchers' timing of a happening one night in the sky when he had been at his farthest west, could he know positively how far west of Cadiz his farthest west had been.

What made the matter of instant concern to their Majesties was the Treaty of Tordesillas with its specification that if either Spain or Portugal discovered land which belonged to the other, it must instantly notify the other, and the other must within a year send an expedition to establish the Line of Demarcation in the new land.

Their Majesties gave ear to Américo's fascinating account of how he had stayed awake all night for several nights to determine his farthest west distance from Cadiz. It was by a method never before attempted, which he had been ingenious enough to make serve his purpose. We venture to believe that their Majesties found it one of the most interesting reports they ever heard.

It very likely began with Américo's telling how in the 2nd Century B.C., a Greek named Hipparchus had established the system of latitude and longitude for marking a position on the face of the earth. Latitude, north-south distance from the equator, as every ship captain knew, could readily be found by noting the altitude of the sun at noon. But no one had known how to find longitude with near approach to accuracy. Since the earth turns completely around on its axis in twenty-four hours, and there are 360 degrees of distance, one hour of time measures fifteen degrees of distance east-west. At the equator, one degree is sixty nautical miles. One minute of time equals a quarter of that distance. What a landsman might consider a trifling error — say ten minutes of time — would at the equator be an error of one hundred and fifty miles — an error that could mean shipwreck. The accurate determination of local time was therefore a pressing problem for navigators.

There had been no way known by which a navigator could tell the difference between his local time and the time back home, for there was no clock that could keep time at sea. On land or on a perfectly steady ship at anchor in calm water, the flow of sand in an hour-glass would measure one hour exactly. But with the rolling and pitching of a ship at sea, the flow of sand in an hour-glass is slowed, and may take anywhere up to sixty-four minutes. The problem of longitude had for centuries seemed insoluble.

Américo set out to solve the problem. He knew he could not ascertain the moment of noon since there were no precision instruments measuring the instant when the midday sun was at its highest. A star's passing of the zenith at night could be more accurately observed. The solution of the problem of longitude would have to be sought in night-time study. A celestial event, a happening in the heavens above, would be visible at the same moment from two places on earth which were distant from each other. The difference in time when that event was observed in the two places would give the longitudinal difference between the two places. Américo looked for a clock in the sky. Stars appear stationary. Planets appear to move, but so slowly that any motion made in a few hours could not be counted by an observer. Only one object in the night sky moved fast enough for Américo's purpose. That was the moon.

Gerard of Cremona in the twelfth century described a method for determining longitude by noting the distance of the Moon from a fixed point in the heavens. This may have helped Américo to conceive of the method which he originated. Whether his idea was entirely original or not, he was the first man in historic record to use the motion of the Moon to measure longitude.

The Moon's appearing to catch up with and pass a planet is what astronomers call a conjunction. The moment of a conjunction could be observed from the western side of the Atlantic and in Spain. The problem was to time the observation in relation to local midnight in both places. If it could be thus timed, the difference in time as observed in two places would tell the longitudinal distance between them.

Américo had with him a copy of the *Almanac* of Johann Müller, called Regiomontano. The *Almanac* told at about what hour on a particular date a conjunction would occur. Astronomers in those days could not predict so precisely as they do now, and the *Almanac* in Américo's possession was often a full hour off. If it was, no matter, for Américo and sky watchers in Spain would be alert the same night and would make note when the conjunction did occur, and would later check with each other's timing. All observers would agree as to what they would call the moment of a conjunction — the instant when the front edge of the Moon appeared to be as far west as the planet. They could determine that moment by having a cord held vertical by a suspended weight, and by keeping one's eyes in line with that cord and the planet, and noting when the front edge of the Moon first touched the line of that cord.

Sky watchers in Spain had mechanical clocks to give their local time.

Américo at the Cape of Watching Without Sleep had only sand glasses. Could he with these establish the precise moment of midnight? No, but he could come close to it, for he was there from about September 14th or 15th to the 20th, close to the Equinox (September 23rd) when nights and days are of equal length. Midnight would occur very close to six hours after sunset as seen at the horizon across the Sea of St. Euphemia. He could safely asume his local midnight was close to halfway between sunset and sunrise, and he could thus get local midnight to within perhaps two minutes of time.

Now in the summer of 1500, while the Admiral was at Court imperiously demanding reinstatement as governor, Américo told their Majesties he had compared his timing of the conjunction at his farthest west with the timing recorded by sky watchers at Toledo, who had clocks to tell them the precise time. When he knew the difference in time, he knew the longitude of his farthest west. But when he compared that longitudinal distance with his estimate of the distance he had sailed, he was forced to conclude that a degree of longitude was much larger than he had held it to be. In July of 1500 he had written: "The reason why I give sixteen and two-thirds leagues to each degree is that according to Ptolemy and Alfragano the circumference of the earth is 24,000 miles or 6,000 leagues, which being divided by 360 comes to 16⅔ leagues for each degree."[1] His league had been four miles. But his studies in subsequent months compelled him to make a new estimate by accepting a greater length of league, and in July of 1501 he wrote: "Each league is four and a half miles."[2] His revised estimate of the length of a league points to his having attained a nearly correct estimate of the earth's circumference — $4½ \times 16⅓ = 75$, and $75 \times 360 = 27,000$ miles. Américo's mile was the Roman mile, and Webster's and Funk and Wagnall's dictionaries give the length of the Roman mile as 4,860 English feet. Américo's 27,000 miles equal 24,852 English miles.

Circumference of earth estimated by	Roman miles	English miles
Eratosthenes (the best of several guesses)	31,500	28,919
Ptolemy	22,500	20,170
Alfragano	28,050	26,819
Regiomontano	28,800	26,509
Columbus	20,400	18,777
Américo (previous to 1501)	24,000	22,081
Américo (after July 1501)	27,000	24,852
Modern science	27,054	24,902

At about the time Américo reported to their Majesties in Granada, Vicente Yanez Pinzón returned from across the ocean. He recounted his having made a landfall on January 20th of 1500 at 10 degrees South. He had from there followed the coast northward, sailing with the ocean current which five months previously had prevented Américo's ship from sailing southward. If Pinzón's estimate of the latitude of his landfall was correct, it meant to Américo that the Cape of Catigara must be further to the South than 8½ degrees South where the map of Ptolemy put it. Where his ships had been turned back by the ocean current, he had been, Américo now perceived, at least a thousand miles to the east of the Tordesillas Treaty Line. Two months after signing that treaty in May of 1495, King Ferdinand and Queen Isabel had called in the mathematician Jayme Ferrer to throw light, if he could, on the correct positioning of the Line of Demarcation. Ferrer, giving 16⅔ leagues to a degree, had estimated that the "370 leagues to the west of the Cape Verde Islands" specified by the Treaty, meant in round numbers 24 degrees. The Admiral Colón refused, as he said, "to be carried away by the new calculations."

When their Majesties informed King Manoel of Portugal that Américo the Florentine with Spanish ships had found land to the West which belonged to Portugal because it was east of the Line, that king immediately asked Américo to head the Portuguese expedition which, according to the Treaty, he must send to establish the Line of Demarcation. King Manoel could not avoid doing this, for Portugal had insisted upon the terms of the Treaty. He offered Américo three ships. As Américo expressed it: "I was summoned, while I was residing in Seville, by the King of Portugal, who entreated me to prepare myself to serve him on this voyage."[3]

Don Cristóbal Colón was still shackled, not to irons but to ignorance. His spectacular career, which had at first appeared to be the most perfectly successful of any adventurer in the world's history, had been based upon erroneous concepts and conjectures. Everyone at Court seemed to think he was now completely out of the running. From the point of view of King Ferdinand he had become a nuisance and should be ignored. If it weren't for that Contract by which their Majesties had tied themselves in with him, they would refuse to have anything more to do with him. But now he was pestering them with repeated requests, almost demands, that they reinstate him as Governor. All they could give him was assurance that his financial rights, his ten percent, would not be taken away. Month after month went by, for him a most unsatisfactory year. Early in 1502 he was comforted by Queen Isabel's telling him that their Majesties had finally decided that Don Bobadilla should no longer be Governor of Española. For a moment Colón thought this meant that his governorship would be restored to him, but he was speedily disillusioned. A new governor for the Indies was appointed — Don Nicholas de Ovando. At this the Admiral almost lost heart. But his characteristic reaction was to make an appeal by speaking of his infirmities, and offering, in spite of them, to undertake another voyage.

Their Majesties accepted his offer and he began his 4th voyage while Américo in Lisbon was preparing to sail on Portuguese ships.

Gentlemen in those days held themselves to a strict code of honor. Américo, of a family of Florentine noblemen who respected that code, would of course not reveal to the King of Portugal knowledge that properly belonged to Spain, nor would he reveal to their Majesties knowledge that properly belonged only to Portugal. Their Majesties in both countries knew they could trust him.

Américo described the purpose of the expedition: "We went solely to make discoveries, and departed from Lisbon with a commission to that effect, and not to seek for any profit."[4] The disclaimer was a realistic statement of fact, and was not motivated by envy of wealth-gathering expeditions. Américo set himself three purposes: 1) to explore to the southward the coast on the Portuguese side of the Treaty Line; 2) by longitude, as correctly as possible, to establish the Line of Demarcation; and 3) to map the stars of the Southern Hemisphere and identify for future navigators the star nearest to the Celestial South Pole — the star with least apparent motion. Dedicated to scientific research, he was thrilled with the feeling that he might be able to make a great contribution to the knowledge of mankind, and so he began his voyage "with the aid of the Holy Spirit," which to him meant the spirit of inquiry, insight, and understanding.

❋ꙮꙮꙮꙮꙮꙮꙮꙮꙮꙮꙮꙮꙮꙮꙮꙮꙮꙮ❋

You show that Américo was an amazingly clear thinker.
What we call a genius.
Did his type of mind impress many people in his day?
No.
But important historically?
A man of the Renaissance.
Like Leonardo da Vinci.
Yes. He and Leonardo knew each other in their early years in Florence.
Leonardo had to be cautious to avoid being accused of heresy.
Yes. It was a century before Galileo.
Did Américo's method of determining longitude impress their Majesties?
Indeed it did. He was later appointed Pilot Major, his duty to teach pilots and issue licenses. But the pilots of Spain opposed him, just as any new idea gets opposed today.
Was his method of finding longitude accepted?
Yes, as the best method for 250 years until John Harrison invented a ship's chronometer which could keep close time at sea.
How close?
To meet the requirements set by the English government — close enough to determine longitude within 30 miles — half a degree — after six months at sea. That is, less than a second a day — better than clocks on land had been.
How close did Américo come?
You will see in Chapter 21.

20

COMPULSION

Their Majesties were determined that their newly appointed Governor should have ample power to enforce obedience and restore order throughout the Indies. They saw to it that Don Ovando was adequately supplied. On February 13, 1502, he set sail for Española with 39 ships and 2500 men.

The Admiral was disgusted, but he now saw that the surest way to regain their Majesties' good opinion and recover the position of which they had unfairly deprived him, was for him to ignore his physical ailments and undertake and accomplish exploration in a direction no one had yet taken. Américo's finding of the long coastline to what he had called Cape de la Vela beyond which he had seen what he called Sea of

Santa Euphemia, suggested to the Admiral a proposal to explore directly to the west from Española and Jamaica. If, as he now expected, he should find and pass through the strait into the Indian Ocean, ḅe would again, as in 1493, be given all he asked, and their Majesties could no longer deny him his rightful Governorship.

He consulted with Queen Isabel and won her support of his project. King Ferdinand was showing increased firmness, and welcomed the opportunity to get the annoying Don Colón well away from the Court for what he hoped would be a long time, preferably forever. Fully aware that the Don had failed to do the exploring he had said he would do, their Majesties issued orders to him on March 14th. These flatly stated what he must do, and what he was forbidden to do. He must explore to the west of Española, and he must not set foot on Española until after he had accomplished that exploring. It was specifically stated, and Governor Ovando was given orders, that he was not to be allowed to go ashore on Española until he returned to that island after completing the exploring. Queen Isabel was now in full agreement with King Ferdinand, as she made the Admiral realize.

His expedition had four ships. The largest, *La Capitana,* capacity about 100 tons, carried 45 men. A smaller ship was the *Santiago de Palos.* There were about 30 men on *La Galega,* and 25 on the smallest of the caravels, *Vizcaino.* All together the crews totalled about 140, more than half of whom were boys rather than men.

The Admiral took his fourteen-year old son Ferdinand with him, and also the Adelantado, when he sailed on May 11th, 1502. At the Canaries, he took on firewood and fresh water. He had a quick crossing to the island Martinique, which he reached on June 15th. On June 18th he came to the harbor of Santo Domingo, and requested permission to bring his ships into the harbor, to have them reconditioned, but Don Ovando refused. At this rebuff, he wrote: "What man ever born, except Job, would not have died of despair — forbidden the land and the harbor which I, by God's will and sweating blood had won for Spain." Perforce, the Admiral went to another harbor. Weather-wise from many experiences with storms, he observed a change in the color of the sky, and movements of the clouds, which told him they were precursors of what the Taino natives of Cuba and Española called a hurakán. Having heard that Don Ovando, who had arrived in Santo Domingo in April, now had twenty-five ships ready to sail to Spain with 200,000 castellanos of gold on board, the Admiral sent to Ovando an urgent message, warning him that a terrific storm was coming, and advising him to hold all the ships in harbor until after the big blow. Ovando laughed at the warning, and immediately sent the large fleet to sea. In his scorn of the Admiral, he had put the Admiral's share of the treasure, 4,000 pesos of gold, about 4,000 ounces, on the smallest and presumably least seaworthy of the ships, the *Aguja*. The fleet had no sooner left the harbor than the hurricane struck. The flagship, with Bobadilla on board, sank with all hands. Twenty ships were lost. Three or four came back into Santo Domingo harbor in a sinking condition. Only one of the ships reached Spain, and that one, let it be said for lovers of the dramatic, was the *Aguja*.

The Admiral had his four ships in a harbor which was somewhat protected from the north and west by high land; but knowing what a hurricane could do, he appointed a rendezvous for them if they were separated. Three of them were swept from their anchorages, and for a time they all lost sight of each other. They managed to survive, however, and all four met again at the rendezvous.

When necessary repairs had been made, the Admiral sailed away to the westward on July 14th. At the Cayman Islands, he took on fresh water, and from them sailed southwestward to the coast of what is now Honduras. On August 14th, he landed and took possession in the name of their Majesties. He found himself trapped on a north coast, and had to get to the east end of it, with wind and current dead against him. He faced an almost impossible struggle, fearing he might never escape from that coast. It took him 28 days, using only daylight hours and anchoring close to land every night, to advance 170 miles — an average speed of only half a mile an hour. When he finally reached the point where the coastline turned to the south, so that wind and current would no longer be against him, he expressed what he felt by naming the cape *Gracias a Dios* ("Thanks to God").

After he had sailed some distance to the south, he learned from the natives that he was coasting land which was an isthmus between two seas, an isthmus which had no water passage across. This was knowledge he did not welcome, since it was contrary to the geography he had been proclaiming for twenty years. He wanted to believe there was a passage through the isthmus to the Indian Ocean. The local Indians who said there was none must be ignorant. He was confident that somewhere further to the south he would find the passage, and confound all his crit-

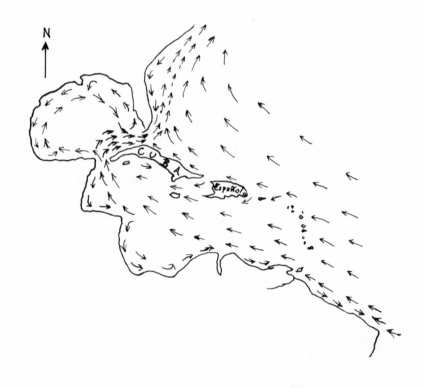

Currents on western side of the Atlantic

ics.

He proceeded southward along the coast of what is now Nicaragua, and southeastward along the coast of what is now Costa Rica. Natives there swam out to the ships. The gold earrings, bracelets, and necklaces which they wore, and which the Spaniards acquired in exchange for baubles, were not pure gold, but an alloy called *guanin*. Extremely disappointed, the Admiral at one point broke off the trading. The Indians attempted to win him over to a desire to continue it by sending aboard two naked girls, one about eight years old and the other fourteen. The Admiral had these two quickly clothed and fed, and he sent them back ashore — intact. This the natives could not understand.

The Admiral's son Ferdinand kept copious notes of everything he saw. In his biography of his father he gave a fascinating account of many incidents. He said the Admiral believed he was near the place where there must be a strait through to the Indian Ocean. With expectation of finding it, he entered every sizeable opening in the coastline. One of them was 6 miles wide and inside was 27 miles across. Another was 7 miles wide and 18 miles deep. He had repeated disappointments, to compensate for which, he made a discovery by linguistic innovation. He transmuted a local name Quiriquitana into Ciamba, because Ciamba had been the name for Cochin-China in Marco Polo's narrative.

The natives very definitely told him the width of the isthmus at its narrowest — nine days' march across. He said the mouth of the Ganges River was only a few days' sail from that other side of that isthmus.

As soon as he became convinced that there was no strait in that isthmus, he did something which revealed his deeper intention. Just as in his voyage of 1498 after leaving the Gulf of Paria, he had turned away from exploration, he now was no longer a geographical explorer. Gold seeking had always been a stronger motivation and, in him, was second only to his most deep-seated ambition, his yearning to exercise princely power. Gold getting now dominated him, although gold could never fill the void after he had been deprived of his Viceroyalty.

Along the coast of what the natives called Veragua, he heard there were gold mines. There inside a river mouth he found an excellent harbor, where he remained for a week enjoying some most profitable trading. For bits of colored cloth and gewgaws, the natives eagerly gave various gold objects which had a higher percentage of gold content than the *guanin*. Among these were disks of polished gold, which probably had some religious significance and may also have been mirrors. Sailing along the coast to the east to Puerto Bello, he traded everywhere for gold, but as he continued on to what he called Retrete, the gold trading was so poor that he decided to return to Veragua. He began the return sailing on December 6th, and immediately faced the most violent and changeable winds he ever encountered. They forced him to change course repeatedly, and for many days he had to sail back and forth to east and west. He afterwards said of this period that he had never seen such high waves. Their vertical upthrust was presumably the coinciding of wind-driven waves with waves ricocheted back from the coast. He was in constant dire peril, close to a rocky shore which was being pounded by immense breakers. There were frequent deluges of tropical rain that kept everyone wet for days on end. Without rest from the struggle to avoid disaster, the Admiral suffered agonies. His old wound opened up. A tornado came bringing a waterspout, a column of water rising from sea to sky. It would rip to pieces any ship it hit, and to keep it from coming close to any of the ships, the Admiral read aloud a passage from the New Testament and held the hilt of his sword as a cross against the whirlwind. When the waterspout passed them by, all the crew believed, as he did, that faith, and the sign of the cross, had saved them. On a day when there was a brief lessening of wind, he sent the boats to shore into the mouth of a small river to get wood and water, but when they were coming back out, one of the boats was swamped, and two men were drowned. Not until January 6th did he get his four ships to anchorage in Veragua just off the bar at the mouth of what he now named the Rio Belén.

Inside the river mouth was the good harbor in which he had previously enjoyed profitable trading for a week. After he now reentered the harbor, he realized that to get much gold, he would have to send men to look for the gold mines, a search which would entail much contact with the natives. The ships' crews, having suffered to the limits of human endurance, were in no mood to treat the natives with kindness or decency. The Admiral's son Ferdinand wrote a running account of what he observed, and he said the Spaniards "committed a thousand outrages, by reason of which the Indians were provoked to alter their manners and to break the peace." The boy Ferdinand seems to have had a limited or prejudiced notion of what constituted "peace."

The fortified settlement which the Spaniards began constructing was attacked. The Admiral seized a tribal chief and his entire family as hostages against further attack. He imprisoned them in a ship's hold. The chief escaped and raised the country against the white men. To foil the Admiral of his intention of using them as hostages, all the other prisoners, women and children, hanged themselves in the hold.

The Spaniards did not find the gold mines, but did find gold-bearing earth. In spite of the satisfaction the Admiral felt at having acquired 300 ducats worth of gold, the Admiral fell ill from the after effects of weeks of struggle, and became apparently delirious, and thought he heard a voice speaking to him. He later wrote down what he imagined he had heard: "O fool and slow to believe and serve thy God, the God of every man! What more did he do for Moses, or for David his servant, than for thee? From thy birth he hath ever held thee in special charge. When he saw thee arrive at man's estate, marvelously did he cause thy name to resound over the earth. The Indies, so rich a portion of the world he gave thee for thine own, and thou hast divided them as it pleased thee. Of those barriers of the Ocean Sea, which were closed with such mighty chains, he gave thee the keys. What more did he do for the people of Israel, or for David who from a shepherd he raised to be king over Judea? . . ." He added: "I heard all this as in a swoon."

Considering the Admiral's words in the light of his parentage, we ask several questions: Did the words "the God of every man" stem from his having had a Jewish mother and Christian father? From his consciousness of having come close to realizing his ambition of gaining princely power, did he still believe God would restore to him his Viceroyalty? Did he add "all this as in a swoon" as cover up?

At the time the Admiral alone on board ship was having this self-encouraging psychological experience, and was finding eloquent words to express without too much appearance of conceit that he had been all his life a specially chosen agent of God, all the men of the expedition were at the fortified settlement desperately defending themselves against attack by the Indians. Of the 140 men, 6 died or deserted, and 12 were killed, 10 of them in the fighting. The Adelantado, "brother" Bartolomeo, was wounded. Don Diego and some of the men constructed a raft with which they escaped over a bar. *La Galega* could not make it over the bar and she had to be abandoned. When the other three ships sailed away from Belén on April 16th, they had only one of the four boats left. After leaving Belén, they found the hull of the *Vizcaino*

Fourth voyage of Columbus

so badly wormeaten, she had to be abandoned at Puerto Bello on April 23rd.

The Admiral was soon persuaded by the pilots and captains to set course for return to Española. Since they were far to the west, he knew they could not sail directly to that island against wind and current. The island of Jamaica, however, according to his estimate, was almost due north of them, and by sailing as close to the wind as they could, they would very likely come to it. He therefore set course for Jamaica, and on May 1st *La Capitana* and *Santiago* sailed away to the north. It was heavy going. On May 10th they sighted and passed the Tortugas (Turtle Islands). On May 13th the Admiral estimated that they were approaching Cuba, which he continued to call the "mainland" in spite of Juan de la Cosa's Map of 1500 which had showed it to be an island. Everyone on the two ships was near to starving, for the only food they had left was oil and vinegar. The hulls of the ships were eaten through with teredo worms, and in spite of constant pumping, the water in the holds was rising. It slowed their progress, and they were so near to sinking that everyone despaired. They had passed between the Caymans and Jamaica without sighting either. Then luckily they sighted the north shore of Jamaica, and on June 25th of 1503 got into a bay and ran the ships ashore close together. They were in what the Admiral named Santa Gloria, and what is now called St. Ann's Bay.

The ships, which would certainly have sunk in another day or two, were of no use except as fortresses. There were no tools on the ships for cutting large timber to build other ships, and no man on them had the know-how for ship building. With no likelihood of being rescued, since no other white men knew of their whereabouts, they were effectively marooned. To survive, they would be dependent upon the natives for food. The Admiral realized that if he let any of the men go ashore, they would enter the natives' houses, take possession of whatever they fancied, possess the women and girls, and enrage the Indians, who would then be glad to see them starve to death. He therefore ordered the men to remain on the stranded ships, except four he sent to do some trading in return for food. Fortunately, they found Indians who were eager to trade, and who in their dugouts brought food to the ships.

The Admiral knew they would never be rescued unless he could get word to Santo Domingo with news of their plight. That could be done only by Indian canoe from the northeastern point of Jamaica against wind and current across 105 miles to the southwestern corners of Española, and from there along the south coast of that island for 350 miles. For this formidable task, the Admiral chose a reliable man, Diego Mendez. Knowing that Ovando would not want to rescue him, he wrote a letter to their Majesties to force a rescue. He instructed Mendez to deliver the letter privately into the hands of someone who would take it to Spain to their Majesties, and to do this without letting Ovando know to whom he had intrusted it, but immediately after the letter was out of his hands, he was to let Ovando know that such a letter was on its way. Thus Ovando's hand would be forced. Ovando would then not dare fail to send rescue.

The Admiral's letter was an appeal to sentiment, with obvious purpose of persuading their Majesties to restore his Viceroyalty: "I came to serve at the age of twenty-eight, and now I have no hair upon me that is not white, and my body is infirm and exhausted. All that was left to me and my brothers has been taken away and sold, even to the cloak that I wore, to my great dishonor. It is believed that this was not done by your royal command. The restitution of my honor and losses, and the punishment of those who inflicted them . . . and have disparaged my admiral's privileges, will redound to the honor of your royal dignity. The highest virtue, unexampled fame as grateful and just princes will redound to Your Highnessess if you do this; and the glorious memory will survive for Spain . . . . I am as ruined as I have said. Hitherto I have wept for others; now have pity upon me, Heaven, and weep for me, earth! Of all things material I have not even a copper coin to offer; in things spiritual, I have even ceased observing the forms here in the Indies. Isolated in this pain, infirm, daily expecting death, surrounded by a million savages full of cruelty and our enemies, and thus separated from the holy sacraments of holy Church, how neglected will be this soul if here it part from the body! Weep for me, whoever has charity, truth and justice! I did not come on this voyage to navigate for gain, honor or wealth, that is certain; for then the hope of all such things was dead. I came to Your Highnesses with honest purpose and sincere zeal, and I do not lie . . . .

"Done in the Indies, in the island of Jamaica, on the seventh of July in the year one thousand five hundred and three."[1]

While from one point of view the Admiral was telling the truth when he said he did not lie, his saying he had "not even a copper coin" skirted the fact that he did have much gold. The garment he mentioned, "the cloak that I wore," meant his gubernatorial robe which Bobadilla had taken from him and had sold. If his statement, "I came to serve at the age of twenty-eight" referred to his coming to Spain in 1485, it was giving a falsified age to support his Genoese cover-up. Knowing Queen Isabel's religious fervor, he was appealing to her, not King Ferdinand, in saying his soul might lose salvation from being "neglected". He revealed his imperious mentality in venturing to tell their Majesties how they as kings should treat him.

Mendez put the letter in his pocket, bought a dugout from the natives, fixed a keel to it so that it would not drift sideways too much, and took with him one Christian and six Indians. Against wind and waves, he undertook what seemed impossible, and failed to make the attempted crossing. Hostile Indians seized him and threatened to kill him, but he escaped and returned to the Admiral.

It looked as though they would never be able to get a message carried to Santo Domingo, and might never be rescued. But the Admiral immediately organized another attempt, with two dugouts, one with Mendez and the other with Bartolomeo Fieschi, Captain of the *Vizcaina*. Each of them took six Christians and ten Indians, the Indians to do the paddling.

To protect the men in the two canoes from hostile Indians, the Adelantado and an armed guard went with them to the northeastern point of Jamaica. From there in the direction of Española was Navassa Island, 78 miles away. On the first day out, in fierce July heat, the Indian paddlers consumed all the fresh water that had been provided for them. During two more days of paddling, one Indian died of thirst. By moonlight on the third night they sighted Navassa, and landed on it in the morning. They found fresh water in pools in the rocks, and some of the Indians drank so much they died. That evening they left Navassa, and with wind and current only slightly against them, since they were now in the lee of Española, they made the 30-mile crossing that night.

After two days' rest, Mendez with six Española Indians went eastward along the south shore. In August of 1503, before he got to Santo Domingo, he went inland to meet Governor Ovando and tell him of the Admiral's plight. Ovando, a self-seeking and most heartless man, was not pleased to hear that Cristóbal Colón was alive. He had been hoping to hear that he had died. Although Mendez told him of the urgent need of sending rescue for the Admiral and his 100 men, he wanted to keep Cristóbal Colón marooned. He was well aware that if Cristóbal Colón were rescued he would be arriving with royal permission to land on Española, and might challenge the governorship. For seven months he would not let Mendez carry news to Santo Domingo of the 100 marooned men in Jamaica. Even after he allowed Mendez to go to Santo Domingo in March of 1504, it was two more months before he would let Mendez procure a ship to rescue Colón.

The marooned men despaired. During the first five months after the two canoes had departed, many of them began to think that the Admiral was serving out a term of banishment, and would not be rescued for perhaps another year. They looked upon the Colón brothers as foreigners — Genoese Italians who did not care what happened to Spaniards. They began to think of mutiny, and in this were egged on by two who wanted to become their leaders, Diego and Francisco Porras. Those who held back through fear of being hanged for mutiny were reminded that they were now on land, not with the Admiral at sea, and that his voyage for which they had signed on, had ended. The Porras couple plausibly argued that Governor Ovando in Española, who had reason to hate Cristóbal Colón, would not call them mutineers if they left the Admiral and crossed to Española. They could say they made the crossing to rescue the Admiral. Thus persuaded, 48 men mutinied on January 2nd, 1504. They left the ships and seized ten dugout canoes and went east to the northeastern point and attempted a crossing, but when they were about ten miles out, a storm forced them to turn back. The waves rose alarmingly, and they feared they would be swamped. To lighten the canoes they threw overboard everything except their weapons. Then they threw overboard most of the Indian paddlers, and chopped off the fingers of those Indians who managed to cling to the gunwales. They kept one Indian on each canoe to do the steering. This was a tactical mistake, for those Indians who thus survived told of the whitemen's cruelty, and their tribesmen withheld food from the mutineers, who had nothing to eat except what they took by force.

The fifty loyal men on the stranded ships were near starvation, for the local Indians, who no doubt heard of what the mutineers were doing, were no longer bringing food in trade. The Admiral then conceived of an idea by which he might regain the confidence and support of those nearby Indians. He knew from Regiomontano's *Ephemerides* that an eclipse of the Moon would occur on February 29th of 1504. He sent invitations to all the chiefs of the region, and when they came on board he told them that God was displeased with them for not having continued to trade, and had become so angry he would, in his divine wrath, bring famine and pestilence upon them. God would soon show them his anger, by a frightening sign. They would see it when the Moon rose that evening. The Indians left, wondering what it could be that God threatened to do. When the eclipse began, they were so fearful, that they came running to the ships bringing food, and they begged the Admiral to tell God that they would continue to bring food. They begged the Admiral to ask God to forgive them. The Admiral let himself be persuaded to pray to God to forgive them, and to show by a sure sign that he had forgiven them. Ostensibly for this he retired to his cabin where he waited until he knew the eclipse would soon end. He then emerged with smiling face, and told the Indians that God had heard his prayer, and had forgiven them, and would let the Moon shine again upon them. They had been so deeply impressed that they kept their promises, and the Admiral and his 50 men were thereafter given food enough to keep alive.

From his timing of the eclipse in relation to the hour when the *Ephemerides* said it would occur, the Admiral estimated his position at Santa Gloria at 7 hours and 15 mintues west from Cadiz, or 109 degrees of longitude. He was actually at 70 degrees west of Cadiz — 39 degrees, or more than 2,000 miles in error. We know he wanted the longitudinal distance to be much larger than it was, and he may have been as dishonest in what he recorded in writing, as he had been in what he had told the Indians. Immediately after giving the Admiral's estimate of his longitude, but without telling of his error, Samuel Eliot Morison says that the Admiral made an entry of "a calculation of latitude for Santa Gloria that is very nearly correct."[2] Whatever implication we may draw, Morison's statement, that the Admiral was able to tell close to correct latitude, strengthens the suspicion that he did not consult with sky watchers in Spain before he estimated his longitude, and that he knowingly declared his longitude to be much greater than it actually was. There can be no doubt that he had decided never to admit that he had failed to give to Spain a quick passage to India.

As week after week and month after month went by without their knowing whether Mendez and Fieschi had succeeded in crossing to Española, fear that they would never be rescued was in all hearts. When Indians reported that the mutineers had failed to make that crossing, hopelessness was intensified. If ten canoes with ten or more men in each to paddle them had failed, then Mendez and Fieschi must have lost their lives in the attempt. And now the mutineers returning to Santo Gloria and stealing food as they came, were stirring widespread enmity against white men among all the Indians. The Admiral felt his control slipping, with mutiny now threatening among his loyal men.

But near the end of March, 1504, after eight months of despair, an approaching ship was sighted. Mendez had succeeded! Rescue had come! These were the first thoughts when the ship turned into Santa Gloria Bay. But hope of immediate rescue was quickly dashed. It was obvious that the incoming caravel was too small to rescue them all. When her captain landed, he said he had been sent merely to inspect and report. He was not friendly disposed, for he had been a supporter of Roldán against the Colóns. He presented the Admiral with two casks of wine and a slab of salt pork, which, he said, were gifts from Governor Ovando. Considering the circumstances, they were no better than a dash of vinegar, and a slap in the face. But he left a welcome message — rescue would be coming as soon as Mendez could charter a ship for the purpose. The Admiral, in a kingly manner, maintaining diplomatic courtesy, wrote a formal letter of thanks to Ovando, though he knew Ovando hated him and wished him dead, and though he hated Ovando as cordially as Ovando hated him. The caravel immediately sailed away.

With assurance of rescue coming, the Admiral believed he could win the mutineers back to obedience. They were camped nearby, and in any case it was necessary to put a stop to their stealing of food and turning the natives against all white men. He tried diplomacy. He had some of his officers take to them a portion of the pork slab and an offer of pardon. Francisco Porras ascribed his offer to weakness, and made excessive demands of specified quantities of food, conditions impossible to fulfill. The parley broke off. The mutineers came marching to do battle. On May 19th, Bartolomeo Colón with all the men who were not too sick to bear arms, went out to meet them. The loyalists had been better fed, and the mutineers lacked will to fight, knowing that even if they won they would be certain of judgment against them when rescue came. There was a brief melee with swords and almost no shooting, because of lack of gunpowder. One mutineer was killed and several wounded. Francisco Porras was captured, and the Admiral promptly put him in irons. All the mutineers surrendered.

There was another long period of waiting, and it was three months after the visit of the pork-slab caravel until a leaking and poorly equipped caravel, the only ship Ovando had permitted Mendez to charter, came to take them all to Española. They left Santa Gloria on June 29th, after having been marooned for one year and five days. It took them 6½ weeks to sail the 425 miles to Santo Domingo, which they did not reach until August 13th. Governor Ovando there made a great show of pleasure at the Admiral's return, and treated him hospitably, but released Francisco Porras. It was obvious to everyone, except to the Admiral himself, that their Majesties would never deem him to be mentally and physically strong enough to act again as Governor. Ovando of course saw that Cristóbal Colón would never again be a rival to himself. Ovando was moved to merciful treatment, not by pity, but by complacency at seeing the Admiral's worn-out physical condition.

Agents of the Admiral had been collecting some of his percentages, and he who had written to their Majesties that he did not have a copper coin, had in Santo Domingo enough financial credit to charter a ship in which he took his two "brothers" and 22 other persons home to Spain. The ship had a long passage of 56 days. She left Santo Domingo on September 12th, and did not drop anchor at Sanlucar de Barrameda up the Guadalquiver River until November 7th of 1504. The Admiral, who had been more than 2½ years away, and completely out of touch with happenings, was looking forward to a meeting with the Queen, whose warmhearted sympathy and understanding had always comforted and sustained him. He anticipated an immediate welcome to Court, but none came. The Queen was ill, and she died 19 days after he landed.

❀ༀༀༀༀༀༀༀༀༀༀༀༀༀༀༀༀༀༀༀༀༀ❀

The Admiral's 4th Voyage! A terrific story! With many crises as though plotted by a Master Dramatist! His sufferings wring one's heart with pity.

Pity? No.

You are heartless!

The Admiral caused his own marooning.

How can you say that?

If he had not made gold his goal in Veragua, he would have started homeward with his four ships in reasonably good condition, and having done his exploring, would have been allowed to land in Española, and then he would have returned to Spain in 1503 and again been welcomed by Queen Isabel.

His troubles were caused by himself?

I admit it seems harsh to criticize a man whose sufferings were so great, but a biographer has no excuse if he fails to tell the truth as he sees it.

Columbus brought on himself all his 4th-Voyage calamities?

All of them — his struggle against changing winds between Retrete and Puerto Bello when he returned to Veragua; then the battle at Belén; the loss of a ship there; the dismay at being out of sight of land on ships certain to sink within a day or two; his being marooned for more than a year, often near starvation, and having to combat mutineers — all were self-inflicted miseries.

21

A CONTINENT BETWEEN TWO OCEANS

Américo sailed from Lisbon on May 15, 1501. Below the Canary Islands his course was southward, his intention being to cross the ocean to a landfall several degrees south of the equator. He put in at Cape Verde for fresh water. While he was there, two Portuguese ships arrived. They had been part of Cabral's fleet, and were returning from India. One of them belonged to Marchioni, a Florentine merchant, and it had several Italians on board, one of them Gherardo Verdi, the brother of one of Américo's men.

Américo gave the weary mariners a hearty welcome and some food such as they had not tasted for more than a year. They gave him spices and much information. They freely answered his questions, telling him much that King Manoel would not have wanted them to divulge. From what they told him, and he was confident they were stating facts as they knew them, he was made to realize there were fallacies in the geography of Ptolemy. It was upsetting to learn that place names on old maps were unreliable. As Américo put it: "If the provinces, and kingdoms, and names of cities, and of islands, do not agree with those of the ancient authors, it is evidence that they are almost completely altered as they come into our Europe."[1] The description given him of everything east of the Cape of Good Hope seemed so distorted as compared with what Ptolemy said, that he concluded that on Cabral's expedition there had been "no cosmographer or any mathematician,"[2] meaning no one able to fix longitude with any near approach to accuracy. We now know that the Portuguese estimate of the longitude of that cape was eleven degrees in error. There was great need for Américo's method of finding longitude.

Since the returning ships could carry letters to Lisbon, Américo at Cape Verde wrote to his patron, Lorenzo di Pier Francisco de Medici, in Florence. His letter dated July 4, 1501, was probably carried by Gherardo Verdi. It would have been confiscated by the Portuguese had they known of it, for it mentioned Cabral's finding land to the west south of the equator, and that was something King Manoel had been concealing for nearly a year. However, after the crews of Cabral's ships got ashore in Lisbon, King Manoel realized that Cabral's landfall could no longer be kept a secret, and so on July 29, 1501, he wrote to tell King Ferdinand about it: "It would appear that our Lord intended that that country should be miraculously discovered, for it lies most conveniently and is indeed necessary to the voyage to India for the repair and watering of ships."[3]

To anyone acquainted with the sea, it would appear fantastic that land on the western side of the Atlantic could be described as lying, "most conveniently" for ships en route from Portugal to the Cape of Good Hope. But so it was. Directions of strong ocean currents in the South Atlantic indicate the directions of prevailing winds, and show how the best sailing route was across to Brazil, and thence south, southwest, and southeast, for a rounding of the Cape of Good Hope.

Américo assembled every scrap of information which the men of Cabral's ship could give him. He learned that Cabral's landfall had been at 18° South; that Cabral had there erected a cross and named the land

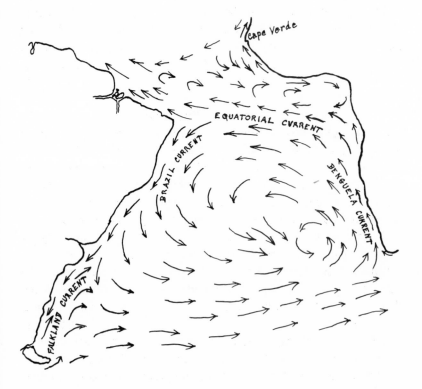

Prevailing winds and currents in the South Atlantic

"Sancta Crucis," and had searched the coast southward until he found a safe harbor which he called "Porto Seguro." Since Américo was headed toward that land, and intended to make his landfall north of Cabral's he wanted to know whether the coastline of Sancta Crucis was continuous with the land he himself had explored two years before. He would investigate the gaps between Cabral's 18° South, Pinzón's 10° South, and his own 5° or 6° South.

He knew it was safe to assume that the latitudes were near to correct. In his letter from Cape Verde he wrote: "The longitude is a more difficult thing, which only a few know how to determine, through much night work and observation of the conjunctions of the Moon with the planets. In the endeavor to ascertain longitude, I have lost much sleep, and have shortened my life ten years, but I hold it well worth the cost, because if I return in safety from this voyage, I hope to win fame throughout the ages. May God not ascribe my ambition to arrogance!"[4]

Sailing southwestward from Cape Verde, he encountered a zone of adverse winds, so that it took him 64 days to cross to the Brazilian elbow — 1520 miles at an average speed of one knot. He encountered "44 days of constant rain, thunder and lightning, so dark that never did we see the sun by day or fair sky by night." He made his landfall at about 6° South, and put into operation an intelligent plan. He kept two ships with him, and sent the third ship southward to Cabral's Porto Seguro, where all would later rendezvous. It was a great convenience to know in advance of such a harbor. With his two ships, he sailed northward until he came to the turn of the coast at a latitude close to his latitude on his farthest south on his previous voyage. There he named Cape St. Rocco (Cabo São Roque in Portuguese) at about 5½° South. He did not attempt to round this cape, because he knew that on the north side of it the ships would be caught by the strong current flowing toward the northwest, the current which had been too fast for his ships to proceed against on his first voyage.

Place names on the earliest maps of the coast of Brazil give us the dates in the church calendar when he discovered the various capes, rivers, mountain peaks and harbors. He named Cape St. Augustine on August 28th. He there went ashore and estimated the latitude at 8° South. Cape St. Augustine is actually at 8° 21' South. Américo probably remained on shore there through September 3rd to observe a conjunction for longitude. Then he went southward, making a coastal chart for King

Manoel. On November 1st, All Saints Day, he entered the "baie de Tuti Santi" (Bay of All Saints — Bahia). After the rendezvous at Porto Seguro, which was at 16°20' South, the three ships remained in consort along the coast to the southwest. The place names given by Américo appeared on the map of Nicolo de Canerio the very next year. Américo discovered and named "Baie de Reis" (Bay of the Kings) on Epiphany, January 6th. This was the Bay of Rio de Janeiro. He gave the name "Pinachullo Detencio" (Craggy Pinnacle) to the spectacular peak now called "Corcovado." Américo was the first man in history to roll down to Rio. At 25° South, he entered a port which he named "Cananor." Years later, this was corrupted to Cananea, the name which the port now bears. But the earliest maps have it "Cananor," and his naming it was most significant. Cananor was a name Américo heard from the men on Cabral's ships at Cape Verde, and it was a name which loomed large thereafter in Portugal. King Manoel wrote in his letter of July 29th to King Ferdinand: "When he (Cabral) was in that Kingdom of Cochin . . . there came a message to him from the King of Cananor, and one from the King of Colum which adjoins it, inviting him to come to them, because he would find a more profitable market there . . . . He made his way to the Kingdom of Cananor, to one of the kings . . . . The king ordered so much spicery delivered to the ships that there was sufficient for a cargo if the ships had been empty." With the cinnamon at Cananor, Cabral completed the ship loading. Cananor was his last port in India.

Américo had this in mind when he followed the coast southwestward to where it turned more sharply to the westward than the southward. When he came to a harbor where his estimate of longitude told him he had reached the Line of Demarcation, and therefore the western limit of land belonging to Portugal, he remembered what Cabral's men had said had been their last port in India, and he gave this last harbor on the Portuguese side of the Treaty Line the name which Cabral's men and King Manoel would appreciate. On top of a cliff on the continental side of the harbor he erected a boundary post, a *padrão* of European marble, bearing the insignia of Portugal.[5] The evidence that Cananor was the last harbor on that coast which Portugal could legally claim is positive and absolute. Cananor was the last place name, or name farthest west on the maps of Canerio, 1502, Waldseemüller, 1507, Ruysch, 1508, and on other maps for a number of years thereafter, and Cananor was properly so distinguished, for it was in fact on the Line of Demarcation. It reveals

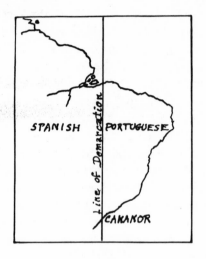

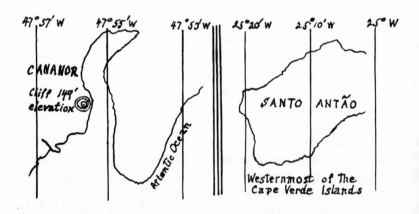

Cananor and the Line of Demarcation

the astonishing precision with which on this occasion Américo deter-mined longitude. He was so close to correct one hesitates to speak of it, because it seems fantastically beyond belief. Let the facts eloquently tell. The Treaty of Tordesillas allowed Portugal "370 leagues west of the Cape Verde Islands." At 16⅔ leagues to a degree this meant 22 and 1/5 degrees, or 22°12'. The modern Hydrographic Chart of the Portuguese Government places the westernmost point of Santo Antão, which is the westernmost of the Cape Verde Islands, at 25° 22' West. The Line of De-marcation therefore would be at 25° 22' plus 22° 12'. or at 47° 34' West. The modern Hydrographic Chart of the Brazilian Government places Cananor (the modern Cananea) at 47° 56' West. Américo was correct to within 22 minutes of longitude, or about one-third of a degree, or (at that latitude) about 20 miles.

Américo was not obligated to give King Manoel any information re-garding land on the Spanish side of the Line of Demarcation. Such in-formation belonged only to their Spanish Majesties. This is why on the earliest maps based upon Portuguese sources, place names ended with Cananor. Beyond Cananor, in Portuguese ships exploring land be-longing to Spain, Américo could not ask Portuguese captains to make detailed studies of the coast. That would be for the Spanish to do. He therefore sailed as rapidly as possible to the southwest, observing only the most obvious features of the coast. By contrast with his slow progress along the Portuguese land from Cape St. Rocco to Cananor at an aver-age speed of only twelve miles a day, his speed beyond Cananor aver-aged sixty miles a day. After the turn of the coast to the west into a great gulf, he found himself at the inner end of what was a mammoth estuary. Where a mouth of a great river (actually two rivers) met the tide, he found the latitude to be 34° South. "Rio Giordan" was the name he gave to the river later called the Plata, or River of Silver.

Some time after 1526 the Portuguese claimed this river as theirs, since discovered with Portuguese ships. But they could not have it, for it was clearly on Spain's side of the Line. The Portuguese did take possession of much land on the Spanish side — in western Brazil.

On two sixteenth-century maps the estuary of the River Plata was called "Mare Americum" (America's Sea). It was not in character for Américo to attach his name to geography. But others did so use it.

Américo wrote: "We ran the course of that land for about 800 leagues."[6] At 4½ miles to a league, this was 3,300 miles, and that is the

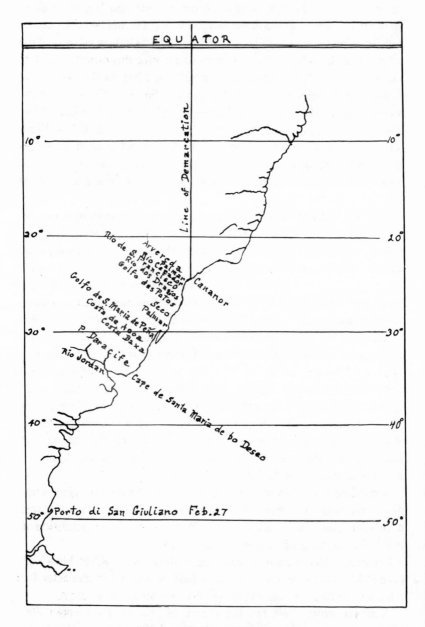

Américo in 1502, on Spanish side of the Line

actual distance following the principal turns of the coast from Cape St. Rocco to the River Plata.

The size of "Rio Giordan" indicated he was not yet near the southern end of the great land. Since there were only a few weeks left before summer in the Southern Hemisphere would be turning into autumn, he decided to sail southward as far as he could in that season, as fast as he could, without closely following each turn of the coast. No doubt he kept in the offing, as sailors call it, or within view of land from the masthead, and with the help of a southward flowing eddy against the far-off-shore northward current. He thus sailed almost a thousand miles to the south of the Rio Giordan. He wrote: "We coursed so far in those seas that we passed south of the Tropic of Capricorn, until the South Pole stood above my horizon at fifty degrees, which was my latitude from the equator." Nearest his farthest south he entered a harbor on February 27, and named it from the church calendar, Porto di San Giuliano (Port St. Julian).

So far as surviving maps show, the name Porto di San Giuliano was first used on the map of 1523, in its Italian form, "Giuliano". Previous to the making of that map, the only recorded voyages to this latitude were those of Américo and of Magellan. While all the accounts of Magellan's voyage tell of his naming of ports, bays, and islands, none of them say that he named the Port of St. Julian. They merely say of it: "We arrived at the Port of St. Julian," or "We entered a port called St. Julian," or "We found ourselves in the harbor of St. Julian." It would appear that they knew its location and name as previously given by Américo, and identified it from its latitude.

Américo wrote: "We navigated 9 months and 27 days in the Southern Hemisphere."' Outward bound he crossed the equator about the 1st of August, and homeward bound about the 27th of May.

From Port St. Julian he sailed back northward out of sight of land, with the aid of the northward-flowing Falkland Current and strong prevailing winds from the southwest, of which he had been apprised by Cabral's men. When he came to within sight of the land, he followed the shore with a close-to-coast northward-flowing eddy, until he came to the island of Santa Caterina, and entered the gulf behind it. Here in preparation for recrossing the Atlantic, in a little river that ran into the gulf, the ships were for the last time beached and heeled over so that their bottoms could be scraped free of barnacles, and worm-eaten planks

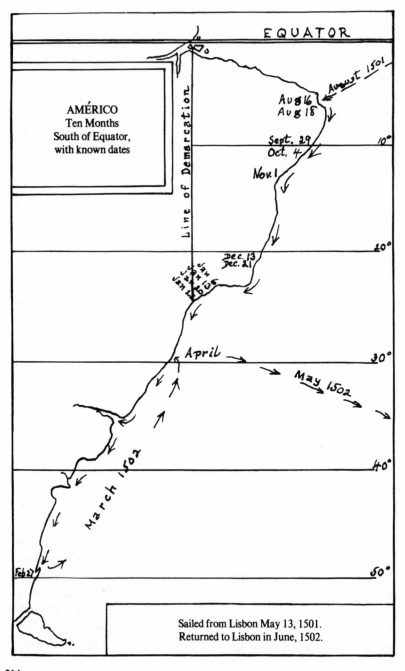

EQUATOR

AMÉRICO
Ten Months
South of Equator,
with known dates

Line of Demarcation

August 1501

Aug 16
Aug 18

Sept. 29
Oct. 4

Nov. 1

10°

20°

Dec. 13
Dec. 21

Jan
Jan
Jan Feb 6

April

May 1502

30°

March 1502

40°

Feb 27

50°

Sailed from Lisbon May 13, 1501.
Returned to Lisbon in June, 1502.

could be replaced, and the seams caulked. He named the gulf "Golfo de Estremo Repairo" and he named the river which was the site of the careening and refitting"Rio dos Voltas" (River of Turning Over, or River of Undergoing Alterations).

From the Gulf of Extreme Repairs he sailed eastward with following winds across the ocean to the African coast, probably to not far north of the Cape of Good Hope, whence he had the aid of a northward-flowing current all the way to Sierra Leone, from where he took advantage of a near-shore northward eddy. He reached Lisbon in the late spring of 1502.

In the thirteen months of the expedition, he had not lost a ship or a man. All returned in good health. Never had there been a voyage with purer motives, unsullied by any seeking for material gain. Some might say that fate seemed to have recognized the highmindedness of Américo's purposes, or that nature had been kind to him. We can reverse that, and say that he had learned enough of the prevailing winds and currents in the South Atlantic from the voyages of Bartolomeu Dias, Vasco da Gama, and Pedro Alvares Cabral, to know how to make good use of what nature provided.

Voyaging for Spain, he had discovered much land that by Treaty of Tordesillas and Papal decree belonged to Portugal. Voyaging for Portugal, he had discovered much land that was Spain's. His two voyages fitted together perfectly, with no wasted effort or needless duplication.

He had expressed to his patron his ambition to be the first to map the stars of the Southern Hemisphere, and identify the Celestial South Pole, for the guidance of all future navigators south of the equator. For this he had "hopes of winning fame throughout the ages."[8] In what he called "a small work," he had assembled a diagramming of the Celestial Southern Hemisphere with accompanying notes on the bright stars with their circuits. He had only the one copy. He made the mistake of showing it to King Manoel. Because it was Portuguese policy not to let the mariners of Spain or other countries have any aid in sailing into the South Atlantic, King Manoel took possession of the work, and did not return it. This was one of the most outrageous things any monarch ever did. Américo could not reproduce the material from memory. Perhaps someday someone will find in the archives of Portugal Américo's "small work."

Américo's charts of the more than 4,000 miles of coastline were also held by the monarch Américo called "This Most Serene King." Portuguese law forbade the exportation of maps, and any maps that did leave Portugal were smuggled out. What Portugal could not keep concealed was Américo's discovery that the great land he had explored was a new continent, a fourth continent. We who know that our planet has seven continents, may find it difficult to realize how startling his announcement was. He had indisputable evidences that he had found an entirely new continent. The gigantic rivers gave indication of the breadth of its interior. The many separate tribes, and many languages they spoke, were too many for what had been reported of Asia. The strange vegetation and variety of birds and animals showed it was a continent different in these respects from Asia. Its extension down to fifty degrees South and beyond, proved that it was not a southern extension of Asia. All the maps of Ptolemy and others, and the voyaging of Marco Polo, indicated that Asia extended to no further south than about ten degrees South.

The final proof that the continent was not part of Asia was in arithmetic based upon longitude. According to Ptolemy, the coast of Cathay (China) was 215 degrees east of Cadiz. By subtraction from 360, the distance from Cadiz westward to the China coast was 145 degrees. The Cape Verde Islands were 20 degrees west of Cadiz. The Line of Demarcation was 22 degrees west of those islands. or 42 degrees west of Cadiz. These 42 degrees subtracted from 145 degrees, left 103 degrees as the longitudinal distance from the Line of Demarcation to the coast of China. At the equator, 103 degrees would be more than 6,000 nautical miles.

By similar computation, from the Line of Demarcation westward to where Ptolemy placed the Cape of Catigara, was about 138 degrees. At the equator, this would be 8,280 nautical miles.

There was no escaping this arithmetic. The new continent was not only not part of Asia, but was thousands of miles from Asia. The great ocean east of China, in which lay the island of Japan, was not the Atlantic, could not be the Atlantic. It was another ocean — an ocean between the new continent and Asia, an ocean broader than the Atlantic. Here was astounding enlargement of the habitable earth— a fourth continent twice the size of Europe, a whole new continent for the people of Europe to colonize.

It is no belittlement of Américo's discovery that Europeans did not quickly welcome the opportunity. The immediate reaction of businessmen in Spain was disappointment and frustration. They wanted to trade

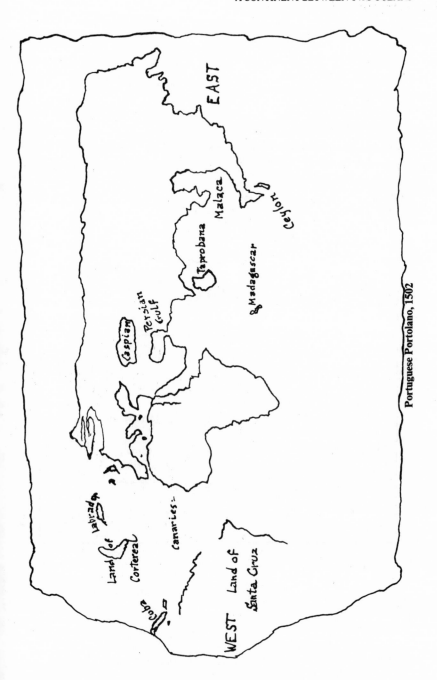

Portuguese Portolano, 1502

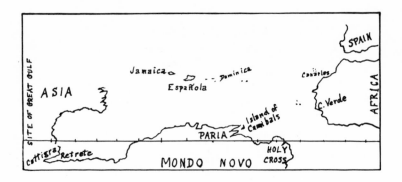

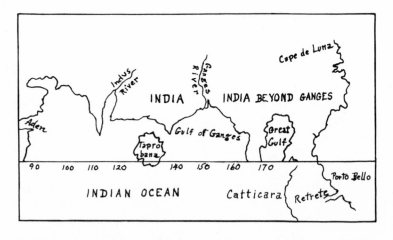

World Map by Bartolomeo Colón, 1503

directly with India. Américo's discovery shattered the dream which Don Cristóbal Colón had given them.

Map makers, on the other hand, immediately accepted the discovery. The first map to show the new continent lying between two oceans was the Portuguese Portolano (Map of Ports) of 1502. Drawn on a whole sheepskin, it showed Asia as definitely ending without any of the New World attached to it. It showed the coast of the new continent in two sections, since there had been a gap between the sections Américo had explored on his two voyages. To the southwest it showed the coast only as far as it belonged to Portugal. It called the continent by the name Cabral had given, Sancta Crucis. While the western end of Cuba was cut off by the edge of the sheepskin, Cuba was labled as an island. For clarity, sailing direction lines and most place names have been omitted from the illustration of the Portolano. Names which are shown have been translated into English.

In sharpest contrast to the new knowledge of world cosmography was the map made in 1503 by Bartolomeo Colón.

Bartolomeo Colón made his so-called World Map of 1503 while marooned on Jamaica with the Admiral, and without any knowledge of what had been discovered in 1502. If he had known what he learned after he was rescued in 1504, he very likely would not have ventured the dishonesty of indicating on his map that there was a strait at Retrete which went through to the Indian Ocean. His map reveals caution in showing the non-existent in two ways, as merely a deep enclosed bay, and as an incompletely explored open-ended passage. By omitting Cuba, Bartolomeo Colón evades the question raised by the Admiral's contention that Cuba was not an island. His map uses the term *Mondo Novo*. This term, "New World," was not first used by Bartolomeo Colón or by the Admiral, or by Américo Vespúcio, or by anyone else during the lifetime of these men. The term was used first, it seems correct to say, by an Orkney fisherman in 1397. It was sent, translated into Italian, in a letter by Antonio Zeno to his uncle Carlo Zeno in Venice. According to Antonio Zeno, the Orkney fisherman said of the mainland extending southward from Nova Scotia: "It is a very great country, and, as it were, a new world" *(grandissimo e quasi un nuovo mondo).* So far as records show, this was the first use of the term "new world" applied to land on the west side of the Atlantic.[9] Bartolomeo Colón's use of it was not an admission of the existence of a previously unknown Western Hemisphere, but as a hitherto unknown southeastern extension of Asia. This was the Admiral's fixed idea. His uncle's map was his face saver. The Admiral in very specific words said that when he was near Retrete, he had been as near to the Indian Ocean as the width of Italy — "the distance Pisa is from Venice." As map maker, Bartolomeo Colón was exceedingly ingenious.

At home in Seville in November of 1504, the Admiral was bluntly met with the reality that map makers would no longer accept the claims which Bartolomeo Colón had attempted to maintain.

Which do you think Américo considered the most important of the three purposes he had in making the voyage for Portugal?

Three purposes?

Yes, you said three — to map the sky of the Southern Hemisphere, to explore the coast, and to fix the Line of Demarcation.

He had a fourth purpose.

You haven't mentioned it.

Wasn't it obvious?

What was it?

To learn all he could about the inhabitants and animals of the great land.

Well then, which of the four purposes did Américo think most important?

The sky mapping, which he believed would win him fame.

He sure misguessed that one!

22

DISCOVERIES

Although the concept of a new continent lying between two oceans and thousands of miles from Asia was being accepted throughout Europe, the Admiral would never relinquish his ideas of geography. He would never admit error. Ever since he first got the idea of crossing the Atlantic, he had twisted facts to conform with theory. He had never really cared about geography, but only in what his mistaken ideas of it enabled him to acquire. He had never been primarily interested in exploration. He had explored only when he believed that by doing it he could prove his contention upon which his Contract with their Majesties had been based. He had been sustained through all the perils and miseries of his 4th voyage, and the marooning, not by any purpose he would reveal to the public, but by his private feeling of royalty, his feeling that he had a right to sovereign power. His insistences had brought him close to achieving his ambition — his becoming an independent governor of an extensive area of islands — almost an empire. If he had not been forcefully dispossessed of his governorship, unjustly as he continued to maintain, he might have become too powerful in his distant islands for their Majesties to unseat him. With a navy based upon the western side of the Atlantic, he would have been in a position to resist trans-Atlantic attempts to depose him. Such was his overwhelming private ambition that it would have been in character for him, if he again became Governor of Española, to plan never again to let the Governorship be taken from him.

Thwarted now of all he had worked for, he continued to pester King Ferdinand with requests for restoration of his Governorship and his percentages. He then found a legal fact which gave him a basis from which to increase his demands. He learned that the maritime law of Castile specified that the Admiral of Castile should have one-third "of all merchandise . . . of whatsoever kind, name or description, which may be bought, bartered, found, acquired or obtained within the limits of the said admiralty." With this legal backing, he began asking for more than ten percent. He demanded a third of all profits brought by ship from the Indies to Spain, with the argument that his being Admiral of the Ocean Sea entitled him to a claim over all activities in the ocean.

His concept of princely rights permitted no retreat, no reduction. With the lordly attitude of a monarch, he saw only what others did to him, and gave little thought to what he did to others. He revealed this in his attitude toward his longtime business acquaintance, Américo the Florentine, who was a gentleman and a scholar, a man who had served Colón always with honesty and fair dealing. The Admiral looked upon him as his friend. He was aware that Américo was well educated, and in his youth in Florence had known such men as Paolo Toscanelli and Leonardo da Vinci, and was now as always in close contact with the leading people in Florence and Seville. The Admiral needed a friendly word at Court and turned to Américo to give it, as we see in a letter he wrote:

To my very dear Son, Don Diego Colón, at the Court.

My dear Son,

Diego Mendez departed here on Monday, the third of this month. Since his departure, I have talked with Américo Vespúcio, the bearer of this letter, who is going to Court on some business connected with navigation. He has at all times shown a desire to serve me, and he is an honorable man. As with many others, fortune has not treated him kindly, and his labors have not been as rewarding as he deserves. He is going with a sincere desire to procure a favorable turn of affairs for me, if it is in his power.

I know not, here, what instructions to give him that will help my cause, for I am ignorant of what will be required there. He goes determined to accomplish for me everything possible. Find out what can be done there to help, and go to work on it, so that he may be fully informed and able to devote himself to presenting my case; and let everything be done with secrecy, that no suspicions may arise. I have told him all that I can concerning the business, and have informed him of all the payments which I have received, and what is due.

This letter is intended also for the adelantado, that he may take advantage of any advice on the subject. His Highness believes that the ships were in the best and richest region of the Indies, and if he desires to know anything more on the subject, I will satisfy him by word of mouth, for I cannot tell him by letter.

May our Lord have you in His holy keeping.

Done at Seville, February 5, 1505.

Thy father, who loves thee better than himself.

Cristóbal Colón.

This letter, which he wrote three months after coming home to Seville from his 4th and last voyage, was an attempt to get help from a man who was now on the Board of Trade in Seville, and was having a hearing at Court such as the Admiral wanted for himself and feared he would not have. Acknowledging that Américo was being more favorably looked upon by King Ferdinand than he himself was, he expressed sympathy with Américo because, as everyone knew, he had not been adequately recompensed for his voyage made for the King of Portugal.

The Admiral, of course, saw another reason for feeling sorry for Américo. Américo was being credited with having discovered what many were now saying was a new continent between two oceans and far distant from Asia. But his announcement that the continent was inhabited only by savages had chilled enthusiasm. Spaniards had been hoping to outdo Portugal by opening immediate trade with the cities of China and India. Although a successful businessman, Américo did not seem to know what Spain wanted. The Admiral thought Américo should have foreseen the unhappy effect his announcement would have. Nothing had ever been so disappointing to Europeans. Américo, the Admiral privately thought to himself, is mistaken if he expects that his announcement of a new continent will bring him honors and fame such as the Admiral had won in 1493. Américo simply did not know how to get ahead in this world. The Admiral would have felt the more pity if he had any idea of what was being done in far-off Italy to injure Américo's reputation.

The Admiral did not know, and no one in Spain knew, what had already happened in Florence. Américo's personal letters to his patron, Lorenzo di Pier Francesco de Medici, contained statements of his private thoughts. They were certainly not intended for publication. In his letter from Lisbon, Américo had written: "What should I tell of the multitude of wild animals, the abundance of pumas, of panthers, of wild cats, not like those of Spain, but of the opposite side of the globe? What should I tell of the many wolves, red deer, monkeys, and felines, marmosets of many kinds, and many large snakes? We saw so many other animals, that I believe so many species could not have been contained in Noah's ark."

Américo had a good reason for believing this, for he knew how limited space was on board ships, and how only a comparatively few species of animals could have been saved from the Flood by Noah's ark. But this casting of doubt on the literal truth of the Bible story was a dreadful heresy. It would be denounced by Church authorities everywhere.

A more startling feature of Américo's description of what he had seen in the new continent was his telling of how he had acquired information about naked cannibals. He said that he had actually resided among them! Pious Christians could not understand why a civilized man would do such a thing, unless it was to satisfy his lasciviousness. Few persons at that time in Europe had discernment enough to credit anyone with what we now call a scientific purpose. What Américo wrote in this matter shocked people when it was published, and of course, was read avidly. In England, it was the inspiration of Sir Thomas More's *Utopia*, 1516, which told of an idealized "Never-Never-Land beyond the equator" where people are free of the corrupting influence of money.

Here is the passage in Américo's purloined and published letter which most deeply moved Sir Thomas More:

"Let us come to rational animals. We found the whole land inhabited by people entirely naked, the men like the women without any covering of their shame . . . . I strove a great deal to understand their conduct and customs. For twenty-seven days I ate and slept among them, and what I learned about them is as follows. Having no laws and religious faith, they live according to nature. They understand nothing of the immortality of the soul. There is no possession of private property among them, for everything is in common. They have no boundaries of kingdom or province. They have no king, nor do they obey anyone. Each is his own master. There is no administration of justice, which is unnecessary to them, because in their code no one rules . . . That which made me the more astonished at their wars and cruelty was that I could not understand from them why they made wars upon each other, since they held no private property or sovereignty of empire and kingdoms, and did not know any such thing as lust for possessions, or pillaging, or a desire to rule, which appear to me to be the cause of wars and every disorderly act."[1]

Nothing could be more opposite to the Admiral's private princely assumptions. Américo's opinion as to the cause of wars was a challenge to every ruler in Europe, and downright subversive, a seemingly reckless defiance of divinely constituted authority. His purpose in interviewing savages was in his day beyond general comprehension, as he well knew when he wrote about it in a private letter. To sleep among naked man-eating savages for purposes of research was centuries in advance of his time. Américo was the first practicing sociologist.

His letters, from Seville in 1499, from Cape Verde in 1501, and from Lisbon in 1502 had been prized by their recipient in Florence, who kept them from the public. But when Lorenzo di Pier Francesco de Medici died in June of 1503, a political boss, Piero Soderini, had risen to power over the Medici. America's letters could no longer be held private, for Soderini saw an opportunity of enhancing his political image in Florence by reshaping Américo's letters to his advantage. Printers saw the possibility of concocting out of them something that would have a ready sale. A small work of a dozen pages was published with the heading, "Albericus Vespucius offers his best compliments to Lorenzo Pietro di Medici." This forgery was titled *Mundus Novus*. It did not fail to feature the sex habits of the savages, and their readiness to copulate with Christians, and by implication the readiness of Christians. It made America's intentions appear deplorable. The last paragraph began with the word "Joker" in Latin: "Jocundus, the translator, is turning this epistle from the Italian into the Latin tongue." *Mundus Novus* was printed by "Master John Otmar, Vienna," August, 1504.

A month later came another and a more confusing forgery. It was entitled "Amerigo Vespucci Letter to Piero Soderini." With some garbled material from Américo's actual letters, and with many contradictions and besmirching details, it made Américo appear as a boaster, a fool, and a liar. Since Cristóbal Colón had made four voyages, it claimed four for Américo, the first in 1497, to put him on the shore of the new continent a year before Colón landed in the Gulf of Paria. It gave Américo a fourth voyage in 1503. This Soderini Letter quickly became a best seller throughout Europe. It was translated into many languages. It was later titled *The Four Voyages*. It was the most outrageous miswriting in history. In Spain, if its contents had been accepted, it would have destroyed Américo. But everyone in Seville and at Court knew he had made only two voyages, the first of them in 1499. Outside of Spain, *Mundus Novus* and the *Soderini Letter* were accepted as geniune. Américo, in Spain, knew nothing of them until after they had been widely disseminated and it was too late to kill them.

There is nothing surprising in Américo's being asked to carry the Admiral's letter to his son Diego Colón at the Court. The Admiral was vexed and festering because he had not received from King Ferdinand an invitation to come to Court. He would, nevertheless, continue to ask that his Governorship be returned to him. If he could not recover the Governorship for himself, he was determined to maintain his demands with the hope that eventually his son Diego would inherit it. Don Diego showed aptitude for practical affairs. He had been a page at Court, and had now become one of the king's bodyguards. As heir to the Governorship, he would marry, with King Ferdinand's approval, or at the king's suggestion, a cousin of the king, Doña Maria de Toledo. She knew, and

King Ferdinand knew, that she would be marrying a wealthy man, or one who would be wealthy.

The Admiral's painful awareness of his own lack of formal education made him want for his sons what he had not. While son Diego showed little aptitude for serious study, son Ferdinand had an inquiring mind, and his father supplied him with plentiful means to buy whatever books he wanted.

We cannot make any accurate estimate of the Admiral's wealth. His ten percent of the first shipment of gold from Española to Seville amounted in present-day purchasing power to many thousands of dollars. In June of 1500 the little *Aguja* carried to Spain the Admiral's 4,000 ounces of gold, and even if they were alloy, their value at present-day prices of gold was in order of one to two million dollars. In ten months of gold collecting in 1501, the Admiral's share at the nineteenth century price of gold was in the order of $600,000, and at recent prices was twenty times that. Morison says that Colón, after returning from his last voyage, had in Española a balance of $180,000, which he had left to meet his expenses there.

On a recent Caribbean cruise, this biographer asked his lecture audience to answer by show of hands whether they believed that Columbus, when he died, was a very wealthy man, or in merely moderate financial circumstances, or in dire poverty. Of the 150 men and women in that audience, only one thought Columbus had been rich, four voted for moderate means, and 145 thought he had died in extreme poverty. How did history get so miswritten? Was it because poverty fitted better with the popular concept of a hero who had to struggle against opposition?

The only effective way to eradicate an error in history is to show convincingly what gave rise to it. Here is how the idea arose that Columbus died in poverty. Soon after writing the letter he asked Américo to carry to Don Diego Colón, the Admiral decided to go in person to the Court to make his demands. But he was in sad physical condition, suffering agonies from arthritis. To travel the hundreds of miles from Seville to the Court in Segovia, he would have a strenuous journey over mountains where there were no roads — only mule tracks. A horse could carry him, but the Admiral knew that riding on horseback up and down steeply inclined mountain paths would be too painful. A horse would be less sure-footed, and not so easy riding as a mule. But nearly 800 years of war against the Moors had caused a shortage of everything in Spain, including mules. A new law forbade any riding on mules. Mules were to be used only as truck carriers and in field work. The Admiral petitioned for special permission to ride a mule to Court. He had to wait for many weeks until the permission came in May of 1505. In that long waiting he could not get a mule, and hasty schoolteachers concluded, he must have been too poor to buy or even rent a mule.

When the permission came, he immediately set out on his journey with every comfort money could provide.

Without Queen Isabel, the Court was for him, a heartless place. He had his under-cover hatred for King Ferdinand, who instinctively disliked him and for financial reasons, did not want to welcome him. Though not given to pity, the king saw from his physical condition that he could not do any more voyaging or cause trouble, and would be merely a nuisance. Since the king had no intention of restoring the Admiral's financial rights, as he would have to do if he restored his Governorship, he gave the Admiral nothing but promises. He could not ask a nobleman to cease to be a nobleman, and so the persistent petitioner Cristóbal Colón remained a Don, and retained his title of Admiral. The Admiral's son Ferdinand wrote that King Ferdinand "received the Admiral courteously, and said he was restoring all his rights and privileges, but it was the king's real intention to take them all away."[2] He offered Colón a steady income if he would renounce his percentages and privileges.

With desperation and in spite of intense suffering, the Admiral followed the Court when it moved to Salamanca, and from there, to Valladolid. In Valladolid, knowing he was dying, he made his last Will. With both of his sons and an attendant priest at his bedside, he died on May 20th of 1506.

Columbus had all the qualities requisite for a popular hero. A handsome man, he had remarkable physical stamina and a daring spirit. He was ambitious, an opportunist, a boaster, an adventurer, conventionally religious, a realist as a mariner, a credulous romantic in regard to lands to which his ships carried him.

Like most people, he respected facts if they served his purpose, and did not conflict with his beliefs. He owed lip service to their Majesties, but he primarily served himself. He, who had temporarily changed the thinking of all Europe, was unprepared to follow along with the development of what he had started. He complained that enemies and circumstances had mistreated him, but he brought his fate upon himself by refusing to explore whenever he could evade doing do, and by his putting first gold, governorship, and princely dream of establishing a line of hereditary rule. Seeds of his failure and suffering were planted in him in his boyhood in Majorca. It all started with his learning that his father had been the rightful heir to a throne.

The Last Will of Columbus was a document of 3500 words in length. A tenth of his estate was to be disposed "to necessitous persons as a tithe." The Executor was also to give money to build a hospital in Santo Domingo. The son Diego was to succeed in title and estate, and in this Columbus still held his dream of a hereditary dominion.[3] If Don Diego had no issue, title and estate would go to the son Ferdinand. As executor, Diego was to distribute the income, giving funds to the Admiral's "brother" Bartolomeo until Bartolomeo had an annual income of at least $20,000 in the purchasing power of gold of a few years ago, and of many times that with recent prices of gold. Bartolomeo,.the Will directed, was to get his share from one-tenth of the estate. From this and several other provisions, we deduce that the Admiral before his death had an annual income of at least $200,000, and perhaps ten to twenty times that. No particular sum was bequeathed to the Admiral's other "brother" Diego, since he was "attached to the Church," for the Admiral had procured for him Holy Orders, and by Church law he could not accept a bequest. The executor's son was instructed to give "brother" Diego "what is right." Son Ferdinand was given a millionaire's annual income. In addition to maintaining an estate in Seville, a house and grounds at the bend of the river opposite the Carthusian convent and at the site of the railroad station (Cordoba trains), Ferdinand Colón purchased more than 20,000 costly manuscripts and early printed books for his library, called the Colombiana.[4] The Admiral's Will left legacies to members of the Genoese Colombo family and the de Harana family, and also money "for the recovery of the Holy Sepulchre." The son Diego would have an income obviously that of a multi-millionaire. The Admiral in his Will mentioned having "a fund in the bank of St. George [the largest bank in Genoa], which gives an interest of six percent, and is secure money."

While the Admiral's estate was being settled, the new concept of world geography was rapidly advancing. In the Rare Book Division of the New York Public Library there is a world map known as the Lenox Globe. It is a copper ball 112 mm., or slightly more than 4½ inches in

(details in flat projection)
shows the new continent between two oceans.

Lenox Globe, 1505 or 1506

diameter, and it has four continents inscribed upon it. It was made in 1505 or 1506.[5] It shows the new continent extending much farther to the south than Africa, and positioned at an immense distance from Asia, with the other ocean west of it wider than the Atlantic. On the Lenox Globe at the latitude of the Strait of Malacca, as measured with a flexible ruler, the Atlantic Ocean is represented by a width of 55 mm., and the other ocean by a width of 97½ mm.

The fact that there was a new continent had been accepted throughout Europe. A group of scholars in a college in northeastern France in the town of Saint-Dié, decided to produce a Cosmography of the World, with a map which would show recent discoveries. One of them, Mathias Ringman, Professor of Latin, went twice to Italy to collect geographical information. Martin Waldseemüller, Professor of Geography, sent inquiries to Spain regarding Cuba. From various sources or hints, he acquired some knowledge of the Florida Peninsula, and put together a fairly accurate outline of the Gulf of Mexico. He copied from Bartolomeo Colón's map the error of showing a strait at or near the location of Retrete. In 1507 he produced a map to show the long coastline from the far north down to a strait, and south of the strait, the new continent. It was a huge map printed in 12 sections to be pasted together, in overall size 4½ by 8 feet. He called it: "A Map of the World According to the Tradition of Ptolemy and the Voyages of Americus Vespuccius." It had also an inset map in gores. In giving the new continent its name Waldseemüller said: "I believe it is very just that it should be named Amerige, after its discoverer, Americus, a man of sagacious mind, or let it be named America, since both Europe and Asia bear names of feminine form." A successful name is a work of art. America was such a perfect invention that it spread into universal usage. In 1538 Mercator applied it also to the northern continent.

It has been said that if Américo had any sense of decency, he would have protested the invention of the name America. The answer to that is that he did not know of it until after the name had been widely accepted, and he could not have changed it if he had wished to do so. The only excuse for protest would have been a feeling of modesty.

Not until more than forty years after the naming of America did anyone advance the argument that "Columbus was first." Ferdinand Colón in his *Life of Columbus* published about the middle of the 16th century wrote: "Anyone could follow the coast, as some were already doing who

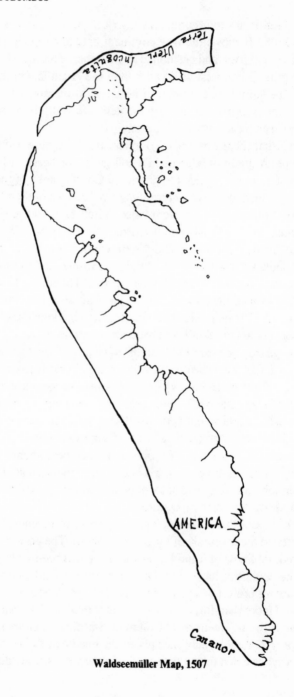

Waldseemüller Map, 1507

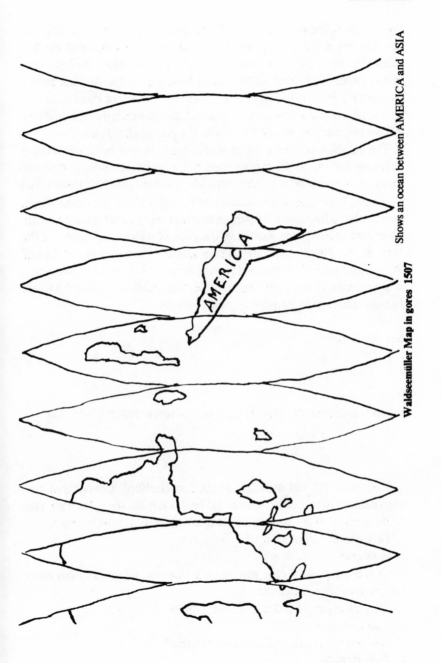

Shows an ocean between AMERICA and ASIA

Waldseemüller Map in gores 1507

improperly called themselves discoverers, not considering that they had not discovered any new land but only followed in the wake of the Admiral after he had shown them the way." Friar Bartolomé de Las Casas in *Las Obras* in 1552 wrote: "It cannot be denied to the Admiral except with great injustice, that as he was the first discoverer of those Indies, so he was also of the whole of our mainland, and to him is due the credit by discovering the province of Paria, which is part of all that land."

The question as to who discovered America is now being reevaluated in the light of recent discoveries concerning the human beings who lived in the New World before Columbus. We now have positive evidence that every physical type, every stature tall or short, every cranial shape, every color, white, black, brown, yellow and every blood type of humanity except possibly one, existed in the pre-Columbian population of the New World. People had come from practically every country of the Old World, and since they included representatives of all types of humanity, it is a mistake to call them "Indians" or "Amerindians," since the whole human race cannot correctly be called Indians.

See the Appendix.

❀ʀʀʀʀʀʀʀʀʀʀʀʀʀʀʀʀʀʀʀʀʀʀʀʀʀ❀

You evade the hot question. In 1982 in Hartford, Connecticut, two men debated whether Columbus did or did not discover America. One of them got so angry he seized a pitchfork and killed the other man.

They had no definitions.

How come?

It is a question of what you mean. Columbus did not do what many people have thought he did.

You are saying he did not discover America?

I do not say it.

But you say Américo discovered America?

Both men did.

You can't credit a first discovery to two men!

Depends on what you mean by "discover." If you mean first to set eyes on, neither Columbus or Américo discovered any land, since many people were in the New World before them If you mean first to publicize, but without identifying, Columbus discovered America. If you mean first to identify and tell the world what something is, Américo discovered America.

As simple as that?

Yes. If a boy captures a butterfly which he does not identify, and a zoologist identifies it as a previously unknown species, after whom is the new species named — the boy or the zoologist?

The zoologist.

Yes. That is why I say Columbus discovered, in the sense of uncovered or publicized, the New World and did it, not in 1492, but when he made the discovery known to Europe, in the year 1493. I also say that Américo, when he announced the existence of a previously unknown continent, discovered America in 1502.

APPENDIX

Arrivals in the New World Before Columbus

Vilhjalmur Stefansson once remarked to this biographer: "Every habitable island on this planet, except two, was inhabited by human beings before the invention of bows and arrows." He said the two exceptions were Spitzbergen and a small island in the Pacific.

From the early Stone Age, people have been carried across by the Equatorial Current from Africa. Many made the crossing involuntarily. Some have crossed the Pacific by the Kurili Islands, and others by Bering Strait. Some crossed the North Atlantic by island hopping. For thousands of years, each new group of arrivals, if not killed off by disease or war, lost its identity through intermarriage with those who had preceded them. Grandchildren of those intermarriages would know only a few words of their ancestors' Old World language. Greatgrandchildren would know none, except perhaps an occasional word which might have seeped into tribal usage. As a result, hundreds of tribal languages were developed by diverse infiltrations. We now have positive evidence that human beings have existed in North America for at least 80,000 years. The more daring of our scholars are beginning to point to about 200,000 years.

Motivations for ocean crossings were flight from war, escape from persecution, desire to acquire materials like copper and tin, eagerness to catch plenty of codfish, and rarely, a desire to explore.

Access to the interiors of continents was made possible by rivers.

The following list of evidences has been casually selected, and is by no means complete.

1700 B.C. A Norwegian king came to trade for copper needed for making bronze. Evidence in Petroglyphs Park, Peterborough, Ontario. See Barry Fell, *Bronze-Age America,* 1982.

5,000 B.C., 814 B.C., and 1310 B.C. — blacks in Brazil and Caribbean. See Ivan Van Sertima, *They Came Before Columbus,* Random House, 1976.

In large areas in the Brazilian rain forest sunlight never penetrates. There are tribes living there who have never seen the sun, the moon, or stars, and perhaps in consequence, have no religion. Blacks from Africa living for thousands of years in that rain forest would lose their skin color. This suggestion of mine should be no shock to Caucasians, since it is rather obvious that many thousands of years ago the ancestors of Europeans were black Africans. A Mayan (Popul Vuh) text says "ancestors came from across the sea where the sun rises" and "There they are, in great numbers, the black men and the white."

An involuntary crossing by the Equatorial Current to Brazil occurred in the 7th century B.C., when one of the ships which the Pharoah of Egypt had sent to circumnavigate Africa, was carried westward. An inscription at Pouso Alto near Paraíba tells the story: "We are Sidonian Canaanites from the city of the Merchant King. We were cast up on this distant land, a land of mountains. We sacrificed a youth to the celestial gods and goddesses in the 19th year of our mighty King Hiram, and embarked from Ezian-geber into the Red Sea. We voyaged with ten ships and were at sea together for two years around Africa. Then we were separated by the hand of Baal, and were no longer with our companions. So we have come here, 12 men and 3 women. . . . " The translation is by Cyrus H. Gordon in *Before Columbus,* 1971.

Egypt was the most advanced nation in ancient times, and it is no surprise that having circumnavigated Africa, an Egyptian Pharoah, Ptolemy III, centuries later wishing to find out how correct Eratosthenes, the Librarian at Alexandria, had been in his estimate of the size of the earth, sent an expedition to circumnavigate the earth. The expedition, sailing eastward, under command of Rata, with Maui as navigator and astronomer, came to land in southern California about 2,000 miles north of the equator, and searched the coast southward in a vain attempt to complete the circumnavigation. In a cave near Santiago de Chile, they left an inscription: "Southern limit of the coast reached by Maui. This region is the southern limit of the mountainous land the commander claims, by written proclamation, in this land exulting. To this southern limit he steered the flotilla of ships. This land the navigator claims for the King of Egypt, for his Queen, and for their noble son, running a course of 4,000 miles, steep, mighty, mountainous, on high uplifted. August, day 5, regnal year 16." The year was 231 B.C. The translation is from *Epigraphic Society Occasional Papers,* Vol.2, No.21, 1974. Address of E.S.O.P. — 6625 Bamburgh Drive, San Diego, Cal. 92117.

9th century B.C. Fifteen miles west of Los Lunas, New Mexico, an inscription in North Phoenician letters, used also at the time by Hebrews, gives the Decalogue. E.S.O.P., Vol.10, Part 1, 1982.

At Bat Creek, Tennessee, an inscription was discovered and published in *Smithsonian Twelfth Annual Bureau Ethnology,* 1984, pp. 382-394. Recently it was recognized as Hebrew in the form of letters of the time when the Romans conquered Jerusalem (70 A.D.) Three Bar Kokhba coins have been dug up not far from Bat Creek: Lousiville 1932, Clay City 1952, and Hopkinsville 1967.

The Atlantic was crossed by all the seafaring people of the Mediterranean. People came to the New World in every century of the Roman Empire. See Pohl, "Did Ancient Romans Reach America?" in *The New Diffusionist,* Vol.3, No.10, January 1975, pp. 23-37. Roman coins, 2,000 of them, have been dug up in North America, more than 200 of them near the mouth of the Hudson River and nearly 200 near the mouth of the Mississippi.

Christian orthodoxy was recorded in pre-Columbian inscriptions in the New World. See *Wonderful West Virginia,* March 1983. Copies obtainable from Dept. of Natural Resources, State Capitol, Charleston, W.Va., 25305.

A few years before 500 A.D. orthodox Christians in North Africa fled from persecution by Vandals and escaped by a long voyage "in the direction of the setting sun" to what they then called *Asqa Samal* ("North Continent"). There is evidence that some of them settled in what is now Cockaponset State Forest in Connecticut. Morocco has a longer Atlantic coastline than any Old World country except Norway, and it embraces the latitude of the Canary Islands, whence, as Columbus knew and demonstrated, prevailing winds blow west to the Caribbean. It was natural for fishermen from Morocco to use that trade wind and then sail north with the Gulf Stream to the fishing banks off Newfoundland. The Vandals in North Africa were crushed in 534 A.D. by General Belisarius serving the orthodox Emperor Justinian of Constantinople. Immediately some of the settlers in the North Continent returned home, and one of them made an inscription at Figuig in eastern Morocco telling of the escape and the timing of the return. How did the settlers in the wilderness of North America know when the Vandal power had been destroyed? How else if not by fishing ships which were crossing annually?

Many landings in North America were made by the Vikings — 1003 Leif Erikson, 1005 Thorvald Erikson, 1010 Thorfinn Karlsefni, etc. down into the 12th century when the Bishop of Greenland and Vinland, the largest diocese of the Roman Catholic Church, crossed from Greenland presumably to dedicate the first church in Vinland. Later, the round stone church at Newport R.I., was built, somewhere between 1275 and 1325 A.D., "in the architecture of the 13th to the 14th centuries," according to Johannes Brøndsted, Curator of the National Museum of Denmark, and recognized leading authority on early European architecture.

Evidences are accumulating that fishermen of western European countries regularly crossed the Atlantic. In 1351 an Orkney fisherman crossed and spent 26 years on the eastern shore of North America, and returned home in 1397 to tell of "Nuovo Mondo" (New World). In 1398, Prince Henry, First Sinclair Earl of Orkney, led an expedition across via Newfoundland to Nova Scotia. Newfoundland was inhabited by fishermen along its coasts. Few ventured into the forested and inhospitable interior. Earl Henry's secretary, Antonio Zeno recorded that ten languages were spoken in Newfoundland, one of them Norse. One of those languages must have been that of the Beotucks, who were descendants from intermarriage of Vikings with savages. From what countries did the other eight languages come? The best guess seems to be Morocco, Portugal, Ireland (the Vikings said the Irish crossed the Atlantic before they did), the Basques, Brittany, the Hebrides, Denmark and Spain. See Pohl, *Prince Henry Sinclair,* 1974.

The Portuguese had the name for cod before Columbus; they named a cape in Labrador before Columbus; there is presently a study being made of the wreck of a pre-Columbian Portuguese fishing ship on the coast of Labrador.

Jacques Cartier, named in history books as the one who officially explored the Gulf of Newfoundland, when he came to islands there in 1535, found fishermen from France there who had already named the islands St. Pierre and Miquelon. Samuel de Champlain, who is credited with first exploration of the south coast of Nova Scotia, in 1601 in Tor Bay found a fleet of French fishing ships. He interviewed the captain of one of them, Captain Savalette, who told Champlain and Champlain's secretary, Marc Lescarbot, that he came from St. Jean de Luz, a fishing port in southern France, and that he had come across "every year for forty years." If Captain Savalette did that, how about his father before him, and his grandfather before that? The Portuguese claim that João Vaz Corte-Real was in Newfoundland in 1472. Columbus knew that Alonso Sánchez from Huelva, a fishing port, had crossed to the Caribbean in 1481.

It would appear that Columbus got his project accepted because of ignorance in Spain as to what fisherman had been doing. Fishermen were of course not telling where they got their fish.

SOURCES AND NOTES

Chapter One: MAJORCA
1. Maria, Nectario, *Cristóbal Colón,* pp. 10-13, 17, 18. On his page 31, Maria cites many corroborating sources.
2. A Roman Catholic scholar, Brother Nectario Maria, on December 10th, 1966, gave a lecture in Cadiz, the title of which was: "Juan Colón alias Cristóbal Colón, alias Christopher Columbus, the Spaniard." That lecture was printed with a preface in which it was said that the telling of the parentage, birth place and actual name of the man the world knows as Columbus "has special significance because in effect it bears the imprimature of the Church. It explains why the Holy Office of the Vatican has turned a deaf ear to the suggestions

and demands of many uninformed persons that Christopher Columbus be made a saint."

3. Maria, Nectario, *Cristóbal Colón,* p. 15.
4. *Ibid.,* p. 16.
5. See chart next page.
6. Desdevises du Dezert.
7. *Ibid.*
8. *Ibid.*

Chapter Two: REVOLT
1. Maria, Nectario, *Cristóbal Colón,* p. 16. Maria says: "Sus tios Juan y Bartolome Colón, hermanos de su madre Margarita, figuren en una revuelta que tuvo lugar en la isla de Mallorca." This in English, "His uncles Juan and Bartolomeo Colón, brothers of his mother Margarita, were conspicuous in a revolt which took place on the island of Majorca." Maria also says they were "not taken prisoners."
2. The revolt of the Catalonians in Barcelona was overcome by King Juan II of Aragon in 1472, when Juan Colón was 12 years of age. The revolt in Majorca may have occurred in that year or a year or two later. It may have occurred in 1472, and if so, that was the year when Juan and his uncle Bartolomeo escaped from Majorca. In 1495, when he was 35, Colón wrote: "I was upon the sea 23 years."

Chapter Three: SEVEN-MILE SWIM
1. *The Life of the Admiral Christopher Columbus,* by his son Ferdinand, tr. by Benjamin Keen, Rutgers University Press, 1959, p. 11.
2. Maria, *Cristóbal Colón,* p. 22, footnote.
3. Desdevises du Dezert, pp. 452-455.
4 Aristoteles, *La filosofia moral de Aristotel.* The *Ethics* translated by Carlos, Principe de Viana. Dedicated to Alfonso III, King of Aragon. Printed by George Coci, a German in Zaragosa (Saragossa) in 1509.
5. Nectario Maria, *Cristóbal Colón,* p. 21, gives the actualities of the naval battle in which Juan Colón with French ships serving Portugal, fought against Italian ships serving Queen Isabel of Castile. Maria cites his sources, as for example, Fernando Gomez de Uribe who confirms the defeat of the fleet of Castile and Aragon near

5.

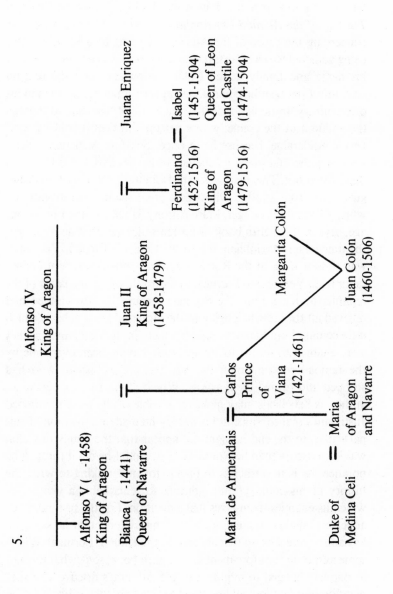

Alfonso IV
King of Aragon

Alfonso V (-1458)
King of Aragon

Bianca (-1441)
Queen of Navarre

Juan II
King of Aragon
(1458-1479)

Juana Enriquez

Ferdinand
(1452-1516)
King of
Aragon
(1479-1516)

Isabel
(1451-1504)
Queen of Leon
and Castile
(1474-1504)

Carlos
Prince
of
Viana
(1421-1461)

Maria de Armendais

Maria
of Aragon
and Navarre

Duke of
Medina Celi

Margarita Colón

Juan Colón
(1460-1506)

Cape St. Vincent on August 13, 1476.

6. Here is the story Colón cleverly concocted and told in Spain years later, as we know since it is how it was told by Ferdinand Colón in *The Life of the Admiral Christopher Columbus,* Chapter V. — "As concerning the cause of the Admiral's coming into Spain, and his being addicted to sea affairs, the occasion of it was a famous man of his name and family, called Colón, renowned upon the sea, on account of the fleet he commanded against infidels, and even in his own country, insomuch that they made use of his name to frighten the children in the cradle; whose person and fleet it is likely were very considerable, because he at once took four Venetian galleys, whose bigness and strength I should not have believed, had I not seen them fitted out. This man was called Colón the Younger, to distinguish him from another who was a great seaman before him. Of which Colón the Younger, Marc Antony Sabellicus, the Livy of our age, says in the eighth book of his tenth decade, that he lived near the time when Maximilian, son to the Emperor Frederic the Third, was chosen King of the Romans: Jerome Donato was sent ambassador from Venice into Portugal to return thanks in the name of the republic to King John the Second, because he had clothed and relieved all the crew belonging to the aforesaid great galleys, which were coming from Flanders, relieving them in such a manner, as they were enabled to return to Venice, they having been overcome by the famous corsair Colón the Younger, near Lisbon, who had stripped and turned them ashore. Which authority of so grave an author as Sabellicus, may make us sensible of the afore-mentioned Justiniani's malice, since in his history he made no mention of this particular, to the end it might not appear that the family of Colón was less obscure than he would make it. And if he did it through ignorance, he is nevertheless to blame, for undertaking to write the history of his country, and omitting so remarkable a victory, of which its enemies themselves make mention. For the historian, our adversary, makes so great account of his victory, that he says ambassadors were sent on that account to the King of Portugal. Which some author in the afore-mentioned eighth book, somewhat further, as one less obliged to inquire into the Admiral's discovery, makes mention of it, without adding those twelve lines which Justiniani inserted. But to return to the matter in hand, I say, that whilst the Ad-

miral sailed with the aforesaid Colón the Younger, which was a long time, it fell out that understanding the before-mentioned four great Venetian galleys were coming from Flanders, they went out to seek, and found them beyond Lisbon, about Cape St. Vincent, which is in Portugal, where falling to blows, they fought furiously and grappled . . . ." This was a clever cover-up by a man who, fifteen years later after the naval battle in which he had participated, was in Spain and needed to conceal the facts of that battle. And so he presented an incident which he said had been omitted from a history book because of malice in a writer who wished to denigrate the Colón family. What the quotation clearly shows is that its author could skillfully imitate the prolixity and opacity of long-winded medieval scholars. What he produced is a masterpiece of obfuscation.

Chapter Five: GO WEST TO THE EAST

1. Samuel Eliot Morison, *Admiral of the Ocean Sea,* p. 38.
2. In view of the physique, hair color and eye coloring, and character of Colom, there is no surprise in the *title* of the book by George Seraphin Canoutas, *Christopher Columbus, a Greek Nobleman;.* . . . St. Marks Publishing Co., 1943.
3. Maria, *Cristóbal Colón,* p. 23, calls it *el valiosisimo pergamino* — "the costly parchment".
4. Manuel Lopez Flores, in research in Huelva and Seville, announced discovery of the parchment without telling how he unearthed it or who had possessed it.
5. In "commentarios realia," published in Lisbon, 1609.
6. Lorenzo y Leal (Dr. D. Baldomero de) in *Cristobal Colon y Alonso Sanchez de Huelva e el prime descubrimiento del Novus Mundus.* Con licencia de la autoridad Eclesiastica Jerez, 1892.
7. Nash, p. 265.
8. Nectorio Maria, in 1978, pp. 25-28.

Chapter Eight: NEW FIRST NAME

1. Columbus, Ferdinand, *Life of the Admiral Christopher Columbus,* p.38.

Chapter Nine: ISABEL
1. Morison, *Admiral of the Ocean Sea*, p. 87.
2. Fernandez-Armesto, *Ferdinand and Isabella*, p. 36.
3. *Ibid*, pp. 11, 12.
4. *Ibid*, p. 29.
5. *Ibid*, p. 108.
6. Morison, *Admiral of the Ocean Sea*, p. 103.
7. *Ibid*, p. 86.
8. *Ibid*, p. 84.
9. Maurice David, pp. 113-118.
10. Morison, *Admiral of the Ocean Sea*, p. 85.

Chapter Ten: CONTRACT AND CREDENTIALS
1. Morison, *Admiral of the Ocean Sea*, p. 96.
2. *Ibid*, p. 97.

Chapter Eleven: ENTERPRISE OF THE INDIES
1. Morison, *Admiral of the Ocean Sea*, p. 110.
2. *Ibid*, p.112.

Chapter Twelve: LARGER THAN NAVARRE
1. *Old South Leaflets*, Vol. 2, No. 33, p. 1.
2. *Ibid*, p. 2.
3. *Ibid*, p. 5.
4. *Ibid*, p. 7.

Chapter Thirteen: FAME
1. Undisputed record in Genoa says Diego Colombo was born in 1468.

Chapter Fifteen: GOLD
1. A recent discovery completely confirms the Majorcan origin of Cristóbal Colón, and his uncle "brother." It is a document of the year 1494 unearthed by Renato Llanas de Niubo in *El Enigma de Cristóbal Colón*, 1973. The document in the handwriting of Conde Juan de Borromeo, of the illustrious Borromeo family, tells us that Peter Martir of Angleria, at that time Treasurer of the Court of the Catholic Kings, knew as a confidential secret that Cristóbal Colón was from Majorca and not from Genoa. A photo copy of the ori-

ginal is given by Nectario Maria on page 12, and the Spanish text on page 13, of his *Cristóbal Colón.* On the 21st of October, 1494, Peter Martir wrote to his protector Conde Juan de Borromeo, and presumably in the same letter included the secret note. Here is an English translation: "I, Juan de Borromeo, having been forbidden to reveal the truth, have been secretly informed by Peter of Angleria, Treasurer of the Catholic King of Spain, confiding to future history that Cristóbal Colón was of Majorca, not from Liguria. And the said Peter of Angleria thinks the astute concealment used by Juan Colón in pretending to be Cristóbal Colón was motivated by political and religious reasons so that he could ask for ships of the King of Spain." Nectario Maria, pp. 10-13.

2. Ferdinand Columbus, *The Life of the Admiral Christopher Columbus,* pp. 147-148.
3. *Idem.*
4. Morison, *Admiral of the Ocean Sea,* p. 670.
5. *Idem,* p. 505.

Chapter Seventeen: SEARCH FOR INDIA

1. Hojeda and Juan de la Cosa, with three pilots, a surgeon, an apothecary and twenty men, and with Fernando de Guevara in command of their companion ship, sailed away from the coast of South America before the end of August and arrived in Española on September 5th, 1499. This is the statement of Navarrete, quoted by Markham in the "Voyage of Hojeda," *Hakluyt Society Publications,* No. 90, pp. 33, 34. Hojeda and La Cosa were back in Spain in the middle of April, 1500.
2. Américo explored much of the coast of Brazil ten months before Pedro Alvarez Cabral landed on its coast on April 2, 1500. Américo by seven months preceded Vicente Yanez Pinzón, who landed on the coast of Brazil on January 20, 1500; and by eight months preceded Diego de Lepe, who landed on the coast of Brazil on February 14, 1500. Américo was the first of record on the coast of Brazil.
3. Américo, *Letter from Seville.*
4. Place names on the maps of Amerigo Vespucci's voyage of 1499 are from Juan de la Cosa's Map of 1500. His map shows two ships sailing between the Brazilian Elbow and the Gulf of Paria, and several

evidences indicate that these were Américo's ships, not Hojeda's. On La Cosa's Map the record of "81" and "60" of the run in leagues of Américo's ships would seem impossible, were it not firmly established by recent observations of the speed of the current on the same course. The "Pilot Chart of the Central American Waters" for March 1926, furnished by the Hydrographic Office of the Navy Department, U.S.A., states that "Second Officer A.R. Payne of the American steamer *Elkhorn,* Captain Smulker, reports that on November 16 and 17, 1924, from Lat. 2° 00' N., long. 46° 15' W., to lat. 3° 05' N., long. 48° 00' W., the current was setting northwest at 2.9 knots; thence to lat. 6° 03' N., long. 52° 04' W., it was northwest, 3.5 knots." Eighty-one leagues at four Roman miles to a league was about 290 English miles. The current accounted for more than 100 of these knots. The sailing speed of Américo's ships was slightly above six knots.

5. Vespucci, *Letter from Seville.*
6. *Idem.*
7. *Idem.*
8. *Idem.*
9. *Idem.*
10. M.F. de Navvarete.
11. Vespucci, *Letter from Seville.*
12. *Idem.*

Chapter Eighteen: SHACKLES
1. Morison, *Admiral of the Ocean Sea,* p. 559.
2. Columbus, Ferdinand, *The Life of the Admiral Christopher Columbus,* said this of the incarceration of his father: "At Santo Domingo, the aforesaid judge, being eager to remain governor there, at the beginning of October, 1500, without any delay, or legal information, sent him prisoner aboard a ship, together with his brother James (Diego), putting them in irons, and a good guard over them, and ordered upon severe penalties that none should dare to speak for them."

Chapter Nineteen: CLOCK IN THE SKY
1. Américo, *Letter from Seville.*
2. Américo, *Letter from Cape Verde.*

3. *Idem.*
4. *Idem.*

Chapter Twenty: COMPULSION
1. Columbus, Christopher, *Lettera Rarissima,* written in Jamaica, July 7, 1503.
2. Morison, *Admiral of the Ocean Sea,* p. 655.

Chapter Twenty-One: CONTINENT BETWEEN TWO OCEANS
1. Américo, *Letter from Cape Verde.*
2. *Idem.*
3. *Idem.*
4. *Idem.*
5. Pohl, *Amerigo Vespucci, Pilot Major,* p. 118 and Note 4, p. 225.
6. Américo, *Letter from Cape Verde.*
7. *Idem.*
8. Américo, *Letter from Cape Verde.*
9. Pohl, *Prince Henry Sinclair. His Expedition to the New World in 1398.*

Chapter Twenty-Two: DISCOVERIES
1. Vespucci, Letter from Lisbon.
2. Columbus, Ferdinand, *The Life of the Admiral Christopher Columbus,* p. 284.
3. In 1538, Virreina Doña Maria de Colón y Toledo renounced in the name of their son Don Juis Colón, the Admiral's grandson, the hereditary titles and privileges over the Indies, to get 25 square leagues from the Emperor Charles V, with the title of Duke of Veragua.
4. After the death of Ferdinand Colón in 1539, his Colombiana Library was in the hands of churchmen, and many years later, it was discovered that three-quarters of the books in it had been disposed of, presumably by fanatics who disapproved of them. For a description of the books Ferdinand had in the French language, see Babelon.
5. F.J. Pohl, "The Fourth Continent on the Lenox Globe" in *Bulletin of the New York Public Library,* Vol. 67, No. 7, September 1963, pp. 465-469.

SELECTED BIBLIOGRAPHY

Altolaguirre y Duvale, *? Colón Español ?, Estudio histórico — critico*. Madrid, Patronato de huérfams de introdeucia é intervencion militares, 1923, 89 p.

Arciniegas, Germán. *Amerigo and the New World*. New York, Knopf, 1955.

Aristoteles, La philosofia moral de Aristotel. The *Ethics* translated by Carlos, principe de Viana. Dedicated to Alfonso III, King of Aragon. Printed by George Coci, a German in Saragossa, 1509.

Babelon, Jean. *La Biblioteque Francaise de Fernand Colomb,* Paris, Edouard Champion, 1913.

Bayerri y Bartomeu Enrique. *Colón tal cual fué, las problemas de la nacionalida y de la personalidid de Colón y en resolución mas justificada.* Barcelona, Porter-Libros, 1961. 80 p.

Boissonnade, Prosper, *Histoire d la Reunion de la Navarre a la Castile.* Paris. Alfonse Picard et Fils, 1893.

Codine, D. Juan. *Guerres de Navarre y Cataluña desde el año 1451 hasta el de 1471.* Barcelona, Imprenta de Torner, 1851.

Columbus, Christopher. *Lettera Rarissima,* written Jamaica, July 7, 1503. — *The Voyages of Christopher Columbus.* Tr. and ed. with an introduction and notes, by Cecil Jane. London, 1930.

Columbus, Ferdinand. *The Life of the Admiral Christopher Columbus,* tr. and annotated by Benjamin Keen. New Brunswick, N.J., Rutgers University Press, 1959.

Curtis, William Eleroy. *The Authentic Letters of Columbus.* Chicago: Field Columbian Museum Publications, 2, Vol. 1, No. 2, May 1895. Pages 193-200 give the Will of Columbus. Certified copy in the Collection of the Duke of Veragua, Madrid, tr. by Jose Ignatio Rodriguez.

David, Maurice. *Who was "Columbus"? His real name and real fatherland:* a sensational discovery among the archives of Spain. New York, The Research Publishing Co., 1933.

Desdevises du Dezert, G. *Don Carlos d'Aragon, Prince de Viane.* Paris, Armand Colen et Cie, 1889. p. 453. (contains catalogue of library of Prince Carlos of Viana).

Donworth, Albert Bernard. *Why Columbus Sailed.* New York, Exposition Press, 1953.

Duryea, Nina Larrey. *Mallorca the Magnificent.* New York, Century Co., 1927.

Fernandez-Armisto, Felipe. *Ferdinand and Isabella.* Birkenhead, Willmer Brothers, 1975.

Gallois, Lucien Louis Joseph. "Toscanelli et Cristophe Colomb," *Annales de geographie* (Pa ris), XI (1902), 97-110.

Goodwin, William B. *The Lure of Gold, being the story of the five lost ships of Christopher Columbus.* Boston, Meador Publishing Co., 1940.

Graves, Robert, and Paul Hogarth. *Majorca Observed.* Garden City, N.Y., Doubleday, 1965.

Kline, Burton. "America Discovered Many Times Before Columbus Came," *World's Work,* L (May, 1925) 135-42.

Las Casas, Fray Bartolomé de. *Brevissima relación de la destrución de las Indias.* (A very short Account of the Destruction of the Indies). 1552. — *Las Obras.* Seville, 1552.

Manzano, Manzano, Juan. *Colón y su secreto.* Madrid, Editiones Cultur e Hispanica, 1976, 742 p.

Maria, Brother Nectario. *Cristóbal Colón alias Christopher Columbus was a Spanish Jew.* New York, Chedney Press, 1971. (Lecture given in Cadiz, Dec. 10, 1966.)
— *Cristóbal Colón,* Madrid, Villena Artes Graficas, Cardenal Herrera Oria, 242.

Morison, Samuel Eliot. *Admiral of the Ocean Sea. A Life of Christopher Columbus.* Boston, Little, Brown, 1942.
— *Portuguese Voyages to America in the Fifteenth Century.* Cambridge (Mass.).

Muller, Johannes (Regiomontanus). *Ephemerides.* Venice, 1484. Editions were published in 1488 and 1492.

Mundus Novus. Vienna. August, 1504; tr. by George Tyler Northup. Princeton, N.J., 1916. Purports to be a letter from Americo Vespucci to Lorenzo di Pier Francesco de Medici.

Nash, William Giles. *America, the true history of its discovery.* London, G. Richards, 1924. 291 p.

Nunn, George Emta. *The Geographical Conceptions of Columbus.* New York, Ayer Co., 1921.

Pohl, Frederick J. *Amerigo Vespucci, Pilot Major.* New York, Columbia University Press, 1944. With new Preface, Octagon Books, 1966.

— Pohl, Frederick J. and Captain Leonard B. Loeb. "Americo Vespucio — Pioneer Celo-Navigator and Geographer," in *United States Naval Institute Proceedings,* Vol. 83, No. 4, April 1957, pp. 396-403.

— "Did Ancient Romans Reach America?" in *The New Diffusionist,* Vol. 3, No. 10, January 1973, pp. 23-37.

— "The Fourth Continent on the Lenox Globe" in *Bulletin of the New York Public Library,* Vol. 67, No. 7, September 1963, pp. 465-469.

— "The Pesaro Map, 1505" in *Imago Mundi,* VII, Stockholm, MCML.

— *Prince Henry Sinclair. His Expedition to the New World in 1398.* New York. Clarkson N. Potter, 1974.

Ptolemaeus, Claudius. *Cosmographia.* Editions of 1474, 1477, 1478.

Sanchez, Alonso, de Huelva. Original document in hands of his descendants discovered in Seville by Don Manuel López Flores.

Steck, Francis Borgia. *Chrisophe Columbo and the Franciscans.* Washington, D.C., 1947.

Sumien, N. *La Correspondence de savant florentin Paolo dal Pozzo Toscanelli avec Cristophe Colomb.* Paris, 1927.

Uzielli, Gustavo. "Toscanelli, Columbo e Vespucci," *Atti* del IV Congresso geografico italiano, April, 1901, pp. 559-591. Milan, 1902.

Van Sertima, Ivan. *They Came Before Columbus,* New York, Random, 1977.

Vespucci Reprints. Texts and Studies, LV.*The Soderini Letter in Translation.* Tr. with Introduction and Notes by George Tyler Northup. Princeton, N.J. Princeton University Press, 1916.

Waldseemüller, Martin. *The Cosmographiae introductio of Martin Waldseemüller* in facsimile, followed by the Four Voyages of Amerigo Vespucci, with their translation into English; to which are added Waldseemüller's two world maps of 1507, with an introduction by Prof. Joseph Fischer . . . and Prof. Frans von

Wieser; ed. by Prof. Charles George Herbenmann. New York, 1907.

Wieser, Franz, Ritter von. Die Karte des Bartolomeo Colombo über die vierte Reise des Admirals. Innsbruck, 1891.

INDEX

J

K

L

W

Z